First-Generation Faculty of Color

First-Generation Faculty of Color

Reflections on Research, Teaching, and Service

EDITED BY TRACY LACHICA BUENAVISTA,
DIMPAL JAIN, AND MARÍA C. LEDESMA

RUTGERS UNIVERSITY PRESS

NEW BRUNSWICK, CAMDEN, AND NEWARK, NEW JERSEY, AND LONDON

LIBRARY OF CONGRESS CATALOGING-IN-PUBLICATION DATA

Names: Buenavista, Tracy Lachica, editor. | Jain, Dimpal, editor. |
Ledesma, María C., editor.
Title: First-generation faculty of color : reflections on research, teaching,
and service / edited by Tracy Lachica Buenavista, Dimpal Jain, and María C. Ledesma.
Description: New Brunswick, New Jersey : Rutgers University Press, 2023. |
Includes bibliographical references and index.
Identifiers: LCCN 2022007399 | ISBN 9781978823440 (paperback) |
ISBN 9781978823457 (hardcover) | ISBN 9781978823464 (epub) |
ISBN 9781978823488 (pdf)
Subjects: LCSH: Minority college teachers—United States. | First-generation
college students—United States. | Education, Higher—Social aspects—United States.
Classification: LCC LC3727 .F57 2023 | DDC 378.1/2089—dc23/eng/20220610
LG record available at https://lccn.loc.gov/2022007399

A British Cataloging-in-Publication record for this book is
available from the British Library.

♾ The paper used in this publication meets the requirements of the American
National Standard for Information Sciences—Permanence of Paper for
Printed Library Materials, ANSI Z39.48-1992.

www.rutgersuniversitypress.org

Manufactured in the United States of America

For all first-generation faculty of color and those who bring the academy within reach, and re-envision it as a just and humane place; we recognize the racial battle fatigue and wounds you endure(d) and offer this book toward our collective healing.

CONTENTS

PART ONE
Research

FOREWORD

During a decades-long first-generation faculty career, the primary focus of my research, teaching, and service has been to advance faculty gender and racial/ethnic diversity in academia. My own educational journey took me from working as a farm laborer to becoming the first in my family to go to college to serving for almost forty years as a professor of education at three large universities in three states (Minnesota, Arizona, and California). In most of my faculty and administrative positions, I was the first Latina, Filipina, or woman of color from a no-collar class to serve. My academic journey, while fraught with challenges reflected in several experiences described in *First-Generation Faculty of Color: Reflections on Research, Teaching, and Service*, provided opportunities for me to publish work that has contributed to increasing the representation of faculty of color, pushing back against narratives that cast differences as deficits, and creating inclusive spaces for the sharing of knowledge and the development of mentoring and networking practices that support the career advancement and development of scholars of color.

As a first-generation, full professor emerita of color and as a former departmental, college, and campus-wide administrator who is one year away from full retirement, reading about the lived experiences of the first-generation faculty of color presented in this volume, not only inspires and energizes me but also gives me tremendous hope for the future of higher education. Each one of these stories gives voice and visibility to challenges faced and addressed by the faculty who impart their narratives. Their narratives point to the importance of networking, mentoring, and family support along their academic journeys. The contributing authors also present examples of safe harbors and counterspaces that serve as points from which to resist oppressive systems that work to negatively judge their work, creating self-doubt and attempting to block their progress. Such spaces provide contexts where first-generation faculty of color have opportunities to gather together, to cultivate, to support, and to validate each other's scholarly work. Within these nurturing contexts, contributing authors describe the creation of new knowledge steeped in their experience and in the experiences of their ancestral and current communities.

While other important and critical scholarship chronicles the experiences of faculty of color (Chen & Hune, 2011; Croom, 2017; Fries-Britt & Turner-Kelley, 2005; Padilla, 1994; Pérez, 2019; Pewewardy, 2013; Turner, 2002, 2015, 2020; Turner & Waterman, 2019; Turner et al., 2008, 2011; Zambrana, 2018), in general, previous work collapses the first-generation experience within a broader generational context and does not tease out the perspectives of first-generation faculty of color. Even though there is no singular monolithic first-generation experience, this practice of conflation makes the unique lived experiences of these faculty essentially invisible. On the other hand, *First-Generation Faculty of Color* is distinctive in that it highlights, as stated by the coeditors, the "experiences of 'first-generation faculty of color,' or minoritized individuals who were first-generation college students and went on to pursue faculty careers."

This is the first book I have read that entirely centers on the experiences of first-generation faculty of color. Most authors note that they write with more urgency and stress as they engage within a society reeling from a racial and health pandemic. Both pandemics further reveal the many inequities experienced by marginalized first-generation faculty of color contributors. Narratives predominantly represent perspectives from faculty currently situated at four-year public campuses, which are also designated as minority serving. One author describes her community college faculty experience and three are located at four-year private institutions. Men and women are featured in this book, with women in the majority. Various racial/ethnic group affiliations are represented, with most writers identifying as Asian American or Latina/o/x. While more work is needed to broaden the institutional, gender, and race/ethnic representation of the first-generation faculty of color community, this doesn't take away from the importance of this work. In fact, taken together, contributing authors create a publication that fills a void in the extant literature on how first-generation faculty of color experience and navigate academia. By bringing these scholars together and providing them with voice and visibility, this volume offers the reader newly created knowledge and potential networking opportunities for others traveling the same or similar journeys. In my view, this publication makes an important and needed contribution to the literature on diversity and the professoriate. Furthermore, this work provides a bridge of insight, as emphasized by the coeditors, within the backdrop of pending faculty retirements and the steady growth of historically minoritized doctoral recipients seeking to enter academia. Institutional leaders and policymakers can use the wealth of knowledge shared in this book to cultivate nurturing work environments that include and value the talent and perspectives of those who are first in their families to become faculty members.

Reflections on Contributing Author Experiences

Chapter authors shared several critical comments and observations about their lived experiences. Given time and space constraints, in this foreword I can highlight only a few of the numerous important insights detailed by each contributor. In this section, I want to reflect on some of those observations that made me think about my own experiences compared with the experiences of first-generation faculty of color who are earlier in their careers. As a first-generation faculty of color who is now retired, comments made in this book made me think about my entry into the professoriate almost forty years ago and some lessons learned late in my career.

The coeditors sought to explore how first-generation identity may or may not change or recede for historically minoritized students as they move along as students and then as faculty in higher education. As Ledesma reports, regardless of degree attainment, a first-generation background uniquely shapes how faculty of color experience and navigate academia. Tension between incorporation and marginalization in the academy (Turner, 2003, 2017) is expressed in these chapters.

I was encouraged from an early age to leave who I am at the doors of educational institutions because that is where my education should begin. Over years of trying to compartmentalize myself, I have learned that my power lies in bringing my whole self to whatever I do. By bringing all of our forms of knowledge to the table, we validate ourselves and our communities of origin. We can withstand critics who believe that these sources of knowledge have little or no value. In my view, the combination of all forms of knowledge creates new knowledge. It is important to acknowledge who we are in total because that influences our approaches to research, the types of questions we ask, the kinds of issues that interest us, and the ways we go about seeking solutions and interpreting our findings.

My first-generation background uniquely shapes how I navigated/continue to navigate my role in the professoriate. However, I tried to fit the mold far longer into my career than the authors describe here. They indicate the importance of former academic mentors in helping them to enter their faculty roles with a more critical and questioning mind. These mentors worked directly with them, providing guidance and support for them as emerging scholars. Mentors are described as encouraging their scholarship and providing safe, collaborative spaces within which to grow as emerging scholars. Mentors are also described as helping them to gain academic experiences, such as copublishing and copresenting. For example, Judith Flores Carmona describes hearing a motivational speech by Cecilia Burciaga, executive assistant to the president of California State University, Monterey Bay (CSUMB), which inspired her to attend CSUMB. Burciaga was instrumental in Carmona's college admission process and in teaching her how to navigate higher education. For instance, Burciaga taught Carmona to defend herself and talk back when encountering microaggressions (Solórzano, 1998) on campus.

Mentors played important roles in my career. In the 1960s, as an undergraduate at the University of California, Davis, I was unaware of scholars who shared a similar racial/ethnic/gender/class background to mine, a farm laborer and a first-generation Latina/Filipina student, but I was strongly influenced by the farm labor and civil rights movements. In the 1980s, as a graduate student at Stanford University, I also met and was mentored by then Stanford associate dean Cecilia Burciaga. Cecilia helped me to overcome self-doubts during graduate school and, while warning me of potential difficulties ahead, bolstered my courage to leave California—where I had been born and raised—to accept my first faculty position at the University of Minnesota. In addition, at Stanford, I was introduced to scholars who, through their publications, guided my dissertation work and future research agenda. Such inspirational mentors influenced me not only to remain in academia but also, as an assistant professor, to try and understand higher education contexts and the experiences of students, faculty, and administrators of color within them.

Interim Dean Appointment and New Learning

The year 2016 brought an unexpected turn in my career. On the heels of my return from an invited paper presentation at the Centre of Excellence for Equity in Higher Education at the University of Newcastle, Australia, I was asked to meet with my provost. He asked if I would consider taking on a new assignment—that of interim dean for the College of Education. Until our meeting, I did not even know that I was being considered and had not sought the position. Provost Mike Lee indicated that he already vetted my potential appointment with several faculty, staff, and other college administrators, including the university president. I was initially so surprised that I thought I had misunderstood the request. When I realized that this was a bona fide request, I still needed to be convinced that I was the right person for the interim position. After our conversation about the college needs and what I might bring to the table during this time of transition, as well as a discussion of the terms for the appointment, including the position description and remuneration package, I accepted the opportunity. Also, a large part of my decision process to accept this position was my trust in and admiration for Provost Lee as well as the fact that my area of decades-long scholarship focused on higher education as a field of study. After I made the decision, I asked, "When do you want me to start?" Again, another surprising challenge—their answer was "Tomorrow!"

Taking on this challenge brought many wonderful things as well as tough problems to resolve. I learned that while a solution is sought after, resolution is what is possible to continue forward progress. I surely made mistakes, but I was learning, and the learning curve was one of the steepest I'd ever encountered, except maybe learning to teach fully online this year. Nonetheless, both times I struggled, both times I realized that this quote about learning something new is so true: "I am not telling you, it's going to be easy. I am telling you that it will be worth it."

Today, I have the privilege of writing the foreword for this new book, coedited by scholars who I consider as esteemed colleagues and who are also first-generation faculty of color. They not only share their narratives about their academic journeys, but also provide a platform to give voice and visibility to others walking along the same or similar paths. They each provide an insight into their learning of something new. One chapter, written by Tracy Lachica Buenavista, sparked my interest because her words caused me to think of one of the memorable factors learned about faculty hiring when I served as an interim dean. It also has a bearing on where I am now as a retired full professor. Buenavista's chapter details "socioeconomic pressures and a financial (il)literacy that shape my first-generation faculty experience. . . . Like many minoritized people, I gained access to the academy, but was/am not able to fully participate." Part of her discussion focuses on retirement. Similar to Buenavista, I entered the professoriate without thinking or knowing about the importance of retirement investments/savings upon leaving the faculty. I was and am still somewhat retirement illiterate. My children will be the first generation to benefit from whatever I am able to pass on to them.

All this brings me to reflect upon my previous role as interim dean in supporting departments as they made the case about the need for new faculty hires. As interim dean, I proposed faculty hires to the provost and we discussed whether or not requests would be honored depending upon, among many other considerations, demands for faculty hiring across the campus. It is a very competitive process. Once a myriad of paperwork was filed, faculty hiring committees went about advertising a job description and deciding on a slate of finalists. Prior to the final hire, I had a one-on-one appointment with each candidate. During our conversation, salary and various perks desired upon hiring were discussed. Because of my plans for retirement and my background as a first-generation faculty member and interim dean, I pointed out the importance of considering the retirement package as well as salary and other potential perks inherent in the position they were each considering whether or not to accept. Most candidates were at the entry-level, assistant professor rank and had not thought about rolling in the retirement package as one of the many elements in their decision-making process.

In short, once the department and the finalist made decisions, then they are communicated to the provost via the dean's office. Further discussion occurs between the dean and provost regarding higher salary or other requests made by the department and/or finalist in order to complete the hiring process. The provost may also express concerns about any potential hire. Most of this discussion occurs informally, in person or by telephone. These types of interactions are very difficult to study, so my learning about higher education institutional hiring practices increased manyfold by serving in this interim position.

Conclusion

In 2018, I was invited to present the graduation keynote address for the School of Education at my alma mater, the University of California, Davis. In it, I provided a personal experience that might have resulted in my deciding to leave Davis, largely due to financial issues. Fortunately, an unexpected intervention caused me to stay. This experience made me realize what thin threads connect first-generation college goers to their campuses. It also exemplified how a simple intervention might prevent such departures. Later, as I conducted research, I heard about, observed, and documented these thin threads and critical interventions many times over in the lived experiences of students, faculty, and administrators of color, most of whom were first-generation. While conducting interviews with faculty and college presidents, they described their support of individuals, but they also described how they used their influence to create inclusive and welcoming campus learning environments—environments where thin threads are strengthened with intentional organizational interventions that serve to provide a foundation for the retention and success of all students, staff, and faculty. Authors featured in *First-Generation Faculty of Color* describe the tensions they face as they work within power structures established primarily to maintain the status quo. In doing so, they provide many examples of the thin threads and critical interventions that kept/keep them engaged in higher education. In chronicling their life journeys and examples of paths taken, they teach, inform, and motivate others.

As racism persists and change seems so far out of reach, many may doubt themselves or wonder if their work is worth the struggle. When asked why I continue to pursue my research, given that the needle has moved very little toward inclusion, I answer with the belief that there is no giving up on a commitment for equity, access, and inclusion in higher education. The work is worth it when considered as part of a broader fight waged for social and racial justice. I also point out how inspired and invigorated I am by the work of scholars, such as those featured here who are achieving the seemingly impossible. This book is part of a growing network creating one of many communities of care and support. Woven together, with each such contributions, one realizes that we are not alone in the struggle.

Caroline Sotello Viernes Turner

REFERENCES

Chen, E. W., & Hune, S. (2011). Asian American Pacific Islander women from Ph.D. to campus president: Gains and leaks in the pipeline. In J. Gaëtane & B. Lloyd-Jones (Eds.), *Women of color in higher education: Changing directions and new perspectives* (pp. 163–190). Emerald Group Publishing Limited.

Croom, N. N. (2017). Promotion beyond tenure: Unpacking racism and sexism in the experiences of Black womyn professors. *Review of Higher Education, 40*(4), 557–583. https://doi.org/10.1353/rhe.2017.0022

Fries-Britt, S. L., & Turner-Kelley, B. (2005). Retaining each other: Narratives of two African American women in the academy. *Urban Review, 37*(3), 221–242. https://doi.org/10.1007/s11256-005-0006-2

Padilla, A. M. (1994). Ethnic minority scholars, research, and mentoring: Current and future issues. *Educational Researcher, 23*(4), 24–27. https://doi.org/10.3102/0013189X023004024

Pérez, P. (Ed.). (2019). *The tenure-track process for Chicana and Latina faculty: Experiences of resisting and persisting in the academy.* Taylor & Francis.

Pewewardy, C. (2013). Fancy war dancing on academe's glass ceiling: Supporting and increasing indigenous faculty role models in higher education. In H. J. Shotton, S. C. Lowe, & S. J. Waterman (Eds.), *Beyond the asterisk: Understanding Native students in higher education.* Stylus Publishing.

Solórzano, D. G. (1998). Critical race theory, race and gender microaggressions, and the experience of Chicana and Chicano scholars. *International Journal of Qualitative Studies in Education, 11*(1), 121–136. https://doi.org/10.1080/095183998236926

Turner, C. S. (2003). Incorporation and marginalization in the academy: From border toward center for faculty of color? *Journal of Black Studies, 34*(1), 112–125. https://doi.org/10.1177/0021934703253689

Turner, C. S. (2015). Lessons from the field: Cultivating nurturing environments in higher education. *Review of Higher Education, 38*(3), 333–358. https://doi.org/10.1353/rhe.2015.0023

Turner, C. S., González, J. C., & Wood, J. L. (2008). Faculty of color in academe: What 20 years of literature tells us. *Journal of Diversity in Higher Education, 1*(3), 139–168. https://doi.org/10.1037/a0012837

Turner, C. S., & Myers, S. L., Jr. (2000). *Faculty of color in academe: Bittersweet success.* Allyn & Bacon.

Turner, C. S., & Waterman, S. J. (2019). Pushing back against deficit narratives: Mentoring as scholars of Color. *Texas Education Review, 8*(1), 138–149. http://dx.doi.org/10.26153/tsw/7044

Turner, C.S.V. (1994, Summer). A guest in someone else's house: Students of color on campus. *Review of Higher Education, 17*(4), 355–370.

Turner, C.S.V. (2002). Women of color in academe: Living with multiple marginality. *Journal of Higher Education, 73*(1), 74–93. https://doi.org/10.1080/00221546.2002.11777131

Turner, C.S.V. (2007). Pathways to the presidency: Biographical sketches of women of color firsts. *Harvard Educational Review, 77*(1), 1–38. https://doi.org/10.17763/haer.77.1.p831667187v7514w

Turner, C.S.V. (2017). Remaining at the margin and in the center. *Journal for the Study of Postsecondary and Tertiary Education, 2,* 121–126. https://doi.org/10.28945/3886

Turner, C.S.V. (2020). "I can only put together thoughts filed away in my brain: Who would pay me to do that?" *Journal of Minority Achievement, Creativity, and Leadership, 1*(1), 3–16. https://doi.org/10.5325/minoachicrealead.1.1.0003

Turner, C.S.V., & González, J. C. (Eds.). (2014). *Modeling mentoring across race/ethnicity and gender: Practices to cultivate the next generation of diverse faculty.* Stylus Publishing.

Turner, C.S.V., González, J. C., & Wong (Lau), K. (2011). Faculty women of color: The critical nexus of race and gender. *Journal of Diversity in Higher Education, 4*(4), 199–211. https://doi.org/10.1037/a0024630

Zambrana, R. E. (2018). *Toxic ivory towers: The consequences of work stress on underrepresented minority faculty.* Rutgers University Press.

PREFACE

To be Black, Indigenous, and People of Color (BIPOC) in the academy is an exercise in grace, strength, and innovation. On an everyday basis, we embody unbelonging while simultaneously being conditioned to seek a sense of belonging in a place that was never meant for us. Our existence as BIPOC faculty is lauded in theory but met with perpetual disdain in practice by the institutions we have infiltrated and exacerbated by the first-generation student identities that shape the survival strategies that have enabled us to persist. This book is a collective *testimonio* of what it means to be first-generation faculty of color, a distinct and complex position experienced by many but rarely ever documented.

Our decision to write this book is an effort to document first-generation faculty of color stories. As critical race theorists, we believe in the power of storytelling to illustrate that faculty of color are not a monolith and how we can experience shared spaces—in this case, the academy—very differently. Writing our stories is an attempt to validate the experiential knowledge and intuition of first-generation faculty of color in the academic diaspora and who are likely away from the families and communities that feed and nurture us. Stories reveal that our isolation within programs and departments, colleges and universities, and academic fields are shared, systemic, and symptomatic of the unforgiving white supremacy that is American higher education. Stories are also what facilitate connection among us when we need community.

Our stories are not our own. Rather, they belong to an extensive community of family, friends, mentors, and students. Together and over generations, we passed down stories as a primary means for survival. As tenured faculty, we believe that storytelling is mentorship, in that it is an accessible and familiar practice to learn and impart lessons critical to thriving in hostile institutions. We are the beneficiaries of such lessons from our mentors, the first generation of first-generation faculty of color, who imagined and laid the foundation for our networks. They sacrificed their own personal and professional lives, and in doing so, gave us permission to live and work differently. If there is one lesson we hope to convey through this collection, it is for emerging scholars of color to give themselves permission to also do things differently. We carry the wounds of intergenerational trauma and as minoritized faculty were modeled (often unhealthy) coping mechanisms by our elders, who navigated their lives under severely different conditions. Learning lessons necessitate breaking ways of being that no longer serve us.

The need for first-generation faculty of color to adapt lessons learned is grounded in the reality that conditions change. The final writing stages of *First-Generation Faculty of Color* happened amid the global COVID-19 pandemic, the Movement for Black Lives, the Mauna Kea movement, and heightened occurrences and awareness of everyday and extrajudicial anti-immigrant and anti-Asian violence. We also witnessed an insurrection at the U.S. Capitol and the U.S. withdrawal from Afghanistan. These are not just social and political events; combined, these are the conditions that broke open the structural fissures of higher education caused by neoliberal divestment, and shape first-generation faculty of color lives.

The first-generation faculty of color who contributed to this collection are, in many ways, first responders to the cumulative crises of contemporary society. We do not use this metaphor lightly and assert our approach to research, teaching, and service are life-affirming, life-changing, and lifesaving for the students, colleagues, and communities we serve both on- and off-campus. Enforced campus closures shut down and decimated support for community-engaged research projects, conference participation, and research sabbaticals, resulting in delayed tenure and promotion timelines for some of us. Like all educators, we pivoted to online instruction, redesigned curriculum and pedagogy, and sometimes dropped all class plans to hold space in the form of weekly support groups for students who relied on the virtual gatherings for a sense of community—a privilege not afforded to our contingent faculty counterparts, many of whom lost employment. We became impromptu social service providers, mutual aid organizers, and campus and community advocates to push for people-first institutional responses to the housing, food, and financial insecurity the pandemic worsened. A few of us, prior to the opportunity to become vaccinated, found ourselves infected with COVID-19 and in several instances, we broke. And all the while, we did this on top of providing material, emotional, and caregiving support to our children and elders, among the most susceptible to becoming sick.

Together and through our stories, we demand that the academy honor the totality of our humanity and recognize first-generation faculty of color as wellsprings of strength and support. We do not argue that our stresses and suffering are exceptional, but we do know that as minoritized faculty, we are disproportionately impacted. This knowledge informs our abject refusal to carry out the business-as-usual approach to research, teaching, and service imposed upon us by the neoliberal university. We did not sign up for this shit. However, what we did sign up for is the opportunity to share other ways of knowing and being such that we collectively participate and achieve local and large-scale wins toward the necessary transformation of American higher education. We hope our stories compel you to join us.

Tracy Lachica Buenavista, Dimpal Jain, and María C. Ledesma

First-Generation Faculty of Color

Introduction

Toward a First-Generation Faculty Epistemology

MARÍA C. LEDESMA

Our lessons as first-generation faculty of color are learned prior to even entering the professoriate. As a doctoral student, I had the unique opportunity to serve as the thirty-second student regent for the University of California (UC), the first Chicana/Latina to hold this post. During my two-year stint as student regent, I visited each UC campus at least twice. These trips included informal visits to acquaint myself with each institution and its specific issues and constituencies as well as more formal visits, such as serving on chancellor search committees and/or participating in other university business. During one of these trips I found myself at UC Merced, the newest of the UC campuses. At the time, the school had enrolled only a portion of their undergraduate student body. As they prepared to expand enrollment and to officially install their new chancellor, I toured the grounds with my fellow student regent.

We walked across the manicured lawns visiting all manner of offices and facilities. At one point we were escorted to the student success center, which housed, among other things, the student counseling services office. Here, we listened as a young white male counselor described the challenges of servicing the school's predominantly first-generation Mexican American and Chicana/o/x undergraduate student body, which hailed primarily from Central California. Rather than explain how the school had tailored their services to support their unique audience, the counselor lamented that not only was their office understaffed and stretched beyond capacity, they also had to spend a lot of time teaching basic skills, including time management and study strategies. He added that counselors also had to convince students that it was not necessary for them to go home every weekend, as so many of them were wont to do. As I listened to the counselor speak, I could not help but think, "He's talking about me!" Never mind that I was a dissertating doctoral student on the cusp of finishing my degree; I still confronted many of the same challenges and insecurities as

1

my undergraduate peers. It was then that I had an epiphany—I would never stop being "first-generation." In that moment, I understood I would move along a continuum, transitioning from one experience to another, but all the while remaining first-generation. For instance, while I was once a first-generation undergraduate, I was now a first-generation doctoral student, and upon gradua-tion I would enter the professoriate as a first-generation pre-tenure faculty. I now write these ruminations as a first-generation tenured professor. But my realiza-tion on that day remains true; I will always be first generation.

In this volume, we explore the under-examined phenomenon of "first generation-ness" and center the lives of "first-generation faculty." First-generation faculty are academicians who were first-generation college students and went on to pursue faculty careers. In so doing, we also expand the discourse of fac-ulty diversity to better consider how education generational status differently shapes how some faculty of color experience academia. Such an examination is important considering the confluence of pending faculty retirements coupled with the marginal but steady growth of historically minoritized doctoral recipi-ents seeking to enter the professoriate (Griffin, 2020). This book provides a timely backdrop to understand contemporary notions of faculty diversity and how insti-tutions can better recruit, retain, socialize, and honor the labor and experiences of faculty who were once themselves first-generation college students.

Some of the questions that guide this book project include, "Does first-generation identity change or recede for historically minoritized students as they move along the higher education pipeline?" "How does first-generation iden-tity shape and frame postbaccalaureate study and professional preparation, especially for those who decide to pursue careers in academe?" And, "How does the 'first generation-ness' of aspiring academicians of color influence their research, teaching, and service experience across various ranks?" As the national discussion around the status and condition of first-generation college students grows, we posit that less attention has been focused on understanding and ana-lyzing the experiences of faculty, who were once themselves first-generation col-lege students. Our hope is that this project builds upon existing conversations and contributes to the development of a first-generation faculty epistemology.

Defining First-Generation

The definition of the term "first-generation" can be deceptively complicated. As Nguyen and Nguyen (2018) observe, numerous critiques abound regarding the broad application of the term first-generation (college) student. Case in point, an institution's percentage of first-generation students can vary drastically depending on how "first-generation" is defined (Nguyen & Nguyen, 2018; Toutk-oushian et al., 2018). Definitions include neither parent having *enrolled* in col-lege (Choy, 2001; Núñez & Cuccaro-Alamin, 1998) or neither parent having *earned* a bachelor's degree (Pike & Kuh, 2005). Furthermore, some posit that generational status depends on whether one or both parents/guardians have *graduated* from a four-year institution (Spiegler & Bednarek, 2013). Contemporary first-generation college student discourse is also U.S.-centric and does not adequately address the issues of "1.5-generation college students," whose parent(s) earned a college degree outside of the United States (Buenavista, 2009, 2013). Precisely because of the fluidity of the definition, what is most consistent within existing scholarship on first-generation students is the inconsistent manner in which "first-generation" is defined and applied. These complexities are magnified when we acknowledge the impossibility of disentangling one's generational status from other social markers, such as class, gender, racial and/or ethnic identity, and citizenship status. For the purpose of this project, we adopt the National Center for Education Statistics' (2020) definition of first-generation student, which describes "first-generation college students as those who are the first in their family to attend college [in the United States]." We also acknowledge the fact that there is no singular, monolithic first-generation experience.

Whatever the definition, with respect to higher education, researchers have long focused their lens on examining the experiences of first-generation undergraduates (Núñez & Cuccaro-Alamin, 1998; Pascarella et al., 2004). This makes intuitive sense, after all, undergraduate study serves as an entry point into most academic and professional pathways. More recently, scholars have also investigated how first-generation graduate students experience graduate study (Holley & Gardner, 2012; Lunceford, 2011). However, as Bechard and Gragg (2020) make clear, much less is known about the manner in which first-generation faculty prepare for and experience faculty life.

Indeed, extant literature on the impact of first-generation status on educational and professional trajectories has focused almost exclusively on the student experience, while generational status as related to the faculty experience has been only marginally addressed. The presumption appears to be that generational status fades into the background as one achieves degree attainment. However, as the contributors of this volume make clear, nothing could be farther from the truth. The experience of being first-generation remains a central and salient identity marker for academicians, especially for Black, Indigenous, People of Color (BIPOC) faculty. It was precisely the lack of attention to the experiences of first-generation faculty of color that inspired the production of this volume.

Whereas scholars have advocated for the need to understand how race, class, gender, sexual orientation, and/or immigration status may complicate dominant faculty-of-color narratives (Gutiérrez y Muhs et al., 2012; Niemann et al., 2020; Turner et al., 2008), the primary objective here is to contribute to existing dialogues concerned with increasing faculty diversity within higher education with special attention to education generational status. This project highlights the experiences of "first-generation faculty of color," or minoritized individuals who were first-generation college students and went on to pursue faculty careers. Collectively, the book contributors confirm that regardless of degree attainment, a first-generation college student's background uniquely shapes how faculty of color experience and navigate academia.

Historically, higher education's relationship with faculty of color has been fraught and complicated (Hartlep & Ball, 2020; Stanley, 2006; Zambrana, 2018). Existing scholarship teaches us that while faculty of color often experience social and political isolation, greater teaching and service obligations, less support and financial resources, racial tokenization within the university, overt discrimination, and overall devaluation within various academic contexts (Delgado Bernal & Villalpando, 2002; Turner, 2002; Turner et al., 2008), faculty of color also play important roles in higher education, including demonstration of innovative classroom pedagogies; the diversification of research agendas, methodologies, and perspectives; valuable mentorship for underrepresented students; and enhanced relationships with communities beyond institutional boundaries (Turner et al., 2008). However, within broader postsecondary narratives, faculty of color are often treated homogeneously.

For these reasons, we embarked on investigating the salience of first-generation status on the experiences of BIPOC faculty; including understanding how first-generation identity informs and shapes research, teaching, and service experiences. Just as the national discourse around the status and condition of first-generation college students gains traction (Chronicle of Higher Education Focus Collection Magazine, 2017), we posit that more attention must be focused on understanding and analyzing the experiences of faculty, who were once themselves first-generation college students. To undertake this task, this volume presents the firsthand accounts of faculty of color, at various ranks, most within the discipline of Education, who speak to the realities of being first-generation faculty.

As this book project has unfolded, it has been curious to see and hear from other first-generation BIPOC faculty who found affirmation in the fact that their experiences were finally being recognized and validated. Whether in early conference presentations or in response to the call for chapters, it has been intriguing to see others come into consciousness about the significance of generational status in shaping opportunity. In this way, beyond a scholarly contribution, this book embodies a community of scholars that institutions of higher education historically excluded, and the ways in which we contend with this reality.

First-Generation Faculty

As reported by the Postsecondary National Policy Institute (2020), according to the National Center for Education Statistics, for the 2015–2016 academic year, 35 percent of undergraduates were the first in their families to go to college. Scholarship examining students' advancement through the educational pipeline suggests that only a small percentage of these undergraduates enroll in graduate study and fewer still go on to ultimately earn a terminal degree; this is especially true for historically minoritized students of color (Pérez Huber et al., 2015). The National Science Foundation's Survey of Earned Doctorates report (2019) describes that between 1994 and 2019, first-generation doctoral recipients have consistently represented a better part of doctoral degree earners. In concert, these data suggest that first-generation graduates constitute a significant portion of the postsecondary population—including representing a rich pool of prospective faculty. As such, it is stunning that not more has been written or said about the experiences of faculty who identify as first-generation.

While research has begun to emerge that centers on the under-addressed topic of first-generation faculty (Bechard & Gragg, 2020), "first-generation faculty" is a concept that the editors of this volume began to theorize some years ago. We define first-generation faculty as academicians who enter the professoriate after having earned their baccalaureate and post-baccalaureate degrees as first-generation students. At the American Educational Research Association 2016 annual meeting, we presented our work as a symposium. We delivered our session, "'First-Generation' Faculty of Color in Higher Education: Voicing Silenced Narratives in Academe," before a standing-room-only crowd and showcased BIPOC faculty who were first-generation college graduates and professors at various ranks in the field of Education. Panelists presented papers on how their first-generation college student experiences continued to shape and frame their lives as academicians. Discussion generated from the conference session, and subsequent projects, helped confirm the need for a framework for understanding and working to better support first-generation faculty of color in higher education. This latter point is especially important; while postsecondary institutions have begun to do a better job of recognizing the presence of first-generation faculty on their campuses, these relationships too often remain transactional. That is, rather than providing tailored support services for their first-generation faculty, institutions instead add to first-generation faculty's workload by recruiting them to mentor first-generation students and/or helm first-generation initiatives (Young, 2016).

Our hope is that our work encourages institutional leaders, policymakers, and practitioners to dedicate time and resources to providing dedicated services to support the recruitment, retention, and promotion of first-generation faculty. Therefore, collected herein are the stories of first-generation academicians who reflect on their path into the professoriate and how their journeys have been shaped as historically minoritized faculty who identify as first-generation.

First-Generation Faculty Voices: Critical Race Theory, LatCrit, and *Testimonio*

In the tradition of critical race theory and Latina/o critical race theory (LatCrit), contributing authors to this volume utilize counter-storytelling (Solorzano & Yosso, 2002) to offer nuanced narratives documenting the unique experiences of historically minoritized faculty, who are also first-generation. Critical race theorists explain that the lives of people of color are shaped by intersecting realities and oppressions (Crenshaw, 1991).

Borrowing from the tradition of critical race theory, most contributors construct their first-generation faculty narratives using critical race autoethnography and *testimonios* to center the experiential knowledge of oft-marginalized people and contextualize larger issues of erasure, contrast, and (in)equity in academia. Indeed, a vast majority of the authors rely on the practice of *testimonios* (Delgado Bernal et al., 2012) to expound upon the too often overlooked and under-addressed experiences of minoritized scholars as they navigate the complexities of faculty life, including negotiating job offers, balancing advising and teaching responsibilities, juggling multiple realities, and crafting a scholar identity, all while attempting to retain and honor their authentic selves. As Delgado-Bernal and colleagues (2012) describe, "Within the field of education, scholars are increasingly taking up *testimonio* as a pedagogical, methodological, and activist approach to social justice that transgresses traditional paradigms in academia" (p. 363). By bridging collective histories of oppression, *testimonios* from first-generation faculty provide an opportunity to (re)center the role of generational status in shaping BIPOC faculty experiences as they prepare for, enter, and attempt to survive within the professoriate.

The resonance of *testimonio* as "product and process" extends beyond the task of helping give voice to those historically silenced or shuttered from mainstream narratives. Delgado Bernal and colleagues (2012) explain how, in some cases, as with this project, *testimonios* help uncover how "group marginalization continues to exist in academia even when one holds a relatively privileged status" (p. 366). This helps explain how and why BIPOC faculty across tenure ranks and across different institutions find themselves existing within competing dualities. On the one hand, first-generation faculty are perceived to have "made it" as salaried professionals, while on another hand they exist in liminal spaces as perceived outgroups or guests in someone else's house (Turner, 1994). And while *testimonios* often shine light on stories of struggle, they also serve as tales of transformational resistance, "talking back, and surviving in academia" (Delgado Bernal et al., 2012, p. 366) as first-generation faculty.

These counter-narratives serve multiple purposes. Not only do they offer catharsis for their authors, they also present testimonials that challenge preconceived notions of what it feels like to function as a first-generation BIPOC scholar within historically white-serving institutions. Citing Delgado (1989) on the importance and urgency of critical race counter-stories, Solorzano and Yosso (2002) make clear that "oppressed groups have known instinctively that stories are an essential tool to their own survival and liberation" (p. 156). As such, these *testimonios* serve the function of not only helping first-generation faculty (re) claim space and voice in academia; they also help others find validation in their struggle and experiences. As Delgado (1989) explains, telling stories is essential for "outgroups" and "groups whose marginality defines the boundaries of the mainstream, whose voice and perspective—whose consciousness—has been suppressed, devalued and abnormalized" (p. 2412). First-generation faculty of color are too often obscured and/or subsumed under a generic "faculty of color" experience. However, as our contributing authors lay forth, generational status matters.

Research, Teaching, and Service

We present this book in three sections—"Research," "Teaching," and "Service"— which represent the three pillars typically ascribed to the faculty profession. Within each section, authors reflect on how being a first-generation faculty member shapes and frames their approaches to their professional duties, which vary depending on their institutional affiliation. For example, for faculty employed at Research 1 institutions, research is by and large more highly valued than teaching and service. By contrast, faculty employed at comprehensive institutions must demonstrate superb classroom pedagogies alongside research and service prowess. Meanwhile, faculty employed at community colleges are subject to the highest teaching and advising loads with the least amount of resources. In most cases, it is still true that historically minoritized faculty, including BIPOC first-generation faculty, experience severe service imbalances. They are often pulled into inordinate amounts of service due to both formal and informal service expectations (Antonio et al., 2000). For first-generation BIPOC faculty, these tensions are especially salient, as they must navigate not only race, class, and gender norms but also the norms around educational generation status, which remain part of the hidden curriculum of faculty socialization.

Research

Within the tripartite of faculty duties that includes research, teaching, and service, it is often research that gets the most attention, the most rewards, and puts the most pressure on new and seasoned faculty to demonstrate their productivity, merit, and material worth to their institution (Griffin et al., 2013). Many faculty of color experience delegitimization and undervaluation for their research due to antiquated modes of evaluation within historically white institutions (Turner et al., 2008). It is the research or scholarly contribution section that frequently gets the most scrutinized when awarding promotion and tenure and has resulted in many faculty of color being pushed out of the academy (Delgado Bernal & Villalpando, 2002). The saying "publish or perish" is so embedded within tenure folklore, we have come to accept that if we do not adhere to an institution's often vague and biased standards, we are expendable and subject to expulsion from the faculty ranks (Miller et al., 2011).

In this section, the authors challenge how we traditionally define research and the need for further exploration into commonly accepted elements of faculty life. Across all five chapters is a call to look beneath the surface as it relates to knowledge production. This includes centering the multiple methodologies, honoring the sanctity of community, and understanding the impact that research has on the sense of self and belonging within and outside the academy.

Authors in this section address key parts of the hidden curriculum of faculty socialization by delving into topics such as exploring the actual academic job search process; scrutinizing the increase of neoliberalism, consumerism, competitive individualism, and surveillance as driving forces in academia; and addressing the lingering critique and devaluation of nontraditional/nonnormative methods and frameworks traditionally employed by BIPOC faculty. Mirroring lessons shared by our contributing authors, we—as editors—adopt an anti-neoliberal stance to research by choosing to list our names in alphabetical order. We reject the notion of competitive individualism, recognizing the equal and shared labor contributed by all three parties in the production of this volume. And while research tends to dominate and overshadow all other requisite faculty duties, teaching experiences are imperative, especially for first-generation BIPOC faculty at comprehensive universities and community colleges.

Teaching

At the heart of first-generation faculty of color experiences is the tension of the classroom serving as a space of both violence and solace. Whereas the curricular content and pedagogies employed by educators of color are noted as important classroom interventions, they are simultaneously weaponized against faculty by students and colleagues alike. Across four chapters in the "Teaching" section of this volume, first-generation faculty of color collectively depict this dichotomy and, in doing so, also expansively conceptualize notions of teaching. Within each chapter, faculty describe how the lessons they learned from their experiences as minoritized students necessarily shape the art of teaching within and outside of the formal classroom. A key contribution of the chapters is a first-generation faculty of color pedagogy that attempts to humanize education, and to blur the line—for students and colleagues alike—between their communities and the institutions in which they are employed.

Institutions of higher education often rely on BIPOC faculty to diversify the curriculum of academic units. They are also known to introduce and utilize culturally responsive techniques to engage an increasingly diverse student body. Faculty of color emphasize—in content and pedagogy—high value on preparing students to participate in a "multicultural democracy" (Hurtado & Alvarado, 2013; Hurtado et al., 2012). Attempts to make classrooms more inclusive expand the discourse of various fields, as well as provide academic validation for minoritized students. Along these lines, authors theorize how first-generation faculty of color necessarily create transformative counterspaces for first-generation students of color to not only survive but thrive. Through their *testimonios*, faculty discuss the need to foster racially conscious spaces, found in such places as racial student organizations and ethnic studies courses, and even in office hours, which can serve as transformational sites. These in turn have the capacity to develop as ecosystems of support centered on student and faculty of color retention. Authors also center and question the disparate treatment of faculty of color, particularly women faculty of color, who still bear the brunt of racist and misogynistic hostilities in the context of teaching. By exposing how the academy continues to disfavor nontraditional voices, particularly those of men of color affected by carcerality, we are reminded of the limitations of teaching evaluation instruments in capturing the richness of the first-generation faculty of color experience. The limitations of standardized white assessment metrics when applied to BIPOC first-generation faculty experiences are further explored by authors' reflections on service.

Service

Literature reveals that historically underrepresented faculty, including first-generation BIPOC faculty, are too often overburdened with formal and informal service obligations (Antonio et al., 2000; Duncan, 2014). The struggle to balance research, teaching, and service expectations is amplified by a combination of factors, including acclimating to often obscure institutional norms and expectations, and negotiating commitments to community, that while laborious, also fuel persistence. Coupled with inhospitable at best, and toxic at worst, campus climates that continue to privilege normative notions of academia, BIPOC first-generation faculty recount their experiences with service.

Contributing authors present four papers that shine light on both traditional understandings of university service requirements, as well as introduce nuanced ways in which service expectations are experienced by first-generation faculty of color. Across all four chapters, authors posit that in order to understand service, we must first understand how university service manifests as a complex entanglement of intersecting identities (race/ethnicity, class, gender, etc.), and commitments to community reciprocity. At the center of this web is understanding the realities of first-generation academicians as literal and figurative bridges between disparate worlds and socioeconomic classes.

As our authors attest, first-generation faculty carry multiple obligations beyond striving for tenure. This includes helping both immediate and extended family remain financially solvent, while at the same time negotiating the still majoritarian culture of academia, which remains mostly blind to their unique needs and experiences. Among their contributions, authors call for postsecondary institutions to adopt critical epistemologies, pedagogies, and practices that complicate and theorize the presence of first-generation faculty in their ranks.

In addition to the formally recognized triad of research, teaching, and service, for BIPOC first-generation faculty, commitment to family and community reciprocity serves as a palpable, if unaccounted for, fourth pillar of faculty life. Indeed, all authors identify family and community as key forces that help motivate their persistence within higher education. In fact, in many cases, BIPOC first-generation faculty endure the enclosure of higher education, not for themselves, but for the benefit and advancement of their kin networks, biological or otherwise. First-generation academicians (re)claim these spaces for all those who remain outcasts, either by choice or by decree.

Indeed, the cover art of our volume is meant to evoke the generations' long collective struggle of BIPOC first-generation faculty shattering the literal and proverbial walls of academia to grant access to others aspiring to enter its ranks. This cover art honors our academic elders while also recognizing the enduring challenge to (re)claim space and belongingness within the academy for those too often erased or ignored within sanctioned postsecondary spaces.

Conclusion

Over the course of the time that it has taken to bring this volume to press, increasing civil unrest has been a constant backdrop. Indeed, this project is bookended by two diametrically opposed events. The first event is the murder of Michael Brown, whose death at the hands of a white Ferguson, Missouri law enforcement officer on August 4, 2014, launched a national response against the long-standing history of police violence against BIPOC people, especially Black men and women. Brown's death, coupled with innumerable state-sanctioned killings of BIPOC people—which peaked again with the murder of George Floyd on May 26, 2020—ushered in the Black Lives Matter (BLM) movement, which took root across postsecondary campuses, nationally and internationally. The second event occurred on January 6, 2021, when thousands of white nationalists from across the nation descended on the U.S. Capitol to interrupt the Joint Session of Congress's formal certification of the election of Joseph Biden as forty-sixth president of the United States. These events, as well as the militarized responses in their wake, or lack thereof, served as palpable reminders of the deep roots of racism and white supremacy that still frame and shape institutional systems and cultures, including postsecondary education, from which the professoriate is not exempt.

In fact, on the heels of the Ferguson uprising and the rise of the BLM movement, calls for increased diversity—and specifically—increased BIPOC faculty representation have been constant. Griffin (2020) observes that as colleges and universities became sites of protest against systemic and structural racism on campuses, students zeroed in on demanding that postsecondary institutions diversify their faculty ranks. Since that time, institutions have responded with renewed focus on supporting faculty of color, including hiring chief diversity officers and implementing cluster hires. These are helpful but insufficient strategies. The demand for faculty diversity is complicated. And as our contributors have laid forth, there is no one generic BIPOC faculty pathway or experience. First-generation-ness matters. Therefore, as postsecondary institutions continue to work toward the future, they would do well to recognize how first-generation academicians experience academia and not collapse all BIPOC faculty into a singular monolithic experience. As our contributing authors have laid forth, along the first-generation continuum, first-generation academicians need guidance, support, and socialization at each stage of their professional journeys.

All postsecondary institutions, irrespective of institutional type, should be invested in understanding and addressing the unique experiences and needs of first-generation BIPOC faculty. Looming faculty retirements coupled with a steady and increasing college-going rates for historically minoritized students, should signal a convergence of interests for institutions to invest in understanding a first-generation faculty epistemology. However, beyond such transactional realities, as detailed by our authors, postsecondary institutions should seek to know more about first-generation BIPOC faculty because appreciating the richness of a first-generation faculty epistemology necessitates understanding the holistic first-generation experience. Our hope is that this book contributes to this conversation.

REFERENCES

Antonio, A. L., Astin, H. S., & Cress, C. M. (2000). Community service in higher education: A look at the nation's faculty. *Review of Higher Education, 23*(4), 373–397. 10.1353/rhe.2000.0015

Bechard, A., & Gragg, J. B. (2020). Microaggressions and the marginalization of first-generation faculty: Professional assimilation and competency development. *Taboo: The Journal of Culture and Education, 19*(4), 140–148. https://digitalscholarship.unlv.edu/taboo/vol19/iss4/8

Buenavista, T. L. (2009, December). Examining the postsecondary experiences of Pilipino 1.5-generation college students. *Association for the Study of Higher Education / Lumina Policy Briefs and Critical Essays No. 8.* Iowa State University, Department of Educational Leadership and Policy Studies.

Buenavista, T. L. (2013). Pilipinos in the middle: Higher education and a sociocultural context of contradictions. In D. Maramba & R. Bonus (Eds.). *The "other" students: Filipino Americans, education and power* (pp. 259–275). Information Age Publishing.

Choy, S. (2001). *Students whose parents did not go to college: Postsecondary access, persistence, and attainment.* National Center for Education Statistics.

Chronicle of Higher Education Focus Collection Magazine. (2017). *How to help first-generation students succeed*. The Chronicle of Higher Education.

Crenshaw, K. (1991). Mapping the margins: Intersectionality, identity politics, and violence against Women of Color. *Stanford Law Review, 43*(6), 1241–1299. https://doi.org/10.2307/1229039

Delgado, R. (1989). Storytelling for oppositionists and others: A plea for narrative legal storytelling. *Michigan Law Review, 87*(8), 2411–2441. https://doi.org/10.2307/1289308

Delgado Bernal, D. (1998). Using a Chicana feminist epistemology in educational research. *Harvard Educational Review, 68*(4), 555–582. doi:10.17763/HAER.68.4.5WV1034973G22Q48

Delgado Bernal, D., Burciaga, R., & Flores Carmona, J. (2012). Chicana/Latina *testimonios*: Mapping the methodological, pedagogical, and political. *Equity & Excellence in Education, 45*(3), 363–372. doi:10.1080/10665684.2012.698149

Delgado Bernal, D., & Villalpando, O. (2002). An apartheid of knowledge in academia: The struggle over the "legitimate" knowledge of faculty of color. *Equity & Excellence in Education, 35*(2), 169–180.

Duncan, P. (2014). Hot commodities, cheap labor: Women of color in the academy. *Frontiers: A Journal of Women Studies, 35*(3), 39–63. https://doi.org/10.5250/fronjwomestud.35.3.0039

Griffin, K. A. (2020). Institutional barriers, strategies, and benefits to increasing the representation of women and men of color in the professoriate: Looking beyond the pipeline. In L. W. Perna (Ed.), *Higher education: Handbook of theory and research* (pp. 277–349). Springer.

Griffin, K. A., Bennett, J., & Harris, J. (2013). Marginalizing merit: Gender differences in Black faculty discourse on tenure, advancement, and professional success. *Review of Higher Education, 36*(4), 489–512. 10.1353/rhe.2013.0040

Gutiérrez y Muhs, G., Niemann, Y. F., González, C. G., & Harris, A. P. (Eds.). (2012). *Presumed incompetent: The intersections of race and class for women in academia*. Utah State University Press.

Hartlep, N. D. & Ball, D. (Eds.) (2020). *Racial battle fatigue in faculty: Perspectives and lessons from higher education*. Routledge.

Holley, K. A., & Gardner, S. (2012). Navigating the pipeline: How socio-cultural influences impact first-generation doctoral students. *Journal of Diversity in Higher Education, 5*(2), 112–121. doi:10.1037/a0026840

Hurtado, S., & Alvarado, A. R. (2013). Diversity in teaching and learning: Affirming students as empowered learners. *Diversity & Democracy, 16*(3). https://www.aacu.org/publications-research/periodicals/diversity-teaching-and-learning-affirming-students-empowered

Hurtado, S., Eagan, M. K., Pryor, J. H., Whang, H., & Tran, S. (2012). *Undergraduate teaching faculty: The 2010–11 HERI faculty survey*. Higher Education Research Institute. http://www.heri.ucla.edu/facPublications.php

Lunceford, B. (2011). When first-generation students go to graduate school. *New Directions for Teaching and Learning, 2011*(127), 13–20. doi:10.1002/TL.453

Miller, A. N., Taylor, S. G., & Bedeian, A. G. (2011). Publish or perish: Academic life as management faculty live it. *Career Development International, 16*(5), 422–445. doi:10.1108/13620431111167751

National Center for Science and Engineering Statistics (NCSES). (2020). *Doctorate recipients from U.S. universities*. Table 34. https://ncses.nsf.gov/pubs/nsf21308/data-tables

Nguyen, T., & Nguyen, B. (2018). Is the "FG student" term useful for understanding inequality? The role of intersectionality in illuminating the implications of an accepted—yet unchallenged—term. *Review of Research in Education, 42*, 146–176.

Niemann, Y. F., Gutiérrez y Muhs, G., González, C. G., & Harris, A. P. (Eds.). (2020). *Presumed incompetent II: Race, class, power, and resistance of women in academia.* Utah State University Press.

Núñez, A., & Cuccaro-Alamin, S. (1998). *First-generation students: Undergraduates whose parents never enrolled in postsecondary education.* U.S. Department of Education, Office of Educational Research and Improvement, National Center for Education Statistics.

Pascarella, E. T., Pierson, C. T., Wolniak, G. C., & Terenzini, P. T. (2004). First-generation college students: Additional evidence on college experiences and outcomes. *Journal of Higher Education, 75*(3), 249–284. doi:10.1353/jhe.2004.0016

Pérez Huber, L., Malagón, M. C., Ramirez, B. R., Gonzalez, L. C., Jimenez, A., & Vélez, V. (2015). *Still falling through the cracks: Revisiting the Latina/o education pipeline.* UCLA Chicano Studies Research Center Research Report, No. 19. https://files.eric.ed.gov/fulltext/ED 574691.pdf

Pike, G. R., & Kuh, G. D. (2005). First—and second-generation college students: A comparison of their engagement and intellectual development. *Journal of Higher Education, 76*(3), 276–300. https://www.jstor.org/stable/3838799

Postsecondary National Policy Institute. (2020). *First-generation students in higher education factsheets.* https://pnpi.org/first-generation-students/

Solorzano, D. G., & Yosso, T. J. (2002). A critical race counterstory of race, racism, and affirmative action. *Equity & Excellence in Education, 35*(2), 155–168. https://doi.org/10.1080 /713845284

Spiegler, T., & Bednarek, A. (2013). First-generation students: What we ask, what we know and what it means: An international review of the state of research. *International Studies in Sociology of Education, 23*(4), 318–337. https://doi.org/10.1080/09620214.2013.815441

Stanley, C. A. (2006). *Faculty of color: Teaching in predominantly white colleges and universities.* Jossey-Bass.

Toutkoushian, R., Stollberg, R., & Slaton, K. (2018). Talking 'bout my generation: Defining "first-generation college students" in higher education research. *Teachers College Record, 120*(4), 1–38.

Turner, C. S. (1994, Summer). A guest in someone else's house: Students of color on campus. *Review of Higher Education, 17*(4), 355–370.

Turner, C. S. (2002). Women of color in academe: Living with multiple marginality. *Journal of Higher Education, 73*(1), 74–93. https://doi.org/10.1080/00221546.2002.11777131

Turner, C.S.V., González, J. C., & Wood, J. L. (2008). Faculty of color in academe: What 20 years of literature tells us. *Journal of Diversity in Higher Education, 1*(3), 139–168. https://doi .org/10.1037/a0012837

Young, M. S. (2016, May 6). Navigating campus together: First-generation faculty can steer first-generation college students toward success. *The Atlantic.* https://www.theatlantic .com/education/archive/2016/05/how-first-generation-faculty-can-help-first-generation -students-succeed/481617/

Zambrana, R. E. (2018). *Toxic ivory towers: The consequences of work stress on underrepresented minority faculty.* Rutgers University Press.

PART ONE

Research

Research with Community, Not on Community. Credit: Alberto Ledesma.

1

Food on the Table

The Hidden Curriculum of the Academic Job Market

DIMPAL JAIN

I've heard stories about my dad's father being a teacher, but it was always in bits and pieces. I knew my mother's father worked for the railway, but parents in the neighborhood would send their kids to him after school for tutoring and academic discipline. My dad's family donated money in my grandfather's name posthumously to a local teaching school in Punjab. We have pictures of a plaque that lists his name on a wall in the school. I know that my dad gave money toward this even when he was struggling financially, and it brought him pride that my grandfather's name would be a permanent fixture in a college, even if my dad never attained a formal college degree himself. Both my parents tell me how proud their parents would be that one of their grandchildren went into the field of education.

I am the first in my family on both sides—across countries and continents—that has earned a PhD. We have other professionals in our extended South Asian family, which includes lawyers, medical doctors, and engineers, but I am the only one with a PhD, the highest educational degree one can earn. My immediate family has mixed educational outcomes, which include one sibling with a master's degree, another with a baccalaureate degree, and one who stopped out of college. We are all first-generation college students. My degree has brought a lot of pressure as well as some skepticism from my family. I recall my uncle asking incredulously how I got into a PhD program? I responded facetiously that it was because I had worn a short skirt to the interview (my mom shot daggers through her eyes at me after that response). Later, when I graduated, that same uncle asked to see my official diploma because he didn't believe that I finished because of my parents' educational status—I was ordered to produce the original hard copy on the spot.

My postsecondary journey as a first-generation college student was always tumultuous, but I succeeded due to peer mentoring, student organizing, and my

17

family's community cultural wealth (Yosso, 2005). What I wasn't prepared for was that the same challenges I experienced as a first-generation college student would extend into my journey through graduate school and the professoriate. Through an autoethnographic method, I explore my journey while on the academic job market, something I was unprepared for as a first-generation doctoral student and early career faculty member. In particular, I pay close attention to the research centered on the experiences of first-generation graduate school students and the hidden curriculum of the academic job market, which includes the job search and selection process. I share how my family and other first-generation academics of color assisted me with the process as I initially approached the academic market and then later as I relocated for a second position as pre-tenure faculty.

First-Generation Graduate Students
and the Hidden Curriculum

Similar to other authors in this book, I subscribe to the definition that a first-generation student is a student whose parent or guardian did not attain a bachelor's degree. The most recent figure from 2015 to 2016 states that over half (56 percent) of undergraduates in the United States identify as first-generation (Center for First-Generation Student Success, 2019). In 2018, 29 percent of doctoral students were first generation (National Science Foundation, 2018). Although first-generation students are not a monolithic group, they do share some traits, experiences, and patterns of enrollment in higher education. When compared to their continuing-generation peers, first-generation undergraduates are more likely to enroll in community colleges, attend college part-time, have dependents, and take out more loans than their peers (Postsecondary National Policy Institute, 2021). They also often identify with the "nontraditional" student community, which includes older returning students, transfer students, foster students, financially independent students, and students with dependents. Last, many, but not all, first-generation students also identify as students of color and come from low-income backgrounds. Yet, much of the first-generation literature focuses on the experiences of undergraduate students, as if students cease to continue to be first-generation as they enter graduate school. As the focus of this chapter is my journey as a first-generation graduate student to a first-generation professor, it is important to examine the limited literature on first-generation graduate student experiences.

Lunceford (2011) offers advice for faculty mentors who are advising first-generation students on the search, application, and preparation process for graduate school. As a first-generation professor himself, he draws from his past experiences of being underprepared and uninformed as he pursued his master's and doctoral degrees. Lunceford offers guidance that is tailored to the first-generation student's graduate school choice process, such as the need to stay close to home, the burden of working while attending school, and how to better connect with faculty outside of the classroom. He cautions faculty that just because they are interacting with graduate students it does not mean that students understand the discipline or how graduate education works.

Gardner and Holley (2011) add to the small but growing body of scholarship that explores the experiences of first-generation graduate students (Roksa et al., 2018; Vasil & McCall, 2017). They interviewed twenty graduate students at two top-tier research universities and explored how they negotiated the graduate school pipeline and their overall satisfaction as a first-generation doctoral student. They found that several students felt they were "breaking the chain" (p. 82) of their family's educational histories; that they didn't know "the rules of the game" (p. 84) for graduate school; that they felt they were living in two worlds between the community and the academy; and that the support of faculty, peers, and other mentors was important. Gardner and Holley recommend that graduate-school advising start earlier in the pipeline, that it be tailored toward first-generation students, and that support groups be formally established for first-generation students while in graduate school.

Related to Gardner and Holly's (2011) finding of students not knowing "the rules of the game" for graduate school is the concept of the hidden curriculum. According to Giroux and Penna (1979), the hidden curriculum is defined as "the unstated norms, values and beliefs that are transmitted through the underlying structure and meaning in both the formal content as well as the social relations of school and classroom life" (p. 22). Essentially, the hidden curriculum includes things that students learn throughout their schooling that are not part of the formal classroom curriculum such as punctuality and conformity, concepts that are valued in a capitalist society and are associated with the social reproduction role of schooling (Giroux & Penna, 1979). In a study conducted with twenty women of color in graduate sociology programs, Margolis and Romero (1995) found that the hidden curriculum manifested mainly in the form of professionalization and socialization. They state:

> Graduate programs socialize students to develop loyalty to and identify with the faculty and other sociologists while distancing themselves from undergraduate students and research subjects. . . . The hidden curriculum receives powerful support from the premium placed on the concept of competition and isolation that are so characteristic of graduate school. (Margolis & Romero, 1995, p. 9)

Margolis and Romero also pay particular attention to how the hidden curriculum reproduces gender, racial, and ethnic hierarchies in graduate school in the form of stigmatization, stereotyping, exclusion, and tracking. The hidden curriculum is a common theme in first-generation scholarship, in addition to other phenomena such as survivor's guilt (Somers et al., 2004) and the imposter syndrome (Bonaparte, 2014).

The Hidden Curriculum of the Academic Job Market

Once you think you've figured out the hidden curriculum of your program, department, and university within graduate school as a first-generation student, the hidden curriculum continues when you are nearing the end of your schooling and enter the academic market in search of a faculty position. I want to stress here that there are many types of positions one can embark upon after they receive their doctorate or master's degree, such as a tenure-track faculty appointment, a postdoc position, a clinical faculty position, an adjunct faculty position, or an administrative or staff position at a college or university. There are also positions as a consultant, a member of a nonprofit organization, or another position serving in private or public industry. With that said, however, I focus on my experience with the job search and selection process for a tenure-track faculty position, which is often considered the pinnacle of advanced doctoral training in the humanities, social sciences, and liberal arts.

Although there is a burgeoning market of guidebooks for academics who are job searching (Hutchinson & Averill, 2019; Kelsky, 2015; Vick et al., 2016), I provide information here on the technical process of academic hiring, as it's often unknown for first-generation faculty. Even the existence of these guidebooks was new knowledge to me, but what I am now familiar with is that the tenure-track faculty job search includes multiple phases over an extended amount of time. Hunt and colleagues (2009) review the typical stages of the academic market within the field of accounting, which can be extended toward faculty in other disciplines. I interpret their steps as the following:

1. Obtain information about the school and apply for the position;
2. Receive contact by the school that expresses interest;
3. Have a phone or video interview;
4. Schedule a possible interview at a professional conference;
5. Have an on-campus interview;
6. Receive a job offer;
7. Engage in negotiations; and
8. Accept or reject the offer.

These steps can vary by discipline and institutional type, and as streamlined and as linear as it may appear, not reflected here are unspoken customs, protocols, and rules along the way. For instance, in Step 1, you may want to contact the chair of the search committee and ask for more clarification regarding the job call. Sometimes that conversation goes well and the chair is happy to discuss the job call, other times the chair is hands-off and does not want to give the appearance of preferential treatment by providing potential candidates any "insider information." There are strict policies and guidelines for creating and posting a faculty job call and most search committees do not want to have any sense of impropriety as they conduct their search (Modern Language Association, 2018).

The tricky thing for the first-generation job applicant is to figure out if they should inquire more in the initial stages of the search and if so, to whom, and how. It can help if their academic advisor or another mentor knows members of the search committee and/or other faculty in that department and can inquire on your behalf or have you make the inquiry referencing their name. This requires, however, that (1) you have a close relationship with this advisor/mentor; (2) that they are well networked within your discipline; and (3) they are well-known and well-respected by others. This is but one small example of how the hidden curriculum operates in the initial step of the job search process. This information is not reflected in the overall steps and can be daunting for first-generation students, who frequently have no generational familial knowledge of how academic job search processes operate and obscure hidden norms and standards.

The scholarship on the academic job market is often written from the perspective of those who are doing the hiring. Attempting to uncover some of the hidden curriculum found within and between the steps, scholars and practitioners have offered advice on how applicants and candidates can best approach the job search process (Vaillancourt, 2013; Vick et al., 2016). The issue, however, is that even this scholarship is often silent on how the academic job search process can be experienced differently for first-generation and/or faculty of color. The professoriate is still dominated by white faculty; in fact, 75 percent of all full-time faculty at degree-granting postsecondary institutions, including tenure-track and nontenure-track, identify as white (National Center for Education Statistics, 2020). Much has been written on how academic hiring committees can recruit and retain diverse faculty members (Gasman, 2016; Smith et al., 2004; Turner, 2002; White-Lewis, 2020), yet there is little to no scholarship that explores the job search process from a first-generation faculty of color's perspective.

Toward this end, I offer my own autoethnographic account of my journey as a first-generation graduate student of color to a first-generation faculty of color. Similar to ethnography and its focus on the study of experience, an autoethnography refers to research and writing about lived experiences through cultural analysis and personal narrative (Boylorn & Orbe, 2016). In order to best describe and recount my experiences with the academic job market, I offer a brief autoethnographic narrative that captures my job search process. I pay particular attention to how I locate myself in the first-generation faculty community as well as engage in self-reflection as I move forward in my academic career.

Food on the Table

In the last year of my doctoral program, I applied for both administrative and faculty jobs in the fall. It was news to me that you had to apply for jobs a year in advance. As I began the academic job process, I was torn between honoring my practitioner roots and exploring my new training as a researcher. I applied to ten positions (seven faculty, three administrative) across the nation that I believed fit my research interests and skill set. Many of the applications called for numerous components beyond the requisite cover letter, curriculum vitae, letters of recommendation, and transcripts such as recent publications, teaching evaluations, sample teaching materials, and separate reflective statements related to diversity and pedagogy. Essentially, each application required numerous hours of labor and resulted in a packet of hard-copy material that I could barely squeeze into one manila envelope.

I did not make it past the first step for the administrative positions, and I made it to only the second step for two out of the seven faculty positions. After juggling all my responsibilities with nothing to show for it by the time spring came, I felt defeated. No job. No fellowship awards. Still writing the dissertation. I wasn't even sure if I was going to commencement. I didn't tell my parents that I was applying for jobs because (1) they wouldn't understand why I was doing it so far in advance and (2) I didn't want them to get their hopes up for something that wasn't a sure thing. My family was very close to me, and I often shared my academic achievements with them. However, I didn't want the pressure of including them in the academic job search process, as it was difficult to explain the multistage application and selection process. I felt like a failure and wasn't sure if I was ever going to make it in academia. After six years of specialized training, I was so uncertain about what was next. I didn't know how much of the hidden curriculum of the application process I had figured out and how much I still didn't know.

It just so happened that after a major professional conference, my advisor and I were on the same flight back to Los Angeles and we sat in the same row together. Through tears and vulnerability, I confided in him about how I felt about my lack of job prospects—I was candid about my perceived lack of employability. I don't think he was aware of how emotionally drained I was. He informed me that a colleague of his just sent him a personal email asking if he could recommend anyone for a postdoc position. He said that he would put my name forward, but the only catch was that the position was in the Midwest. At that point, it wasn't "a catch" from my perspective; rather, it was a potential job. Upon my return to Los Angeles, I applied for the postdoc position and, on a whim, applied to a late-posted job call for a tenure-track position at a private institution in the Central Valley region of California. I was unsure of my chances for either as it was already May and at that point most, if not all, institutions had made their selections for the academic year. As it turned out, I was invited for campus visits for both positions in June, which is essentially unheard of. In short, I had been fast-tracked to Step 5.

The on-campus interviews lasted several days for both positions. My flight and accommodations were taken care of. I was told to treat the campus visit as a marathon and not a sprint, meaning that I had to preserve my energy through the duration of the long interview process. I learned that you have an itinerary that often includes meetings with faculty, staff, students, and departmental, college, and university leadership. Everyone has a copy of your CV before they meet with you and ask questions about your research and why you're interested in joining their campus. You are also required to do a teaching and/or research presentation—often referred to as the "job talk"—which is commonly open to the university community. You present your work and leave yourself open to inquiry and possible criticism. You shake several hands, eat small bites at several meals, and make sure that in your schedule you make time to use the restroom in between appointments. There is no moment that you are not "on." Your feet ache. Your voice becomes strained. Everyone is watching, everyone is listening, everyone is making a judgement if they want you as a colleague, and the entire ordeal is exhausting.

The process is high-stakes, and as a potential first-generation faculty member you have no reference point for this, no prior experience, and no elder in your family you can call for specific advice. You are often the only person of color in the room and have never had so much attention focused just on you. You have only your other first-generation friends who are all fumbling through the process themselves, taking notes, and sending pep talks your way. The feeling is overwhelming and the entire time you realize how much scrutiny you are under and how few other first-generation academics of color are able to make it to this point. You tap into your reserves of energy and tell yourself that it is not luck that brought you here, but rather, it's a result of your training and your ability to fulfill the job description at an exceptionally high level. There is a fine line that you occupy between being humble and being confident and pretending that the academic interview process is familiar and comfortable.

After both on-campus interviews, to my surprise, I was offered both positions. I worked really hard to prepare for both visits, but I was surprised that in a short time I went from having zero job prospects and crying on a plane to having two offers and having to make a difficult choice at the end of the academic year. Upon the advice of my friends, mentors, and my advisor, I took the tenure-track position and was able to negotiate for my salary and other resources. After a year, I had made it to Step 8 of the academic job search model. I was employed. After a year and a half into the position, however, I was growing restless and the university's campus racial climate had increasingly become untenable. I remember that my advisor, who is also a first-generation professor, wisely told me that my first job post-PhD wouldn't be my last job. He was right.

I applied for two other faculty tenure-track positions where my research and pedagogy were a good fit. I knew faculty at both universities and had more confidence that I would make it past Steps 2 and 5. I secured campus visits for both and felt more prepared for the grueling schedule and multiple modes of inquiry. At this time, my friends and I had also created an informal support group where we would coach each other with interview questions and rehearse our job talks in front of one another. With their help, I was selected for both positions and once again had to make a hard decision between a research-intensive university in another state, or a more primary teaching position back in Southern California. This time I clued in my family.

I told my parents and siblings after I had the campus visits, however, because again I didn't want them to get their hopes up if I wasn't selected for either position. To provide a common job-seeking analogy, I recall telling my mom that when I had visited my friend out of state (the excuse I used for why I went away for a trip), I filled out a job application at a counter and they liked me and wanted to hire me. I also told her the same thing happened when I took a trip to Los Angeles. With little expectations of how she might respond, I asked my mom for advice on what job I should take. I had asked numerous others, including senior colleagues, mentors, and academic friends, and was creating a thorough pro/con list in my head.

The first thing my mom asked was if I was going to make more money than the current position I had, because according to her, it did not make sense to leave a job for a lesser-paying job. I told her that yes, I would make more money—both positions were paying me more and the out-of-state one had the higher salary offer. "Good," she said, "that means you can put food on your table." And then she asked, "OK, so where are you going to enjoy this food more? Who will be at this table with you?" I was silent. Dumbfounded. I had never thought about it on those terms.

So much of the advice I had been receiving from others revolved around which institution was more prestigious, what perks could I get for travel or research, how would my research time be protected, and how serious this choice was for my long-term career. The negotiations hadn't started yet and I was a wreck. Yet my mom essentially asked where would I be happier? Who was going to eat this food with me that I can now afford? Where would I enjoy the company of those who joined me for the meal? My mom, in all her immigrant wisdom, knew that my social and emotional happiness was just as important as my professional happiness. Without using the exact terminology, she was advocating for a strong sense of work–life balance. After that conversation, my choice was clear: I chose the teaching-intensive institution. All the professional advice from people with multiple degrees and years of formal workplace experience couldn't replace the sage wisdom of my momma. I never felt luckier to be a first-generation professor than at that moment.

Conclusion

I come from a tradition of immigrant hustle, from grandfathers who shared their love of teaching, from a mother who understands that happiness doesn't always equal money, and from a father that believes in the promise of formal higher education even though he himself never experienced it. By not involving my family in my initial academic job search process, I was starting to slide down the dangerous slope of not respecting their insight just because they lacked familiarity with academia. The hidden curriculum of graduate school and the academic job market—the things I didn't know or didn't know how to do—had left me not only with internal self-doubt but also made me doubt my family's cultural wealth. So many of us are pushed out of the job process at multiple steps for reasons that are largely political and personal, never professional. This lack of knowledge is also contributed to the scant research dedicated to this topic. I would like to see more formal studies that provide first-hand accounts of candidate's job processes along with empirical research on how institutions view and select their candidates (White-Lewis, 2020).

What would have helped me—as well as fellow first-generation faculty of color like me—would have been more direct guidance during graduate school with how the academic job market operates, essentially pulling back the curtain on this hidden curriculum. Similar to how it is assumed that upon graduation, doctoral students automatically know how to teach in a college classroom, it is also assumed that we know the ins and outs of the academic interview process without any formal support. A series of workshops could be held for key stages, including the job search, the application materials, the initial phone or video interview, the on-campus interview, and negotiations. Ideally, first-generation faculty of color that teach in the program would lead these workshops. Also, for program benchmarks such as qualifying exams, an additional component could be for students to submit their teaching philosophy statement or diversity statement, which are now common requirements for faculty applications. Last, graduate student organizations, with the assistance of faculty, could lead mock interviews for students who are currently on the market and invite other students to observe and participate.

Without receiving any of this formal support I have described, I know that my journey is unique and that I am one of the few first-generation faculty of color who was able to secure a tenure-track position not only once, but twice. I also have earned tenure, which in itself is becoming increasingly difficult in today's neoliberal capitalistic academic market that continues to resist the hiring of faculty of color and persistently relies on obscuring the practices, customs, and rituals that allow us to fully join and remain in the professoriate. It is only through sharing our autoethnographic stories that we will begin to uncover the hidden curriculum of the academic job market.

REFERENCES

Bonaparte, R. (2014). Higher education and first-generation students: Cultivating community, voice, and place for the new majority by Rashné Rustom Jehangir. *Journal of Higher Education, 38*(1), 171–174. https://doi.org/10.1353/rhe.2014.0037

Boylorne, R. M., & Orbe, M. P. (Eds.). (2016). *Critical autoethnography: Intersecting cultural identities in everyday life.* Routledge.

Center for First-Generation Student Success (2019). *First-generation college students: Demographic characteristics and postsecondary enrollment.* Center for First-Generation Student Success. https://firstgen.naspa.org/files/dmfile/FactSheet-01.pdf

Gardner, S. K., & Holley, K. A. (2011). "Those invisible barriers are real": The progression of first-generation students through doctoral education. *Equity & Excellence in Education, 44*(1), 77–92. https://doi.org/10.1080/10665684.2011.529791

Gasman, M. (2016, September 16). An Ivy League professor on why colleges don't hire more faculty of color: "We don't want them." *Washington Post.* https://www.washingtonpost.com/news/grade-point/wp/2016/09/26/an-ivy-league-professor-on-why-colleges-dont-hire-more-faculty-of-color-we-dont-want-them/

Giroux, H. A., & Penna, A. N. (1979). Social education in the classroom: The dynamics of the hidden curriculum. *Theory & Research in Social Education, 7*(1), 21–42. https://doi.org/10.1080/00933104.1979.10506048

Hunt, S. C., Eaton, T. V., & Reinstein, A. (2009). Accounting faculty job search in a seller's market. *Issues in Accounting Education, 24*(2), 157–185. https://doi.org/10.2308/iace.2009.24.2.157

Hutchinson, H., & Averill, M. B. (2019). *Scaling the ivory tower: Your academic job search workbook.* MarshFlower Publishing.

Kelsky, K. (2015). *The professor is in: The essential guide to turning your Ph.D. into a job.* Three Rivers Press.

Lunceford, B. (2011). When first-generation students go to graduate school. *New Directions for Teaching and Learning, 127,* 13–20. https://doi.org/10.1002/tl.453

Margolis, E., & Romero, M. (1998). "This department is very male, very white, very old, and very conservative": The functioning of the hidden curriculum in graduate sociology departments. *Harvard Educational Review, 68*(1), 1–32. https://doi.org/10.17763/haer.68.1.lq3828348783j851

Modern Language Association. (2018). *Guidelines for search committees and job seekers on entry-level faculty recruitment and hiring.* https://www.mla.org/Resources/Career/Career-Resources/Guidelines-for-Search-Committees-and-Job-Seekers-on-Entry-Level-Faculty-Recruitment-and-Hiring-as-well-as-Postdoctoral-Applications

National Center for Education Statistics. (2020). *Characteristics of post-secondary faculty.* https://nces.ed.gov/programs/coe/indicator_csc.asp#info

National Science Foundation. (2018). *Doctorate recipients from U.S. universities.* National Science Foundation. https://ncses.nsf.gov/pubs/nsf20301/

Postsecondary National Policy Institute. (2021). *First-generation students in higher education.* https://pnpi.org/first-generation-students/

Roksa, J., Fedlon, D. F., & Maher, M. (2018). First-generation students in pursuit of the PhD: Comparing socialization experiences and outcomes to continuing-generation peers.

Journal of Higher Education, 89(5), 728–752. https://doi.org/10.1080/00221546.2018 .1435134

Smith, D. G., Turner, C. S., Osei-Kofi, N., & Richards, S. (2004). Interrupting the usual: Successful strategies for hiring diverse faculty. *Journal of Higher Education, 75*(2), 133–160. https://doi.org/10.1080/00221546.2004.11778900

Somers, P., Woodhouse, S. R., & Cofer, J. E., Sr. (2004). Pushing the boulder uphill: The persistence of first-generation college students. *NASPA Journal, 41*(3), 418–435. https://doi .org/10.2202/1949-6605.1353

Turner, C.S.V. (2002). *Diversifying the faculty: A guidebook for search committees* (2nd ed.). Association of American Colleges & Universities.

Vaillancourt, A. (2013, January 2). What search committees wish you knew. *Chronicle of Higher Education.* https://www.chronicle.com/article/What-Search-Committees-Wish /136399

Vasil, M., & McCall, J. M. (2017). The perspective of two first-generation college students pursuing doctoral degrees in music education. *Journal of Music Teacher Education, 27*(2), 1–15. https://doi.org/10.1177/1057083717717464

Vick, J. M., Furlong, J. S., & Lurie, R. (2016). *The academic job search handbook* (5th ed.). University of Pennsylvania Press.

White-Lewis, D. K. (2020). The façade of fit in faculty search processes. *Journal of Higher Education, 91*(6), 833–857. https://doi.org/10.1080/00221546.2020.1775058

Yosso, T. J. (2005). Whose culture has capital? A critical race theory discussion of community cultural wealth. *Race, Ethnicity and Education, 8*(1), 69–91. https://doi.org/10.1080 /1361332052000341006

2

Neoliberal Racism and the Experiences of First-Generation Asian American Scholars

VARAXY YI AND SAMUEL D. MUSEUS

Over the past few decades, the increasing diversity of college students has led to higher education researchers, policymakers, and practitioners calling for a greater focus on students and faculty from underserved backgrounds and cultures. This increased diversity has led to a rise in the enrollment of first-generation college students[1] though this population faces unique challenges (Garza & Fullerton, 2018; Pascarella et al., 2016). As a result, postsecondary leaders are tasked with creating support systems to address challenges that these students face. Additionally, programs and practices that specifically focus on first-generation students have become widespread.

As college campuses have increased their supports for first-generation college students, there has also been a growing interest in engaging faculty who were once first-generation college students themselves. Some institutions have launched efforts to highlight stories of first-generation faculty, including their challenges and successes. While literature on first-generation college students is growing, discourse about first-generation college students who enter and navigate academia are more difficult to find. Conversations about the experiences of racially minoritized faculty who come from first-generation backgrounds are virtually nonexistent.

In this chapter, we reflect on and examine our experiences as Asian American faculty members with first-generation college student backgrounds utilizing an intersectional lens. We provide an overview of the concept of intersectionality and the systems of oppression that are the focus of our analysis and that have

---

[1]. While there is no uniform definition regarding first-generation status, for the purposes of this chapter, we define first-generation college students as "an individual who is pursuing a higher education degree and whose parents or guardians do not have a postsecondary degree" (Peralta & Klonowski, 2017, p. 635).

so heavily shaped our experiences, as well as personal narratives demonstrating how these systems mutually shape our experiences navigating academia. We utilize intersectionality and related frameworks to interpret these experiences, conclude with recommendations for future research, and also offer final reflections. Our hope is to provide a window into how Asian American faculty who originate from first-generation college student backgrounds experience the culture of academia, and its resulting challenges.

Theoretical Frameworks and Systemic Oppression

It has been almost three decades since Crenshaw (1991) asserted that one of the limitations of identity politics is that they frequently conflate or overlook differences within groups. She also noted that this limitation is problematic because it fails to capture how multiple systems of oppression and corresponding social identities shape individual and group realities. Over time, scholars have asserted the need to understand the unique experiences at these intersections (Berger & Guidroz, 2009; Crenshaw, 1989, 1991; Museus & Griffin, 2011).

Building on the work of previous scholars (Crenshaw, 1989, 1991; Shields, 2008), we define *intersectionality* as relationships among multiple systems of oppression and positionalities that lead to multiple subject formations (Shields, 2008). *Structural intersectionality* can describe how multiple systems of oppression intersect to oppress and shape the experiences of individuals (Crenshaw, 1991). In contrast, *political intersectionality* refers to how multiple identity groups to which a person belongs pursue different and sometimes conflicting political agendas, which can result in challenging conditions for those who are situated at the intersection of those groups.

Systemic Racism

The reality that white supremacy plays a significant role in shaping higher education systems and the experiences of Asian Americans within them is well-documented (Buenavista, 2018; Museus et al., 2015; Museus & Park, 2015). The permeation of white supremacy and how people of Asian descent are racialized and dehumanized are deeply embedded in the history of Western society (Said, 1978). For example, historically, Western explorers depicted the people of Asia as tyrannical, deceitful, sexually deviant, and strange. Such racist depictions of Asians as a *yellow peril*—or menace and danger to white civilization—continued to influence how people in Western nations viewed Asians into the twentieth century (Espiritu, 1993; Lowe, 1996).

Although Asian Americans continue to be racialized as a foreign threat in some contexts, it could be argued that the dominant monolithic racial trope of Asian Americans became the model minority myth (Yi et al., 2020). This stereotype suggests that Asian Americans are universally successful and do not face racism-related challenges (Museus & Kiang, 2009; Osajima, 1995; Suzuki, 1977). The model minority myth is deployed to reinforce white supremacy in multiple ways. For example, the stereotype perpetually masks inequities *within* Asian American communities, fuels fallacies that Asian Americans are impervious to racial challenges and do not require support, and rationalizes the exclusion of Asian Americans from conversations about race (Lee, 2006; Museus, 2014a; Ngo, 2006). Moreover, this stereotype reifies racism targeted toward other communities of color and pits Asian Americans against these other racial groups (Matsuda, 1996; Yu, 2006).

Furthermore, we must also note that ethnic groups across Asian America are racialized in disparate ways. For example, while East Asian Americans (e.g., Chinese, Japanese, Korean) are generally racialized as model minorities, Southeast Asian Americans (e.g., Cambodian, Laotian, Hmong, Vietnamese) are often also constructed as deviant minorities (e.g., dropouts, welfare sponges, gang members) in some contexts (Lee, 2006; Museus & Park, 2015; Ngo & Lee, 2007). Similarly, South Asian Americans may be racialized as terrorists (Ali, 2016). Therefore, racialized experiences across Asian American subgroups can vary significantly.

Neoliberalism

The neoliberal regime emerged as a reaction to the civil rights movements of the 1960s and 1970s that challenged white supremacy and heteropatriarchy in society (Goldberg, 2015). In response to this resistance, conservative elites sought ways to silence progressive demands to hold both public and private institutions responsible for contributing to democracy (Giroux, 2007). To do so, they pushed for the deregulation of markets and mass privatization, which became increasingly supported in the 1980s, marking the rise and solidification of neoliberal ideologies throughout society (Inwood, 2015). Thus, the origins of neoliberal ideology were a mechanism to suppress the increased democratization of the civil rights era and social movements that were demanding a more equitable system.

Neoliberalism is sophisticated, evolving, and contextual. However, building on previous scholarship (Adsit et al., 2015; Burford, 2017; Darder, 2012; Davies, 2005; Giroux, 2008, 2011; McChesney, 1999; Muehlebach, 2013), Museus and LePeau (2019) identify the following common key elements of neoliberalism:

- *Consumerism:* Prioritization of consumer choice, which can contribute to a culture in which the value of people, behaviors, and agendas are assessed and determined by their potential to generate revenue. Thus, the neoliberal order valorizes those who do work that can generate significant revenue.
- *Competitive Individualism:* Neoliberalism emphasizes free-market individualism and competition, which reify beliefs in meritocracy, and engenders

an environment in which people are rewarded for prioritizing their own self-interests over the collective.

- *Surveillance:* Neoliberal forces engender a false sense of individual auton-omy, as they lead to dehumanizing systems of surveillance (e.g., monitor-ing and reporting) that are designed to ensure that people comply with rules of the system, thereby eradicating trust.
- *Precarity:* As the neoliberal regime shifts responsibility to individuals, the latter wind up in increasingly precarious positions in which they are pres-sured to fight for survival.
- *Declining Morality:* Neoliberal structures increase and reinforce the focus on profits and fiscal sustainability, while eroding beliefs that society's institutions have a responsibility to ensure and advance the public good.

Systemic racism and neoliberalism converge to create cultures that pose many challenges for faculty of color—especially those who come from first-generation backgrounds. Within colleges and universities, neoliberalism fuels academic capitalism, or institutions' active efforts to integrate into the global economy (Slaughter & Rhoades, 2004). As a result, colleges and universities increasingly pressure faculty to operate with and assess them based on neoliberal logics. Most central to the current discussion is the reality that these systems create cultures that pressure or force faculty of color to leave their home communities behind, engage in individualistic competition, be an all-knowing expert to increase their own market value, and always maximize productivity (i.e., quantifiable outputs, such as publications, citations, and grant revenue). In the following sections, we share our narratives, and then revisit these elements of racist neoliberal cultures to discuss how they can be engaged to understand our experiences.

Varaxy's Story

As a Khmer American woman and child of refugees, my education has been shaped by the first-generation student experience. For every transition into a new environment as the first, I am met by old acquaintances—anxiety and feelings of doubt about whether I belong. I have rarely felt belonging in academic spaces; more often feeling lonely, overwhelmed, isolated, and conflicted. As I transi-tioned into a faculty position in 2018, I became more aware of the ways I am expected to participate in academia. I still struggle with neoliberal forces that attempt to lead me astray from my values of collectivism and community. My past and present efforts to resist these forces help to honor my values as a Khmer American scholar.

It has been difficult to feel comfortable in my own skin when in academia, especially when the rules of engagement are at odds with the ways I have been socialized. I have been raised to think of the collective and in interdependent terms. Coming from a collectivist family, culture, and community, moreover, the independent, individualistic, and excessively competitive nature of academia has created much dissonance. I constantly feel at odds about how to participate. Simultaneously, I often engaged in inaccessible, scholarly language that reinforces distance and separation between me and my community. There is an irony that I pursued this field to support and advance my community and yet, in many ways, it fosters isolation. This reality continues to test my resolve as a Khmer American scholar.

Engaging academia as a first-generation college student has been, and is, difficult. I remember the terrifying experience of sitting in a class as a first-year doctoral student with limited experience within academia. I often fought an internal battle with my subconscious, struggling between my default inclination to sit, listen, and soak up knowledge and the expectation that I contribute, question, and critique. After all, academia favors those who speak out and often who are the loudest. I wanted to contribute my perspectives, but I could not shake the feeling that my experiences did not matter or were not relevant because they were rarely reflected in the curriculum. As I developed critical and racial consciousness, it was still very rare for me to have deep, nuanced conversations about the experiences of Southeast Asian American communities outside of my own small circles. I still feel this as faculty.

I coped by learning to be independent and strategic in seeking out resources and opportunities. Consequently, I developed a complex regarding the desire to figure things out on my own instead of seeking help. During my dissertation phase, I often felt paralyzed by messages in academia that questioned the value of my work and contributions. I spiraled in indecision, anxiety, and self-doubt. I was not yet confident that my knowledge and ways of knowing mattered. Consequently, I would more often choose self-isolation to try to figure things out on my own rather than seek support. There was a constant pressure to get things right before getting it out. While these experiences strengthened my resourcefulness and resilience, it was often a double-edged sword because I felt so very alone.

There was pressure to participate in ways to prove myself, my value, and my worth, which, paired with my desire to make a difference, only served to increase my anxiety. I spent many sleepless nights focused on advancing research. I was constantly presenting at conferences along with finishing coursework and holding graduate fellowship positions. For a period of five years I did little besides work, certain that these were the necessary actions and behaviors of a "good" and "productive" scholar. Meanwhile, I felt guilty that I was unable to afford to attend important family and community functions.

Furthermore, competition seemed to be fostered through scarce resources—fellowships, grants, and even faculty mentors. The scarcity mind-set, which alters and destroys relationships, influences much of our behaviors in academia. The goal was always to produce the most publications, win the most awards and grants, and grow the size of one's professional network. But what use was individual accomplishment if it did not move the collective?

Moving the collective became my guiding purpose. This guide helped me to resist some of these rules of engagement as I made intentional choices about how to show up in academia. I prioritized uplifting the collectives I belonged to (e.g., research team and Women of Color) through sharing resources, hidden curriculum, and vulnerabilities. I also resisted messaging about what one should be willing to give up for the elusive tenure-track position. I decided I was unwilling to give any more of myself in pursuit of a position that would continue to keep me isolated from my family. I decisively resisted advice to cast a wide net because I was unwilling to twist myself to fit an institution. At present, I am at a minority-serving institution near my family. I have a clear understanding as to what I need to do to earn tenure. Though I am still beholden to neoliberal standards, I feel freer to pursue the work that is important to me.

The neoliberal academy presents clear rules for engagement and asks me to give of myself in ways I am no longer prepared to give. This has been the result of hard-earned lessons and seeing alternative models of showing up. Collectivism and care for the work can protect against scarcity and its negative consequences. I also envision something different for myself as I actively resist this often competitive, cutthroat game that measures me based on the volume of what I produce or the revenue I generate. Instead, I have chosen my own measuring stick, altering the rules to fit my values and beliefs. Therefore, in academia, I choose to show up in community and never alone.

Sam's Story

When I entered the field of higher education, I did so with one purpose in mind—to help change the system so that it is more equitable. Throughout the course of my career, that mission has remained, but the surrounding context has shifted and reshaped it. I have found myself increasingly embedded in a system of constraints that shapes how I produce this work. This discovery is partly a function of the ever-increasing neoliberal pressures with which we are bombarded, and partially a result of my increasing awareness of them.

I identify as Uchinanchu (Indigenous Okinawan) and a second-generation Asian American in the United States. As such, cultural extermination and assimilation have always been central to my understanding of how oppression works and my own experiences. But I also come from a low-income background and was a first-generation college student. These identities are intertwined inextricably and deeply shape my realities, making it especially difficult to navigate a system that is steeped in whiteness and increasingly forces our assimilation into the corporatized cultures of academia. It is through this intersectional lens that some of the most difficult challenges that I have encountered in the academy can be understood.

I remember the first time I took a graduate course, and the inadequacy that I felt. It was some time before this feeling was replaced with the realization that I brought something valuable to the table—a perspective from a first-generation Asian American that was far too often absent from the discourse. I also remember leaving home for the first time to attend a graduate program that I chose because of its ranking, prestige, and funding packages, and the emotional toll that accompanied leaving my family and the Asian American community in Minnesota. This was the first time, but definitely would not be the last, that my soul would see scars as a result of the conflict between the cosmopolitan world of academia and the commitment to racially minoritized communities that have given my life purpose.

Like so many others, I have felt how the culture of academia constantly works to eradicate my commitment to equity. The neoliberal regime only allows equity work that reinforces it. In this increasing neoliberal world, I have been bombarded with messages that I never do enough, that my worth is only as good as the amount of money it generates, and that the competitive cultures that emanate from the neoliberal regime will ensure that there will be no shortage of people who see academia as competition that they must win for their own survival.

Perhaps one of the most salient ways in which the culture of academia socializes us into systems of oppression and kills our souls is through neoliberal forces pulling us increasingly farther away from our communities. Prior to tenure, this pull manifests in academic review processes channeling our energies and time away from service to communities and toward peer-review productivity. After receiving tenure, this pull can shift with increased pressure to make work relevant to larger audiences with power in order to grant monies and other forms of revenue for our institutions. Around the time I earned tenure, I created a new theory that explained how more equitable campus environments offer conditions for diverse college student populations to thrive and an assessment operation to administer survey that could assess environments at campuses that wanted to use data to advance their diversity and equity efforts. I became increasingly embedded in toxic neoliberal realities. Navigating these systems as a former first-generation college student—who was not raised to be competitive and individualistic—was difficult, to say the least. An increasing amount of my energy had become focused on the revenue I needed to generate in order to sustain the operation and to support graduate students working in it. As a result, my interactions with those around me became more transactional and less humanized, and I concentrated less of my energy on working with my communities.

There is a silver lining in these clouds. Despite all the ways in which systemic forces constantly work to force us to assimilate, sever ties with our communities, and reconstruct our identities in harmful ways, those of us who are in this field advocating for justice within the academy are able to survive because of our communities and can find our way back to them. These communities allow us to look past the world as it is and provide possibility and hope for how the world can be. For many of us, they demonstrate how we can create more humanized, holistic, collective, and relevant spaces and systems. Perhaps this is why so many of us, when we clash with oppressive forces, retreat into those communities—because they feed our souls, and in doing so, allow us to survive and even thrive. The beauty of this reality is that we have the power to (re)create these communities in spaces we choose, both outside and within the academy. Most of us who fight for justice do the former on a regular basis, but we can also focus our energies on creating research teams, collaborative networks, and individual interactions that embody the hope and love that exist within our most loved spaces. Envisioning and constructing this alternative reality might be the greatest act of resistance to systemic racial and neoliberal forces that have so profoundly shaped our lives.

At the Intersection of Racism and Neoliberalism

Neoliberal racism creates conditions in which faculty of color are forced to choose between academia and their communities. Higher education heavily values professional mobility and individuals who are willing to go where the jobs exist (Rhoades et al., 2008). This prioritization of mobility itself is a culture-bound assertion that does not reflect the values of place, family, and community that are important to those from many racially minoritized and working-class origins. As our narratives underscore, such cosmopolitan values place immense pressure on first-generation faculty of color—in particular, to be ready and willing to weaken ties with their home communities in order to maximize their potential for professional success. This conflict is particularly problematic given that many first-generation faculty of color enter the academy to advocate for their communities and, in turn, are motivated by them.

Neoliberal systems and academic capitalism pressure everyone to value prestige and potential for revenue generation over everything else. Such pressures engender academic cultures that value individuals who are experts and portray to know it all—despite the irrefutable reality that any one person has very limited knowledge and capacity. As Varaxy discusses in her narrative, this culture compels first-generation faculty of color to feel that they must avoid making mistakes and look like they know all within their respective scholarly areas of expertise. Such pressures can also lead to imposter syndrome, which signifies that environmental conditions lead first-generation faculty of color to question whether they have enough intellectual capacity and drive to survive, be successful, or have an impact (Brems et al., 1994). Our narratives demonstrate how these pressures can and sometimes do create significant conflict for those of us who originate from communities that value the perspectives of those around us, are taught to listen to these viewpoints, and are socialized to avoid silencing others.

Portraying that we know everything increases our value in the knowledge economy. Doing so to be perceived as an expert is a tactic used to compete in a hypercompetitive culture. Those who are viewed as knowing it all gain an advantage over their more modest peers, as they are more likely to be perceived as legitimate, and gain greater access to financial resources, prestigious institutions, and connections to privileged and highly resourced networks. At the same time, they are complicit in reinforcing neoliberal systems and values. For those who come from communities in which humility is a core value with an emphasis on the collective (Kim, 2007; Yeh & Huang, 1996), conforming to the expert identity can further strain relationships with their communities. As our narratives show, this conflict causes constant dissonance as we navigate the professional world.

Implications for Research

In terms of research implications, it is important to recognize that first-generation status does not dissipate as first-generation Asian American faculty advance into higher levels of academia. Thus, it is important that researchers develop an understanding of the larger pipeline for first-generation students, including the experiences of faculty of color from first-generation backgrounds in graduate preparation programs and navigating the academy. Future research, for example, could develop a deeper understanding of how neoliberalism and racism intersect to mutually shape graduate preparation and socialization among first-generation graduate students of color. Second, further exploration of the experiences of first-generation Asian American faculty is warranted. Given the increasing numbers of Asian immigrants and refugees in the United States, the number of first-generation Asian American faculty is likely to increase. Unfortunately, empirical research focusing on their experiences, challenges, and successes is virtually nonexistent. Third, future studies should explore the experiences of first-generation Asian American faculty across different institutional contexts to better understand both the challenges they face and how they survive and succeed. Further attention to the specific strategies that first-generation Asian American faculty employ to be successful in academia can enhance existing knowledge of this population.

We must seek ways to transform the academy so that it better fosters and maintains more humanized educational environments for first-generation Asian American faculty and other first-generation faculty of color. While neoliberalism and academic capitalism favor mass production and revenue generation, such priorities often result in dehumanization, mistrust, and competition, which are conditions that almost always negatively affect the well-being of first-generation Asian American faculty and other first-generation faculty of color. Humanized educational environments are characterized by support systems that connect faculty to people who care about them and are committed to their success (Museus, 2014b). Fostering such environments requires seeing first-generation faculty as individuals with histories, backgrounds, and experiences that are inherently valuable to the pursuit of education in the academic community, rather than determining their work based on their productivity potentials.

Reflections

As first-generation Asian American faculty existing and functioning in a time that neoliberal racism continues to exert immense influence and pressure to contribute to the academic capitalist knowledge-learning regime, we prioritize engaging in collaborative work that honors our collectivist orientations and that prioritize community uplift. We are creating epistemological, spiritual, and physical spaces to help us resist the neoliberal academy. This collaborative work keeps us centered and focused on why we entered academia in the first place— to pursue equity for our communities. We are not naive enough to suggest that we can completely avoid conforming to neoliberal pressures; however, being mindful of how and for whom we conduct our research will keep us focused and able to resist them.

We commit, and encourage others, to continuously reflect on our positions and positionalities as first-generation faculty. Though constant surveillance, competition, and heightened precarity can potentially cause us to become jaded in our work, the willingness to engage these environmental realities through shared reflection and vulnerable stories must be normalized. Honesty and vulnerability about our challenges is one way to excavate and undermine the stronghold neoliberalism has on our behaviors as faculty. In thinking about how we can make a difference, not just for our ethnic and racial communities, but also for our academic community, we must expose the challenges we face in the neoliberal academy. This includes stories about the ways we have reinforced neoliberal logics and been impacted by neoliberal racism. Doing so will not only counter the consumerism and competitive individualism pervasive in the academy, but also eliminate feelings of being alone.

REFERENCES

Adsit, J., Doe, S., Allison, M., Maggio, P., & Maisto, M. (2015). Affective activism: Answering institutional productions of precarity in the corporate university. *Feminist Formations*, 27(3), 21–48. https://doi.org/10.1353/ff.2016.0008

Ali, A. I. (2016). Citizens under suspicion: Responsive research with community under surveillance. *Anthropology & Education Quarterly*, 47(1), 78–95. https://doi.org/10.1111/aeq.12136

Berger, M. T., & Guidroz, K. (2009). *Intersectional approach: Transforming the academy through race, class, and gender.* University of North Carolina Press.

Brems, C., Baldwin, M. R., Davis, L., & Namyniuk, L. (1994). The imposter syndrome as related to teaching evaluations and advising relationships of university faculty members. *Journal of Higher Education, 65*(2), 183–193. https://doi.org/10.1080/00221546.1994.11778489

Buenavista, T. L. (2018). Model (undocumented) minorities and "illegal" immigrants: Centering Asian Americans and U.S. carcerality in undocumented student discourse. *Race Ethnicity and Education, 21*(1), 78–91. doi:10.1080/13613324.2016.1248823

Burford, J. (2017). What might "bad feelings" be good for? Some queer-feminist thoughts on academic activism. *Australian Universities' Review, 59*(2), 70–78.

Crenshaw, K. (1989). Demarginalizing the intersection of race and sex: A Black feminist critique of antidiscrimination doctrine, feminist theory, and antiracist politics. *University of Chicago Legal Forum, 1989,* article 1. https://chicagounbound.uchicago.edu/uclf/vol1989/iss1/8

Crenshaw, K. (1991). Mapping the margins: Intersectionality, identity politics, and violence against women of color. *Stanford Law Review, 43*(6), 1241–1299. https://doi.org/10.2307/1229039

Darder, A. (2012). Neoliberalism in the academic borderlands: An on-going struggle for equality and human rights. *Educational Studies, 48*(5), 412–426. https://doi.org/10.1080/00131946.2012.714334

Davies, B. (2005). The (im)possibility of intellectual work in neoliberal regimes. *Discourse: Studies in the Cultural Politics of Education, 26*(1), 1–14. https://doi.org/10.1080/01596300500039310

Espiritu, Y. L. (1993). *Asian American panethnicity: Bridging institutions and identities.* Temple University Press.

Garza, A. N., & Fullerton, A. S. (2018). Staying close or going away: How distance to college impacts the educational attainment and academic performance of first-generation college students. *Sociological Perspectives, 61*(1), 164–185. https://doi.org/10.1177/0731121417711413

Giroux, H. (2007). *The university in chains.* Paradigm Publishers.

Giroux, H. (2008). *Against the terror of neoliberalism: Politics beyond the age of greed.* Paradigm Publishers.

Giroux, H. (2011). The disappearing intellectual in the age of economic Darwinism. *Policy Futures in Education, 9*(2), 163–171.

Goldberg, D. T. (2015). *Are we all postracial yet?* Polity Press.

Inwood, J. F. (2015). Neoliberal racism: the "Southern Strategy" and the expanding geographies of white supremacy. *Social & Cultural Geography, 16*(4), 407–423. https://doi.org/10.1080/14649365.2014.994670

Kim, B. S. (2007). Adherence to Asian and European American cultural values and attitudes toward seeking professional psychological help among Asian American college students. *Journal of Counseling Psychology, 54*(4), 474–480. https://doi.org/10.1037/0022-0167.54.4.474

Lee, S. J. (2006). Additional complexities: Social class, ethnicity, generation, and gender in Asian American student experiences. *Race Ethnicity and Education, 9*(1), 17–28. https://doi.org/10.1080/13613320500490630

Lowe, L. (1996). *Immigrant acts: On Asian American cultural politics.* Duke University Press.

Matsuda, M. (1996). *Where is your body and other essays on race, gender, and the law.* Beacon Press.

McChesney, R. W. (1999). Introduction. In N. Chomsky (Ed.), *Profit over people: Neoliberalism and global order* (pp. 7–16). Seven Stories Press.

Muehlebach, A. (2013). On precariousness and the ethical imagination: The year 2012 in sociocultural anthropology. *American Anthropologist, 115*(2), 297–311. https://doi.org/10.1111/aman.12011

Museus, S. D. (2014a). *Asian American students in higher education.* Routledge.

Museus, S. D. (2014b). The culturally engaging campus environments (CECE) model: A new theory of success among racially diverse college student populations. In M. B. Paulsen (Ed.), *Higher education: Handbook of theory and research* (pp. 189–227). Springer.

Museus, S. D., & Griffin, K. A. (2011). Mapping the margins in higher education: On the promise of intersectionality frameworks in research and discourse. *New Directions for Institutional Research, 2011*(151), 5–13. https://doi.org/10.1002/ir.395

Museus, S. D., & Kiang, P. N. (2009). Deconstructing the model minority myth and how it contributes to the invisible minority reality in higher education research. *New Directions for Institutional Research, 2009*(142), 5–15. https://doi.org/10.1002/ir.292

Museus, S. D., Ledesma, M. C., & Parker, T. L. (2015). *Racism and racial equity in higher education.* Jossey-Bass.

Museus, S. D., & LePeau, L. A. (2019). Navigating neoliberal organizational cultures: Implications for higher education leaders advancing social justice agendas. In A. Kezar & J. Posselt (Eds.), *Administration for social justice and equity in higher education: Critical perspectives for leadership and decision making* (pp. 209–224). Routledge.

Museus, S. D., & Park, J. J. (2015). The continuing significances of racism in the lives of Asian American college students. *Journal of College Student Development, 56*(6), 551–569. https://doi.org/10.1353/csd.2015.0059

Ngo, B. (2006). Learning from the margins: Southeast and South Asian education in context. *Race Ethnicity and Education 9*(1), 51–65. https://doi.org/10.1080/13613320500490721

Ngo, B., & Lee, S. J. (2007). Complicating the image of model minority success: A review of Southeast Asian American education. *Review of Educational Research, 77*(4), 415–453. https://doi.org/10.3102/0034654307309918

Osajima, K. (1995). Racial politics and the invisibility of Asian Americans in higher education. *Journal of Educational Foundations, 9*(1), 35–53.

Pascarella, E. T., Pierson, C. T., Wolniak, G. C., & Terenzini, P. T. (2016). First-generation college students: Additional evidence on college experiences and outcomes. *Journal of Higher Education, 75*(3), 249–284. https://doi.org/10.1080/00221546.2004.11772256

Peralta, K. J., & Klonowski, M. (2017). Examining conceptual and operational definitions of "first-generation college student" in research on retention. *Journal of College Student Development, 58*(4), 630–636. http://doi.org/10.1353/csd.2017.0048

Rhoades, G., Kiyama, J. M., McCormick, R., & Quiroz, M. (2008). Local cosmopolitans and cosmopolitan locals: New models of professionals in the academy. *Review of Higher Education, 31*(2), 209–235. http://doi.org/10.1353/rhe.2007.0079

Said, E. (1978). *Orientalism.* Pantheon.

Shields, S. A. (2008). Gender: An intersectionality perspective. *Sex Roles, 59*(5–6), 301–311. https://doi.org/10.1007/s11199-008-9501-8

Slaughter, S., & Rhoades, G. (2004). *Academic capitalism and the new economy: Markets, state, and higher education.* Johns Hopkins University Press.

Suzuki, B. H. (1977). Education and socialization of Asian Americans: A revisionist analysis of the "model minority" thesis. *Amerasia Journal, 4*(2), 23–51. https://doi.org/10.17953/amer.4.2.x203l74863857108

Yeh, C. J., & Huang, K. (1996). The collectivistic nature of ethnic identity development among Asian-American college students. *Adolescence*, *31*(123), 645–661.

Yi, V., Mac, J., Na, V. S., Venturanza, R. J., Museus, S. D., Buenavista, T. L., & Pendakur, S. L. (2020). Toward an anti-imperialistic critical race analysis of the model minority myth. *Review of Educational Research*, *90*(4), 542–579. https://doi.org/10.3102/0034654320933532

Yu, T. (2006). Challenging the politics of the "model minority" stereotype: A case for educational equality. *Equity & Excellence in Education*, *39*(4), 325–333. https://doi.org/10.1080/10665680600932333

3

A Nanny's Daughter in the Academy

MARIA ESTELA ZARATE

While the research on first-generation faculty is limited, a related body of work shows that women, faculty of color, and working-class faculty face greater challenges in the professoriate. Collectively, the work depicts how hiring, tenure, and promotion policies in higher education institutions reinforce preexisting social hierarchies of oppression (Delgado Bernal & Villalpando, 2002). Examining faculty career persistence along these categories of privilege and oppression (i.e., class, race, ability, and gender) is helpful to understand how to dismantle institutional barriers that hinder first-generation faculty experiences.

At the same time, to fully understand the trajectories of first-generation faculty, it is important to document and examine their lived experiences, using a range of paradigms to analyze the intersecting forms of oppression that hinder and facilitate their success (Museus & Griffin, 2011; Pifer, 2011). For example, some first-generation faculty, like myself, are not able to position ourselves in only one category of exclusion. While I may face similar challenges as other women faculty, the similarity of our experiences is limited by the ways that our other identities are positioned in systems of power (Carroll, 2017; Machado-Casas et al., 2013). White faculty or faculty who are not first-generation faculty likely have fundamentally different relationships with institutions and draw on resources I cannot access as a Chicana first-generation faculty. Indeed, first-generation faculty have complex and intersecting identities and diverse experiences that merit deeper examination.

Because no one theory alone can fully capture the broad range of experiences that characterize first-generation faculty, scholars are then challenged to identify, amalgamate, or create theories that frame and conceptualize first-generation faculty experiences. As a scholar in the field, I suggest that my peers and I continuously explore frameworks and theories and expand disciplinary boundaries to name and understand the complex trajectories, identities, and experiences of diverse first-generation faculty (Cruz, 2018; Gonzales, 2018). For me, Chicana feminist epistemology (Delgado Bernal, 1998) is one framework that has legitimated my lived experiences in the academy as a source of theoretical explorations and knowledge (Delgado Bernal & Villalpando, 2002). In the following, I use my *testimonio* as a first-generation undergraduate and doctoral student and faculty—in dialogue with Romero's (1997, 2011) account of Teresa, a maid's daughter—to frame how I navigated and survived the academy.

Building Our Own Theory

Thus we need *teorias* that will enable us to interpret what happens in the world, that will explain how and why we relate to certain people in specific ways. (Anzaldúa, 1990, xxv)

Existing theoretical frameworks attempting to explain faculty attrition in the academy, such as resiliency theory, organization socialization, occupational segregation, and job satisfaction (August & Waltman, 2004; Marschke et al., 2007; Turner et al., 2008), do not fully portray the lived experiences of faculty who have been historically excluded from these institutions. As an alternative, Anzaldúa (1987, 1990) calls for theories and frameworks that break from liberal paradigms that reify binary thinking, pursue objectivity standards, and ignore structural oppression. Delgado Bernal (1998), and later Calderón and colleagues (2012), propose alternative methodologies grounded in Chicana feminist epistemologies, placing the complexities of hybrid identities and borderland existence at the center of inquiry. This way of creating theory eschews Western colonial research criteria that minimizes researcher bias and subjectivity. It more accurately represents the lived reality of those outside the sphere of institutional power. In Chicana feminist epistemology, stories told by racialized women and queer people are the basis for theory. From this epistemological standpoint, concepts and frameworks—such as pedagogies of the home, nepantla/nepantlera frameworks, borderland sites, *mestizaje*-as-method, and *testimonio/testimonialista* (Delgado Bernal et al., 2012; Oliva et al., 2013)—have emerged to portray oppression, resistance, and survival of women and queer people of color.

In this chapter, I draw on *testimonio* as methodology, and join a collective of *testimonialistas* (Castillo-Montana & Torres-Guzmán, 2012; Sánchez & Ek, 2013) calling attention to the contradictions and conflicts of educational institutions. A *testimonio* is a way "of bearing witness and inscribing into history those lived realities that would otherwise succumb to the alchemy of erasure" (The Latina Feminist Group, 2001, p. 2). As an oral and narrative method, *testimonios* have been used to capture the oppression, trauma, and survival of women and queer people who exist in hostile spaces that subjugate their history, wisdom, and knowledge. In using a *testimonio*, I assume that my story is only one account of a larger system of subjugation and that others similarly positioned share similar experiences (Reyes & Curry Rodriguez, 2012). Finally, a *testimonio* is not untethered storytelling; rather, it is a narrative located in a broader sociopolitical context. Here, my *testimonio* takes place in institutions of higher education, gatekeepers to social mobility, and viewed through the lens of a broader socioeconomic hierarchical arrangement—the live-in domestic laborer and the employer.

A Lived Framework of a Maid's Daughter

Romero's (1997, 2011) rich account of a woman, Teresa,[1] whose mother was a live-in maid, is the basis for a framework that explains my survival in the academy. Teresa grew up living in the maid's quarters of her mother's white employer's home until early adolescence, when she was moved to the employer's living quarters. She describes this arrangement as living in two worlds with two identities, the maid's daughter in the employer's home and the privileged private-school girl living in one of the most desirable neighborhoods in Los Angeles. On the one hand, Teresa cleaned neighbors' houses, cared for neighbors' children, and deferred to the educational and discipline decisions that the employer made for her. On the other hand, she attended private schools paid by the employer, vacationed with wealthy families, and interacted with upper-class peers. Every day, she negotiated the boundaries of race, class, and gender, and fought to remain grounded in her mother's cultural values. In Romero (1997), Teresa reflects on how these contrasting experiences shaped her identity, privilege, and personal and professional decisions the rest of her life. Years later, she is still unable to disentangle the privilege associated with living with a wealthy family and the pain from surviving on the margins of their world.

Romero (1997) accurately points out that Teresa's story is a "microcosm of power relations" in our stratified society. As such, it is an apt metaphor to understand how those traditionally excluded from universities, such as first-generation faculty, negotiate their position in the academy. Teresa's account provides a "lived framework" to examine my own schooling trajectory, beginning as an undergraduate at a predominantly white and elite institution to an assistant professor in a predominantly white and male department. In this *testimonio*, the academy is the employer, its members are the family, and I am the maid's daughter. Using this lived framework, I draw comparisons between Teresa's experience—living in the margins of a seemingly benevolent family—and my own schooling experiences in a community that is not entirely mine.

---

1. Teresa is the pseudonym in Romero (1997). In Romero (2011), her pseudonym is Olivia.

My Trajectory to the Academy

Like many other Mexican families in the 1970s, my parents, sister, and I arrived in Houston, Texas, to a "port-of-entry" neighborhood with rows of deteriorating shotgun homes. My father's third-grade-level education and my mother's high school education limited their employment options to entry-level service jobs. Yet, they persevered in their machinist and nanny jobs to incrementally improve our living conditions over time. My sister and I began our schooling as English learners in a bilingual classroom and endured learning a new and unfriendly language. In line with the dominant bilingual education model at that time, my sister and I transitioned to English-only instruction in the third grade. However, unlike most of our English learner peers, we were reclassified and enrolled in a gifted and talented program. This allowed us to embark on a road less frequently traveled by immigrant children and enter the margins of privilege.

In our family, *la escuela* (school) and *la tarea* (homework) took precedence over nearly everything. My parents' educational expectations and support were not tangible and concrete like college access models depict parental encouragement and support. Their support was sometimes contradictory, subtle, and came in ways that only later I recognized as encouragement: like the purchase of a desk lamp instead of a car oil change. Yet, there was never any question in my mind that my parents expected a *carrera profesional* (white-collar job) from my sister and me— *una carrera donde puedas andar limpia* (a career where we didn't have to get dirty)— and avoid the physical exhaustion of their machinist and nanny occupations.

While attending a selective high school with mostly white, upper-middle-class classmates, I began to comprehend the limitations of my designated position in the socioeconomic hierarchy. I observed my classmates work after-school in jobs that my parents coveted and fill their weekends with ballet season tickets and private music lessons to enhance their college applications. I also came to learn that poverty wasn't the only thing stacked against me—my racial identity also appeared to be a liability. Teachers, administrators, and peers whispered about affirmative action and racial quotas in college admissions, inserting doubt about my suitability for selective colleges. Students of color were rarely present in honors and advanced placement courses, and the curriculum never strayed from the Western canon. Teachers dismissed openly racist incidents as teenage indiscretions.

At the same time, a *Tejana* high school counselor became my protector and guide. She gave me permission to sit in her office and cry. I watched her subvert rules on my behalf. And she guided my family through the complex world of being college-bound. In many ways, she was like Teresa's mother, bringing me to the threshold of the employer's house, the academy. As Teresa did with her mother, I outgrew her protection in college as I searched for new heights beyond her sphere of influence.

By the time I had enrolled at Rice University, it was clear to me that my academic trajectory was unique among Latinx students in the United States. Unfortunately, college was like high school—equally hostile, predominantly white, wealthy, and with few opportunities to gain critical consciousness. It was in college that I observed privileged peers and faculty use convoluted rhetoric and contorted logic routes to promulgate simplistic, reductive, and racist ideology. Amid the national anti-affirmative action discourse and English-only movements of the 1990s, my presence was frequently questioned with subtle questions about "qualifications." Student-run publications flippantly labeled the mostly Mexican-origin janitorial staff "wetbacks" and "gnomes." I was so angry at the institution that I had no choice but to engage in daily battles to survive and win.

Going to graduate school at the University of California, Los Angeles (UCLA) was a reprieve from the overt racist, classist, and sexist language and policies I experienced during undergrad years. To be sure, UCLA's graduate program can continue to strive to achieve adequate representation of students and faculty of color and in pushing more critical perspectives in its curriculum. And there were covert ways in which class and status were communicated and enforced. On the other hand, a sizable group of students persistently pressed for more critical perspectives and articulated the needs of students of color and first-generation students. Although these pleas remained largely unfulfilled, I was relieved to find peers and mentors with similar visions of equitable and just education.

Unfortunately, the department I joined for my first tenure-track position was a throwback to the hostile, racist, sexist, and classist experiences of my undergrad college. As the only Latina or Chicana faculty in the school, and with no African American or Black representation, the exclusion, verbal violence, and trauma that I experienced were both overt and covert. Different rules and expectations applied to me, and I felt intellectually alienated and unsupported. Senior colleagues belittled the research community I belonged to, spoke derisively of queer applicants and applicants of color, and were outspoken about their deficit views of students of color. If I spoke, I was immediately silenced. And I was advised to use only quantitative methodologies to secure tenure. To survive, I left the institution. I concede this *testimonio* is, in part, a way to reclaim the narrative of my departure as a survival strategy from institutional trauma.

A Nanny's Daughter in the Academy

Who Belongs in the Family?

Teresa's mother's employer had the power to determine who could be a part of their family; Teresa felt she and her mother were bystanders in that decision. The privilege that is gained from belonging to a family with resources is so priceless, we are told, that a maid's daughter doesn't have agency to select their "family." Instead, the family has the power to select the laborer.

The undergraduate and graduate school admissions process is similar, where institutional representatives decide when and who can become part of the exclusive family, often using ambiguous and inconsistent selection criteria (Killgore, 2009). Similarly, faculty search committees are seemingly omnipotent because they are tasked with deciding who can join the family (Sensoy & DiAngelo, 2017). Not all applicants are privy to insider information that discloses how to gain access to the employer's family. A maid's daughter must then rely on the benevolence of a college counselor, an admissions counselor, or a subversive member of the search committee to provide piecemeal insider information (Holland, 2015). Other times, an external force, such as affirmative action policies, requires the "family" to take in a maid's daughter. Indeed, selection process appears to be meritorious, with requirements that seem neutral and objective, yet curiously function to reject and exclude those who may interrupt the existing structure of the employer's "family" (Killgore, 2009; Sensoy & DiAngelo, 2017).

Part of the allure of gaining entry to the employer's family is the myth of their compassion and commitment to Teresa's well-being and social mobility. Teresa's employers appear to be liberal, viewed as "tolerant" for opening their home to the maid's daughter, and were praised for their "kindness." Similarly, a maid's daughter in the academy is evidence of the employer's commitment to "diversity." And in appreciation for their "generosity," she is expected to validate the academy's shallow support for "diversity" by making aesthetic appearances in committees, events, and glossy brochures. This is akin to higher education institutions commodifying "inclusion" and "diversity" with superficial policies promoting interest convergence (Anderson, 2005; Harris et al., 2015). For example, university publications often featured my picture—both as a student and later as faculty—sometimes my face was lightened, and sometimes my picture even appeared in brochures of departments and colleges where I was not a student or faculty. Like Teresa, my image was displayed at events and on websites to demonstrate employer benevolence and commitment to "diversity." The universities tokenized my presence and commodified me for an aesthetic purpose (Muñoz et al., 2017).

Unseen and Unheard

As domestic workers, Teresa and her mother performed the labor-intensive and tedious roles that the family members did not want to do. As a quasi–family member, Teresa was expected to accept her role quietly, undetected. Teresa's mother dutifully adhered to her role, partly in fear of angering the employer and losing their housing. In comparison, first-generation students and faculty are similarly granted access to elite institutions on the unstated condition that they do not disturb or significantly alter the employer-maid relationship (Turner,

1994). As a student, when I joined protests or called attention to an injustice, my own parents and school personnel alike criticized me for "not focusing" on my studies, for not valuing the financial aid that was invested on my behalf. In hostile class discussions, overtly racist comments reinforced my status. Curriculum ignored my lived reality. Later, as pre-tenure faculty, my maid's daughter status was often reinforced in faculty and committee meetings, where I was expected to remain silent to instances of overt sexism and racism.

When Teresa claimed a more vocal and independent role in the family, arguments with the employer's family ensued, followed later by estrangement. Similarly, when I sought to explain how students perceived the department's racial climate, a white senior male colleague verbally assaulted me in a faculty retreat and a senior faculty ostracized me. I had stepped out of my ascribed role, had broken a tacit agreement to remain invisible. Like the estrangement that Teresa experienced, the verbal assault was a reminder that I did not fully belong to the family. Mitchell (2018) aptly "know-your-place-aggression," describes the emotional, verbal, and physical violence women and people of color experience when they attempt to claim space in predominantly white institutions. In granting me quasi-family status in the academy, I was expected to be both appreciative and grateful for their tolerance, as well as reminded of my location in the family if I stepped outside those bounds.

Although Teresa had access to some of the same privileged resources as the employer's children, such as attending private school or joining them on vacations, there always remained a gap that reminded her she was the maid's daughter. As a student and faculty at elite institutions, I was also granted access to some employer resources. I had access to the same courses and instructors, libraries, office, funds for textbooks and computer, salary, sabbatical, and other resources spelled out in policy handbooks. But there were other types of knowledge, practices, and support that reminded me that I was not fully part of the family. For example, my college roommate's father, who was faculty at another college, reviewed her written assignments. In contrast, I struggled to meet college-level writing expectations. As new faculty, I learned a colleague self-financed a professional development program to improve her productivity, a resource no one told me about until years later; and my own department would not fund this expense for me. More recently, I did not know to ask for a stipend to complete summer administrative duties and was thus not offered a stipend, whereas a male counterpart in the same department asked for and received a stipend for the same work. This lack of support was a reminder that I wasn't a full-fledged member of the family. As the daughter of a live-in maid, I did not know I could ask for more resources nor how others leveraged their support; and when I did ask for support, I was dismissed. At the end, differences in access to resources and support undermine the rhetoric of diversity and equity (Harris et al., 2015) and reveal the power differentials that exist in employer-maid relationships.

Resisting Erasure

In exchange for quasi-familial status, the employer expected Teresa to assimilate to their norms and values. There was an implied, if incorrect, assumption that Teresa and her mother desired to shed their culture, to be like the employer's family. Belonging to the academy is similarly conditioned on shedding identities and behaviors that upset patriarchal, white, neoliberal ideals of the academy (Cruz, 2018). This process of erasure begins with a curriculum that privileges Eurocentric knowledge (Delgado Bernal & Villalpando, 2002). As an undergraduate, my education largely omitted all non-Eurocentric and nonpositivist knowledge and scholarship. But I sought ways to nourish and claim my cultural history, because for Chicana first-generation faculty like me, persistence in the academy is dependent on our ability to resist erasure and maintain our cultural anchors (Pérez, 2019). I listened to Tejano music, visited my family in Mexico, took courses that focused on scholarship and literature from scholars of color, and joined Latinx organizations on campus. These "counterspaces" of resistance are important to cultural maintenance and survival of the academy (Solorzano et al., 2000).

In the long term, Teresa persevered in maintaining her Chicana identity by intentionally seeking social interactions with Chicanx working-class peers and adults. For this, the employer questions her commitment to education. In the academy, individuals who remain grounded, personally and professionally, in marginalized, working-class, or immigrant communities are questioned about their commitment to the profession (Quijada Cerecer et al., 2011). Choosing to prioritize time with family, students, or public service in lieu of writing publications is viewed as inconsistent with professional expectations. My commitment to my career was questioned when I rejected subsidized university housing close to campus. My white colleagues could not fathom that I needed to live in a space that reinforced my ethnic and cultural roots, even if it meant driving 1.5 hours each way. Choosing to live in South Los Angeles allowed me to breathe at the end of a day on campus. Attending exercise classes with working-class Latina women in my neighborhood gave me the courage to face the next faculty meeting. Partly as an antidote to the hostility of my colleagues, I needed to be nourished by the spaces and the people that were familiar to me.

A Borderland Mestiza

As the daughter of a live-in maid, Teresa negotiated multiple social boundaries and rules that varied by context. Her home life included other domestic workers, working-class Mexican families, and wealthy white neighbors. At school and work, she interacted with upper-class, working-class, white, and Chicano peers. She was caregiver to neighbor's children, managed an ice cream parlor, and went to a selective university where she became an activist. In this variable landscape, Teresa was sometimes outsider and sometimes insider, and constantly "has to interpret the social cues and social settings correctly" (Romero, 1997, p. 196). Indeed, she was Anzaldúa's (1987) borderland *mestiza*, navigating boundaries while sustained by her ancestors' culture and knowledge. Teresa's position can also illustrate Du Bois's (1995) double-consciousness, always looking at her and her mother's lives "through the eyes of others" (p. 45), never quiet living up to either ideal.

As a first-generation student and faculty, I similarly learned that all interactions were situated in unstated norms that reproduced hierarchies of power. I became hyperaware of the mode of interaction that was applicable at home versus the academy. I learned when to strategically mimic male assertiveness or when to play pleasant and agreeable woman. Although humility was valued in my family, I learned that in male-dominated settings, I needed to be subtly arrogant and seek opportunities to boast about my accomplishments. As untenured faculty, I learned that I was expected to remain silent at faculty meetings, to express my opinions only if I concurred with the three senior male faculty. Now, as a tenured full professor, I still monitor my language and speech, attentive to the context and expectations of the audience.

Failure to discern and observe the rules of each context can have dire consequences for a maid's daughter. For Teresa and her mother, their housing and employment were at stake. For a maid's daughter in the academy, the institution can similarly withhold resources or alienate her. The academy has a range of tools at their disposal to deliver the message of "know-your-place aggression" (Mitchell, 2018), even post-tenure. For example, leadership positions are awarded to others while requests for uncompensated labor mount for the maid's daughter, failure to comply are viewed as uncooperative behavior, speaking up for an injustice is viewed as an attitude problem, and advocating for critical curriculum is viewed as "imposing" my value system.

But Teresa and her mother did not submit to all the employer's rules. From her mother, Teresa learned to strategically acquiesce to some employer demands but consciously critique and subvert other rules. I similarly observed my parents strategically accommodate and reject demands from their employers and used this strategy in the academy. This is where our resistance is borne: we outwardly conform and accommodate but covertly resist. One way that I undermined the colonization process of schooling was by learning to speak like the employer, but I maintained my native language and speech to subvert other situations. Nonetheless, resistance to erasure and the struggle for survival in spaces not created for me has, at times, eroded my confidence and desire to claim my space. Living in between two worlds at war with one another takes its toll (Anzaldúa, 1987; Du Bois, 1995).

Implications for My Research

As a first-generation, working-class, immigrant Chicana faculty, the academy remains a contradictory space for me, a place where I simultaneously have the privilege to intellectually examine institutional oppression while struggling to be a legitimate member of the institutional family. Yet, from this tension arises a new consciousness—a *mestiza* consciousness, as Anzaldúa (1987) labels it—that gathers "its energy from continual creative motion that keeps breaking down the unitary aspect of each new paradigm" (p. 102). As a borderland *mestiza* living in both the employer's and my *gente*'s (people's) family, I borrow epistemologies from multiple dimensions of my personal and professional lives to generate scholarship and research grounded in lived realities.

The "alchemy" (Anzaldúa, 1987) of my family's histories, my community's collective experiences, and my scholarly training inform my approach to research. This amalgamation of experiences is what Delgado Bernal (1998) calls "cultural intuition." She argues that the Chicana researchers' cultural intuition can shift the epistemological foundations of education research to generate research that addresses and is grounded on the lived experiences of its subjects. When confronted with methodological dilemmas, dead-end findings, or the inadequacy of current theories, I draw on my "cultural intuition" as a first-generation, working-class, immigrant Chicana to seek different methodologies, explore or create frameworks, and straddle disciplinary boundaries in order to shift the epistemological foundations of research.

For example, the genesis of the idea to analyze longitudinal trajectories to college by gender in Zarate and Gallimore (2005) emerged from a *conocimiento* (consciousness) exercise in a Women's Studies class while in graduate school. In that activity, I identified distinct schooling patterns between women and men in my family, which then compelled me to analyze trajectories separately for girls and boys in the sample—a sample that shared immigration and migration experiences with my family's immigration history. This shift allowed starkly different trajectories to emerge for boys and girls, indicating that differences in schooling experiences were hidden when gender was only a control variable or an interaction term, as it is commonly included in quantitative analysis. The back-and-forth and blending between disciplines, methodological traditions, and past and future histories of immigration yielded a finding that eschewed the tired trope of deterministic underachievement for Latinx immigrant youth.

In much of my research, there is a story of my own resistance and history embedded in methodological and theoretical framing of the subjects. The struggles that accompany the institutional exclusion that I experience allow me to imagine and create new paradigms that are neither theirs nor exclusively mine. The unique positioning of first-generation faculty in the academy allows us to ground our research on real-life questions and experience. In education research, this standpoint allows us to capture the contradictions of the schooling process and illustrate how our community negotiates hierarchies in our educational processes. In turn, this allows for identifying how power is distributed in systems and institutions and targeting our collective resistance to the systems that seek to keep us out.

REFERENCES

Anderson, G. M. (2005). In the name of diversity: Education and the commoditization and consumption of race in the United States. *Urban Review, 37*(5), 399–423. https://doi.org/10.1007/s11256-005-0017-z

Anzaldúa, G. (1987). *Borderlands/La frontera: The new mestiza.* Aunt Lute Books.

Anzaldúa, G. (1990). Haciendo caras, una entrada. In G. Anzaldúa (Ed.), *Making face, making soul, haciendo caras: Creative and critical perspectives by feminists of color* (pp. xv–xxviii). Aunt Lute Books.

August, L., & Waltman, J. (2004). Culture, climate, and contribution: Career satisfaction among female faculty. *Research in Higher Education, 45*(2), 177–192. http://dx.doi.org/10.1023/B:RIHE.0000015694.14358.ed

Calderón, D., Delgado Bernal, D., Perez Huber, L., Malagón, M., & Velez, V. N. (2012). A Chicana feminist epistemology revisited: Cultivating ideas a generation later. *Harvard Educational Review, 82*(4), 513–540. https://doi.org/10.17763/haer.82.4.l518621577461p68

Carroll, D. (2017). A faculty women of color micro-invalidations at white research institution: A case of intersectionality of institutional betrayal. *Administrative Issues Journalist, 7*(1). https://doi.org/10.5929/2017.7.1.2

Castillo-Montana, M., & Torres-Guzman, M. E. (2012). Thriving in our identity and in the academy: Latina feminist epistemology as a core resource. *Harvard Educational Review, 82*(4), 540–559. doi:10.17763/haer.82.4.k483005176882ln5

Cruz, J. M. (2018). Brown body of knowledge: A tale of erasure. *Cultural Studies—Critical Methodologies, 18*(5), 363–365. https://doi.org/10.1177/1532708617735131

Delgado Bernal, D. (1998). Using a Chicana feminist epistemology in educational research. *Harvard Educational Review, 68*(4), 555–582. https://doi.org/10.17763/haer.68.4.5wvl034973g22q48

Delgado Bernal, D., Burciaga, R., & Carmona, J. F. (2012). Chicana/Latina *testimonios*: Mapping the methodological, pedagogical, and political. *Equity & Excellence in Education, 45*(3), 363–372. https://doi.org/10.1080/10665684.2012.698149

Delgado Bernal, D., & Villalpando, O. (2002). An apartheid of knowledge in academia: The struggle over the "legitimate" knowledge of faculty of color. *Equity and Excellence in Education, 35*(2), 169–180. https://doi.org/10.1080/713845282

Du Bois, W.E.B. (1995). *The souls of Black folk.* Penguin Putnam.

Gonzales, L. D. (2018). Subverting and minding boundaries: The intellectual work of women. *Journal of Higher Education, 89*(5), 677–701. https://doi.org/10.1080/00221546.2018.1434278

Harris, J. C., Barone, R. P., & Patton, L. D. (2015). Who benefits? A critical race analysis of the (d)evolving language of inclusion in higher education. *NEA Higher Education Journal, (D),* 21–38. https://studylib.net/doc/8907492/who-benefits%3F--a-critical-race-analysis-of-the--d-

Holland, M. M. (2015). Trusting each other: Student-counselor relationships in diverse high schools. *Sociology of Education, 88*(3), 244–262. https://doi.org/10.1177/0038040715591347

Killgore, L. (2009). Merit and competition in selective college admissions. *Review of Higher Education, 32*(4), 469–488. https://doi.org/10.1353/rhe.0.0083c

The Latina Feminist Group. (2001). *Telling to live: Latina feminist testimonios.* Duke University Press.

Machado-Casas, M., Cantu Ruiz, E., & Cantu, N. E. (2013). *Laberintos y testimonios*: Latina faculty in the academy. *Educational Foundations, 27*(1–2), 3–14.

Marschke, R., Laursen, S., Nielsen, J. M., & Rankin, P. (2007). Demographic inertia revisited: An immodest proposal to achieve equitable gender representation among faculty in higher education. *Journal of Higher Education, 78*(1), 1–26. https://doi.org/10.1080/00221546.2007.11778961

Mitchell, K. (2018). Identifying white mediocrity and know-your-place aggression: A form of self-care. *African American Review, 51*(4), 253–262. https://doi.org/10.1353/afa.2018.0045

Muñoz, S. M., Basile, V., Gonzalez, J., Birmingham, D., Aragon, A., Jennings, L., & Gloeckner, G. (2017). (Counter)narratives and complexities: Critical perspectives from a university cluster hire focused on diversity, equity, and inclusion. *Journal of Critical Thought and Praxis, 6*(2), 1–21. https://doi.org/10.31274/jctp-180810-71

Museus, S. D., & Griffin, K. A. (2011). Mapping the margins in higher education: On the promise of intersectionality frameworks in research and discourse. *New Directions for Institutional Research*, (151), 5–13. https://onlinelibrary.wiley.com/doi/10.1002/ir.395

Oliva, M., Rodríguez, M. A., Alanís, I., & Quijada Cerecer, P. D. (2013). At home in the academy: Latina faculty counterstories and resistances. *Educational Foundations, 27*(1–2), 91–109.

Pérez, P. A. (Ed.). (2019) *The tenure-track process for Chicana and Latina faculty: Experiences of resisting and persisting in the academy.* Routledge.

Pifer, M. J. (2011). Intersectionality in context: A mixed-methods approach to researching the faculty experience. *New Directions for Institutional Research*, (151), 27–44. https://onlinelibrary.wiley.com/doi/10.1002/ir.39

Quijada Cerecer, P. D., Ek, L. D., Alanis, I., & Murakami-Ramalho, E. (2011). Transformative resistance as agency: Chicanas/Latinas (re)creating academic spaces. *Journal of the Professoriate, 5*(1), 70–98. https://caarpweb.org/wp-content/uploads/2016/11/5-1_Quijada Cerecer_p.70.pdf

Reyes, K. B., & Curry Rodríguez, J. E. (2012). *Testimonio*: Origins, terms, and resources. *Equity and Excellence in Education, 45*(3), 525–538. https://doi.org/10.1080/10665684.2012.698571

Romero, M. (1997). Life as a maid's daughter: An exploration of the everyday boundaries of race, class, and gender. In M. Romero, P. Hondagneu-Sotelo, & V. Ortiz (Eds.), *Challenging fronteras: Structuring Latino and Latino lives in the U.S.* (pp. 195–209). Routledge.

Romero, M. (2011). *The maid's daughter: Living inside and outside the American dream.* New York University Press.

Sánchez, P., & Ek, L. D. (2013). Before the tenure track: Graduate school *testimonios* and their importance in our profesora-ship today. *Educational Foundations, 27*(1–2), 15–30.

Sensoy, Ö., & DiAngelo, R. (2017). "We are all for diversity, but . . .": How faculty hiring committees reproduce whiteness and practical suggestions for how they can change. *Harvard Educational Review, 87*(4), 557–580. https://doi.org/10.17763/1943-5045-87.4.557

Turner, C.S.V. (1994). Guest in someone else's house: Students of color. *Review of Higher Education, 17*(4), 355–370. https://doi.org/10.1353/rhe.1994.0008

Turner, C.S.V., González, J. C., & Wood, J. L. (2008). Faculty of color in academe: What 20 years of literature tells us. *Journal of Diversity in Higher Education, 1*(3), 139–168. https://doi.org/10.1037/a0012837

Zarate, E., & Gallimore, R. (2005). Gender difference in factors leading to college enrollment: A longitudinal analysis of Latina and Latino students. *Harvard Educational Review, 75*(4), 383–408.

4

On Navigating with Flavor

A Reluctant Professor on the Pathway Here

DARRICK SMITH

The pathway from K–12 to the faculty ranks of the academy is riddled with narratives of struggle and triumph. As an autoethnographic narrative that seeks to demonstrate a reflexive analysis of coping and survival mechanisms in academia, I emphasize racial positionality along with conspicuous invisibility to highlight experiences with informal rituals of communal and cultural celebration as crucial preparatory aids toward the navigation of higher education. I utilize an asset-based framing of late twentieth-century urban culture and the associated tools and perspectives that can be internalized as a result of being socialized in such environments.

A Flavorful Way of Being

When initially asked to explain my experience as a first-generation college graduate and professor, a visceral emotion of distance and alienation vibrated powerfully in my body. Being a perpetual minority in predominantly white institutions can do that to a person. Such a feeling immediately stimulated what I can only describe as a defense mechanism of thoughts, images, and corresponding emotions that recentered my body into a warm state of grounded comfort. The thoughts and images that my mind conjures up when faced with alienating and thus dehumanizing spaces are those of an adolescence and childhood that gave me a sense of self and pride in the people from which I have come. Much of what I will mention has been diluted over time for me; as I have gotten older, spaces have been gentrified, city ordinances have targeted the pathways to such communal activities, and I have been less entrenched. Still, it is the essence of what I consider "cultural magnificence" that cannot fully disappear and, as such, cannot be purged from my being as a compilation of memories, relationships, rituals, phrases, symbols, and perspectives that make up the core of who I am as I engage with the world around me.

What it really is—the color. And I don't just mean the people of color and the saturation of humanistic hues as I move through every element of a diverse, Black city. That is incredibly important. But I mean to refer more specifically to the colors of life and that emit from such a context. This is more than what some scholars (academically) describe as "coolness" (Hall, 2009; Kirkland & Jackson, 2009) as these are not simply behaviors or demonstrations of inclusion or anti-establishment. This is closer to "black girl magic" or Iton's "black fantastic" (Crawford, 2014; Iton, 2010; Snyder, 2014) in that they represent an incredibly powerful manifestation of culturally located selves enacting behaviors of mutual empowerment through celebration and congregation. They are the behaviors, expressions, and frameworks that are present in organizing spaces where necessary actions and ideologies challenge invisibility and enduring circumstances of marginalization.

It is these communal spaces and norms of cultural expression that are powerful beyond what words can accurately describe and what poetry comes close to articulating in many forms and variations. It is indeed what many have referred to over the last four decades in African American vernacular as "flavor," "soul," or what Howard C. Stevenson (2003) refers to as "cultural ways of being." This flavor is what I would recall being one of the more important elements that helped to shape my concept of self. To be even more specific, the multitude of ways in which pride in being in one's "skin" was routinely expressed created a space for understanding the myriad ways that people live their lives. And in doing so, such expressions represented to me the plethora of forms in which communities and individuals can express a love for being alive while in very precarious social, political, and economic situations.

So when I imagine some of the core sustaining factors that have helped me move through this educational system, I also reflect on how these factors helped me make sense of this educational system as a professor. Now, there are several ways that I can discuss these colors of expression and this "flavor" that—in very particular environments—we get to smell, touch, and see sparkling before us. As the bodies, voices, movements, and the creations that are produced from all of this wonderfulness shapes the social world far beyond the Black communities of the United States, the flavor can garner much, well-deserved attention from the public and scholars alike. Unfortunately, an academic can make something so difficult to describe seem both manageable and simultaneously bland as one attempts to present a picture that is segmented and staged for analytical discourse. But in this case, because I am talking about myself and my experience, I will try to avoid falling too deeply into this trap and write as I feel.

A (Not "the") Black Lens

There is something special about growing up in a very Black community. At the time of my adolescence, my city was over 48 percent Black. What that means is that I got a chance to be immersed in my culture as a majority population throughout my childhood. So gatherings at the city's Lake were predominantly Black gatherings. Sundays in the city were routine opportunities to see Black people in their "Sunday best" formal clothing as they moved throughout the city from church services to Sunday brunches. As I caught public transportation throughout my days, I had the chance to routinely encounter, and thus normalize in my mind the experience of Black working professionals as they commuted to work and addressed professional needs throughout their day. As an adolescent, I got to experience African American teachers scattered throughout my primary and secondary education. Even though they were not numerous in my mind comparatively to the diverse array of ethnicities that made up the faculty teams throughout my education. My parents would host their family, friends, and coworkers at our home. These were people who were also often, but not always, Black and professional people who worked in a variety of different fields. My relatives worked as lawyers, dentists, autoworkers, and organizational managers, and in other routine jobs. As a child, I wasn't allowed to sit in on the adult conversations, but I enjoyed listening from the periphery to topics ranging from politics to sports to relationships.

But perhaps what made these experiences personify Black flavor is the routinized, pervasive, expansive, and multigenerational frequency of racial discourse. It would be impossible to count the number of times I was coached, unsolicited, to the ways that this white world will try to interrupt my progress. Conversations that range from an analysis of national politics to history lessons regarding the intertwined realities of our current global economic system and the significance of the transatlantic slave trade. These were discussions had by teenagers, senior-aged elders, and everyone in between. Such dialogue could occur spontaneously on the phone, on the bus, on the train, in the classrooms of our schools, in the counseling offices with social workers, and just about every other social space you could imagine.

The understanding of Black oppression and the need for continual resistance was a normalized discussion and influenced how one might choose their reading material, develop their music selection, and understand the nightly news and civic politics. And it is within this framing of Black Oakland existentialism that people would hop out of cars when seeing an old friend from grade school and embrace them with joy and smiles. It is within this framing and understanding that one can stop in to a local barbershop or hair salon and experience narratives and social commentary sparked with outbursts of laughter, passion, and empathetic nods and gestures—all manifested and centered in Black bodies and culture.

This is the environment that shaped me. This is the environment in which I normalized the idea that if I were to be targeted as a Black man, it was because of the strength, creativity, diversity of skills, and worldview that I may have, not because there is something deficient about where I come from or my identity.

This is the social and communal context that influenced me to place more value on the richness of the community from which I came than on the academic institution where I work. No university or system of higher education could develop the flavor and soul from which I came—they can only attempt to explain it.

Moving Through

Predominately white institutions are historically structured, intended, and operated with the intent to exclude all that I described here. Thus, in essence, they are places that have established their viability and reputations off of my absence. If left unchallenged, there would never be any space for me and for folks that remain invested in rich, flavorful environments like the one that I have described.

Another piece is understanding that while they may be different spaces, the same instincts for survival and resistance are needed in higher education when confronting what is often a culture of exploitation and compliance (Martinez et al., 2017). All those things still play out in very similar ways at the university as they would on the street—it's just less violent or overtly confrontational. You have bullies on the streets and you have bullies at the university. You have professionals manipulating and exploiting other people to elevate their own status. You have people trying to con you for various reasons—either to give them money or to make you believe that they are something that they're not, or that they are more important than they actually are. You have people cliquing up to influence what's going to happen on the block or what's going to happen on their side of town or in order to form alliances to strategically undermine others. All that happens at the university level, and having experience with these issues previous to the institution constitutes a form of "knowing" that many might dismiss as irrelevant in an academic environment (Bernal & Villalpando, 2002).

Being a Black man in academia doesn't leave you much choice when it comes to your options as to how to navigate the tension between your cultural self and the culture of the academy. Much of the beautiful elements of being a professor can be diluted or lost when regarding the intersection between my identity and my professional role. Most particularly, much of the beauties that I can even imagine would not be ones that were a result of an intersection between my identity and spaces of higher education. On the contrary, the powerful and positive elements that deeply resonate with me are the aspects of my job that inspire my love for teaching, learning, and connecting with good people. However, if one considers the intersection between my identity and my role as an associate professor at an American university, what I have experienced is much of what could be expected, given the historical exclusionary nature of higher education.

This is not to assert that I am disappointed, nor deprived of the many privileges that come with achieving tenure at a four-year university in the United States. The privileges of tenure and teaching schedules that afford me the opportunity to engage in alternative means of development are special aspects of the profession. I'm sure that to many of my colleagues, the status that accompanies the role of the tenure track professor and its associated titles are also privileges that could be seen as beautiful elements of my job. Some people revel in the sound of the word "doctor" followed by their last name as people address them in both formal and informal spaces. One could even suggest that those pursuing a role in the professoriate have used visions and dreams of such interpersonal exchanges as sources of motivation throughout their journey.

Predictable Discomfort

Scholars who have written on the struggles that people of color face in the academy discuss the ways in which marginalized identities experience various forms of marginalization in higher education that lead to psychological, emotional, and often physical health concerns (Diggs et al., 2009; Eagan & Garvey, 2015; Harrell, 2000; Turner, 2002). The ramifications of moving through institutions as a marginalized identity often manifests in what has been called "cultural taxation" (Tierney & Bensimon, 1996)—an added layer of fatigue from labor that results from the social, political, and cultural positionality of a faculty member and their sense of obligation to their racial / ethnic community. The pressures that I might bring to the space on my shoulders can add a significant amount of anxiety to every task I take on as I equate my success or failure with my overall capacity to honor my community, family, and ancestors. For others, this pressure could also include or be replaced by pressure to challenge stereotypes or institutional culture of deficit thinking toward marginalized identities (Arnold et al., 2016; Pittman, 2010).

Researchers have noted the potential and lived challenges for Black faculty at predominantly white universities. Discussions of tokenism (Kelly, 2007; Niemann, 2016; Tasker, 1977) have expanded and connected to include explorations into the psychological impact of being Black in the academy (Butner et al., 2000; Dade et al., 2015; Dancy et al., 2018). Researchers have also captured experiences and identified mechanisms when dealing with racial tension and microaggressions in the academy (Haynes et al., 2020; Louis et al., 2016; Smith, 2004). Additionally, studies have also revealed the added labor burdens that Black faculty members may assume in view of insufficient student support mechanisms as a result of their sharing of identities with some of their institutions' most marginalized students (Edwards & Ross, 2018; Haynes et al., 2020; Tuitt, 2012). All of these and several other issues can be attributed to the small numbers of Black faculty in American universities (Kelly et al., 2017).

Conspicuous Invisibility

There is something of emotional significance that comes along with being in a professional service discipline that focuses on issues that impact the Black community and names the Black community in much of the discourse, but yet is filled with researchers, scholars, and instructors that are not of African American heritage. The experience, while not new or novel, can be described as a conspicuous invisibility or "being there without being there" (Quinlan 2008, p. 1480). For me, such an experience can evoke emotions that include anxiety, alienation, frustration, and bitterness. While the notion of "conspicuous invisibility" is a term often associated with qualitative methodology, here I am referring to its use as a dynamic with a racialized social, political, and existential context that marginalizes bodies of color. In this way, as Stevenson and colleagues (2003) articulate, "conspicuous invisibility is the persistent, pervasive, and perpetual systemic imaging of Black men as problematic and the systematic blindness or refusal to acknowledge and remember African-American male talent and potential" (p. 62).

Again, my experience with conspicuous invisibility is one that is situated within a context of self-proclaimed social justice educators and institutions. In such a context, I can speak to my experience as manifesting in three ways:

1. My experience as a Black man in this society is validated but only when attached to pain and suffering.
2. My presence as a marginalized man of color on faculty is touted as an example of the institution's commitment to diversity and the inclusion of historically oppressed voices. Yet when we experience conflict with students from more privileged identities or need support that might be traditionally given to faculty of more privileged identities, our presence and voice become dispensable.
3. While there is much reference to the cultural value, and historical symbolic significance of the African American struggle against poverty, state-sanctioned terrorism, white supremacy, and so on, there is very little alignment in regard to the value of integrity, respect, healthy communication, or courage that could be identified as important staples of survival and progress in working-class communities.

The ways in which I experience conspicuous invisibility are not new in the academy for faculty staff or students from marginalized identities. What I am discussing here is not a result of what I believe to be malicious or racialized intent, nor would I agree that it is the result of what others may deem as unconscious bias. I am privileged to be surrounded by incredibly intelligent scholars who have made it their life's mission to analyze and dissect dynamics of power and the ways that social and political systems impact people. In such an environment, where oppression and allyship are regularly discussed, however, the existential realities of repression don't seem to shift the aesthetic of the academy. Too often, the behaviors and perspectives that define academia seem largely unchanged as the world of social change and activism become merely inserted into it. It is my impression that there is an inherent disconnect that is not only permissible, but almost required within higher education as many of us seek to move marginalized voices and experiences to the center of academic discourse in the social sciences. But how could this be any different?

In research, conspicuous invisibility emerges as part and parcel of a larger institutional dynamic of enclosure in the academy. Researchers and authors have identified the ways in which academia at large and higher education in particular, have long served a purpose of establishing and maintaining privilege and economic stratification in our society. Whether it be through the perpetuation of white supremacy, admissions perks to elite families, or antilabor politics, the university has often been noted as a learning space that is largely unwelcoming to marginalized bodies and the ideologies that promote their empowerment (Saunders, 2007).

The notion of enclosure is just one more potential ramification of the ways that the academy has historically occupied these positions. The notion of enclosure represents the accumulation and securing of land, materials, or other resources of value from those whose labor produced it (Kamola & Meyerhoff. 2009). Originally a Marxist term referencing structures of feudal resource accumulation, researchers note that enclosure in the academy can manifest in different forms that, for the most part, align with neoliberal social, political, and economic phenomena (Federici, 2009; Hall, 2013; O'Donovan, 2014; Riemer, 2016). Some examples of enclosure in higher education include the normalization of neoliberal policies restricting admissions and particular areas of course content, the problematic, access-oriented issues inherent in academic publishing, increased costs that restrict access to education, the establishment of policies that further limit faculty and staff labor power, and for-profit imperatives that shift institutional goals away from student learning (Bollier, 2002; Coles & Scarnati, 2014; Peekhaus, 2012).

Conspicuous invisibility emerges as one considers these aforementioned dynamics while adding a common element of social science research to the list—a dynamic of extraction without intervention. This is to mean a problematic, fundamental aspect of research protocols that not only allows, but rather expects researchers to study individuals and groups but not intervene upon the troubling situations that are often the focal point of their inquiry. Furthermore, once data is extracted and ideas are developed, there are additional expectations that insights or potential problem-solving ideas be encrypted into an academic language and submitted for publishing in literary locations foreign to the communities that served as research "subjects."

In essence, this dynamic represents a positioning of subjects as conspicuously present as targets for inquiry but simultaneously renders them invisible as human beings engaged in ongoing efforts to cope, adapt, or exist in their current social reality. In this dynamic, the subjects of social science inquiry are often expected to remain as a reservoir for knowledge and frameworks for those who do not share their positionality or experience. Clearly they are there, but fundamentally they are not expected to benefit from the inquiry in which they participated. As a Black, first-generation professor, this fundamental aspect of academia represents one of the core areas of tension in my work.

When I think about the challenges that I face in academia, I find it hard to separate the context, phenomena, attitudes, and institutional operations from the experiences that I have off-campus in the world. Being raised in a Black household in a city with a history of Black political activism and cross-cultural working-class organizing, I was mentored and socialized to expect elite spaces to manifest cultures of white supremacy and colonialism. My trek through the U.S. educational system to where I am now has been riddled with near daily reminders and experiences of systemic, racial marginalization and targeting, and the forms of internalization that are necessary within my own community for an oppressive democratic structure to thrive.

In the midst of this inherently disconnected, unappreciative, and highly colonizing space, it makes sense that I would experience such emotional turmoil as a person who is rooted in the exact opposite set of ethics under which higher education operates. Researchers have noted the coldness and capitalist culture upon which the academy stands (Patton, 2016; Thompson & Louque, 2005). Without needing to go into great detail here, I will just say that the realities of the dehumanizing essence of higher education remains relevant even when educators take on causes and establish spaces that advocate for social justice or its disciplinary adjuncts of anti-imperialism, decolonization, and parallel projects of liberation pedagogy. I would say that what I have experienced is the result of what emerges out of this amalgamation of well-meaning educators interested in social justice and an entire system of higher education that establishes its prestige on the distance from ethnic, marginalized populations or the centering of their concerns.

Conclusion

I try to navigate the academy as the Black man on the margins like I navigated Oakland—just trying to be myself and stay true to what's important to me. This idea reigns over everything. It reigns over everything I do at my institution or at any of these places of higher education. Academics don't get violent and they often lack or have been disconnected from the type of flavor that makes me feel seen. There's a lot of passive-aggressive talk and folks can always try to have you or your position terminated, but because I am from where I'm from, I always have a backup plan and it's hard to genuinely fear anyone in academia.

In my eyes, the worst a colleague or senior member of administration could do is try to fire me, humiliate me, or lower my status. But to me, my true status

would never rely on any university, department, or the culture of higher education. You could demote my status among a community of researchers all you
want. But when you are from a place of flavor, smiles, and love in the face of
oppression, such status seems less significant. So the worst you could do is
make me leave this white space or make me less appealing to institutions
that are dehumanizing and unappealing to me. That's no punishment. See,
what I come from doesn't function by the words of those at the university. If
this place were to say to my community, "He's a terrible researcher," I imagine
my folks would reply, "We didn't elevate Darrick to go *ask more questions for you.*
We elevated him to help *answer questions for us.* If y'all think he's not a good
researcher, we don't care about that. That's not how he serves us."

So that's my whole perspective. It's important to be grounded in the richness that constitutes the flavor from which you came. For those of us from violent cities, we know that right alongside such violence existed a persistent, rooted
baseline of love and appreciation. The oppressive social context of political and
economic targeting was not just something you had to "overcome," but something that gave you tools and skills and experiences that many Americans might
struggle to even imagine. Essentially, the violence and the flavor gave me strategies and frameworks for success that academia did not. I have pride in who I am
and the people who share similar experiences and skin tones. There is a flavor
of life, expression, resilience, and success that academia can't provide. I am honored to have grown up with it. If I remember to always value and stay grounded
in that, there's really not much any institution can do to distract me from
remaining who I am supposed to be, or what I am supposed to do.

REFERENCES

Arnold, N. W., Crawford, E. R., & Khalifa, M. (2016). Psychological heuristics and faculty of
   color: Racial battle fatigue and tenure/promotion. *Journal of Higher Education, 87*(6),
   890–919. https://muse.jhu.edu/article/634189
Bernal, D. D., & Villalpando, O. (2002). An apartheid of knowledge in academia: The struggle over the "legitimate" knowledge of faculty of color. *Equity & Excellence in Education,
   35*(2), 169–180. http://dx.doi.org/10.1080/713845282
Bollier, D. (2002). The enclosure of the academic commons. *Academe, 88*(5), 18–22. https://
   www.jstor.org/stable/40252215
Butner, B. K., Burley, H., & Marbley, A. F. (2000). Coping with the unexpected: Black faculty
   at predominately white institutions. *Journal of Black Studies, 30*(3), 453–462. https://
   www.jstor.org/stable/2645946
Coles, R., & Scarnati, B. (2014). *Beyond enclosure: Pedagogy for a democratic commonwealth.* Ket-
   tering Foundation. https://www.kettering.org/wp-content/uploads/HEX-2014-final.pdf
   #page=71
Crawford, M. N. (2014). Uncovering the Black fantastic in Black body politics. *Souls, 16*(3–4),
   166–182. https://doi.org/10.1080/10999949.2014.968956
Dade, K., Tartakov, C., Hargrave, C., & Leigh, P. (2015). Assessing the impact of racism on
   Black faculty in white academe: A collective case study of African American female

faculty. *Western Journal of Black Studies, 39*(2), 134–146. https://lib.dr.iastate.edu/edu_pubs/128

Dancy, T. E., Edwards, K. T., & Earl Davis, J. (2018). Historically white universities and plantation politics: Anti-Blackness and higher education in the Black Lives Matter era. *Urban Education, 53*(2), 176–195. https://doi.org/10.1177/0042085918754328

Diggs, G. A., Garrison-Wade, D. F., Estrada, D., & Galindo, R. (2009). Smiling faces and colored spaces: The experiences of faculty of color pursing tenure in the academy. *The Urban Review, 41*(4), 312–333. https://doi.org/10.1007/s11256-008-0113-y

Eagan, M. K., & Garvey, J. C. (2015). Stressing out: Connecting race, gender, and stress with faculty productivity. *Journal of Higher Education, 86*(6), 923–954. https://doi.org/10.1080/00221546.2015.11777389

Edwards, W. J., & Ross, H. H. (2018). What are they saying? Black faculty at predominantly white institutions of higher education. *Journal of Human Behavior in the Social Environment, 28*(2), 142–161. https://doi.org/10.1080/10911359.2017.1391731

Federici, S. (2009). Education and the enclosure of knowledge in the global university. *ACME: An International Journal for Critical Geographies, 8*(3), 454–461. https://acme-journal.org/index.php/acme/article/view/843

Hall, R. (2013). Academic activism in the face of enclosure in the digital university. *Power and Education, 5*(2), 186–199. https://doi.org/10.2304/power.2013.5.2.186

Hall, R. E. (2009). Cool pose, Black manhood, and juvenile delinquency. *Journal of Human Behavior in the Social Environment, 19*(5), 531–539. https://doi.org/10.1080/10911350902990502

Harrell, S. P. (2000). A multidimensional conceptualization of racism-related stress: Implications for the well-being of people of color. *American Journal of Orthopsychiatry, 70*(1), 42–57. https://doi.org/10.1037/h0087722

Haynes, C., Taylor, L., Mobley, S. D., Jr., & Haywood, J. (2020). Existing and resisting: The pedagogical realities of Black, critical men and women faculty. *Journal of Higher Education, 91*(5), 698–721. https://doi.org/10.1080/00221546.2020.1731263

Iton, R. (2010). *In search of the Black fantastic: Politics and popular culture in the post–civil rights era.* Oxford University Press.

Kamola, I., & Meyerhoff, E. (2009). Creating commons: Divided governance, participatory management, and struggles against enclosure in the university. *Polygraph, 21,* 15–37.

Kelly, B. T., Gayles, J. G., & Williams, C. D. (2017). Recruitment without retention: A critical case of Black faculty unrest. *Journal of Negro Education, 86*(3), 305–317. https://doi.org/10.7709/jnegroeducation.86.3.0305

Kelly, H. (2007). Racial tokenism in the school workplace: An exploratory study of Black teachers in overwhelmingly white schools. *Educational Studies, 41*(3), 230–254. https://www.jstor.org/stable/10.7709/jnegroeducation.86.3.0305

Kirkland, D. E., & Jackson, A. (2009). "We real cool": Toward a theory of Black masculine literacies. *Reading Research Quarterly, 44*(3), 278–297. https://doi.org/10.1598/RRQ.44.3.3

Louis, D. A., Rawls, G. J., Jackson-Smith, D., Chambers, G. A., Phillips, L. L., & Louis, S. L. (2016). Listening to our voices: Experiences of Black faculty at predominantly white research universities with microaggression. *Journal of Black Studies, 47*(5), 454–474. https://doi.org/10.1177/0021934716632983

Martinez, M. A., Chang, A., & Welton, A. D. (2017). Assistant professors of color confront the inequitable terrain of academia: A community cultural wealth perspective. *Race, Ethnicity & Education, 20*(5), 696–710. https://doi.org/10.1080/13613324.2016.1150826

Niemann, Y. F. (2016). The social ecology of tokenism in higher education. *Peace Review*, *28*(4), 451–458. https://doi.org/10.1080/10402659.2016.1237098

O'Donovan, Ó. (2014). The commons, the battle of the book and the cracked enclosures of academic publishing. *Community Development Journal*, *49*(suppl_1), 121–130. https://doi.org/10.1093/cdj/bsu021

Patton, L. D. (2016). Disrupting postsecondary prose: Toward a critical race theory of higher education. *Urban Education*, *51*(3), 315–342. https://doi.org/10.1177/0042085915602542

Peekhaus, W. (2012). The enclosure and alienation of academic publishing: Lessons for the professoriate. *tripleC: Communication, Capitalism & Critique. Open Access Journal for a Global Sustainable Information Society*, *10*(2), 577–599. https://doi.org/10.31269/triplec.v10i2.395

Pittman, C. T. (2010). Race and gender oppression in the classroom: The experiences of women faculty of color with white male students. *Teaching Sociology*, *38*(3), 183–196. https://doi.org/10.1177/0092055X10370120

Quinlan, E. (2008). Conspicuous invisibility: Shadowing as a data collection strategy. *Qualitative Inquiry*, *14*(8), 1480–1499. https://doi.org/10.1177/1077800408318318

Riemer, N. (2016). Academics, the humanities and the enclosure of knowledge: The worm in the fruit. *Australian Universities' Review*, *58*(2), 33–41.

Saunders, D. (2007). The impact of neoliberalism on college students. *Journal of College and Character*, *8*(5). https://doi.org/10.2202/1940-1639.1620

Smith, W. A. (2004). Black faculty coping with racial battle fatigue: The campus racial climate in a post–civil rights era. In D. Cleveland (Ed.), *A long way to go: Conversations about race by African American faculty and graduate students* (4th ed., pp. 171–190). Peter Lang.

Snyder, G. F. (2014). On post-Blackness and the Black fantastic. *Souls*, *16*(3–4), 330–350. https://doi.org/10.1080/10999949.2014.968952

Stevenson, H. C. (2003). Commentary: The conspicuous invisibility of Black ways of being: Missing data in new models of children's mental health. *School Psychology Review*, *32*(4), 520–524. https://doi.org/10.1080/02796015.2003.12086216

Stevenson, H. C., Davis, G. Y., Carter, R., & Elliott, S. (2003). Why Black males need cultural socialization. In H. C. Stevenson (Ed.), *Playing with anger: Teaching coping skills to African American boys through athletics and culture* (pp. 61–86). Praeger.

Tasker, L. (1977). New directions in political socialization. *Sociology*, *11*(1), 218–219. https://doi.org/10.1177/003803857701100144

Thompson, G. L., & Louque, A. (2005). *Exposing the "culture of arrogance" in the academy: A blueprint for increasing Black faculty satisfaction in higher education*. Stylus Publishing.

Tierney, W. G., & Bensimon, E. M. (1996). *Promotion and tenure: Community and socialization in academe*. State University of New York Press.

Tuitt, F. (2012). Black like me: Graduate students' perceptions of their pedagogical experiences in classes taught by Black faculty in a predominantly white institution. *Journal of Black Studies*, *43*(2), 186–206. https://doi.org/10.1177/0021934711413271

Turner, C.S.V. (2002). Women of color in academe: Living with multiple marginality. *Journal of Higher Education*, *73*(1), 74–93. https://doi.org/10.1080/00221546.2002.11777131

5

What Are We Willing to Sacrifice?

Mental Health among First-Generation Faculty of Color

OMAR RUVALCABA

In a publication by *Inside Higher Ed*, Dr. Aguilar, a Latinx faculty at the University of Southern California, shared his frustration with microaggressions at a conference where attendees confused him for hotel staff twice (Aguilar, 2018). Dr. Aguilar went on to contemplate what faculty of color may sacrifice as they work to be accepted in academia. Dr. Licón, a Latino assistant professor in Latin American and Latinx Studies at the University of Wisconsin–Eau Claire, shared an anecdote that suggests that faculty of color may be sacrificing their health to participate in the Ivory Tower. Dr. Licón's parents had worked in assembly plants most of their adult life so that their children could focus on school and get good jobs—which to his parents meant jobs that did not require breaking their backs and instead working in an air-conditioned office. Ironically, he now has a history of back pain due to sitting long hours during graduate school and now in his office (G. Licón, personal communication, July 13, 2018). In this chapter, I focus on the possible mental health compromises made by first-generation faculty of color. As faculty of color, we experience unique types of stress in joining primarily white institutions. Grit and resilience may help scholars persevere in the face of academic stress and help explain how some faculty of color succeed in academic context despite multiple barriers (Duckworth et al., 2007), but this deficit approach places the responsibility on the individuals and champions exceptions rather than focusing on understanding structural barriers. As a field, psychology has neglected consideration of the possible health consequences of persisting and succeeding in spaces that push faculty of color out.

Due to a lack of literature regarding how stressors (e.g., microaggressions) and perceived discrimination relate to first-generation faculty mental health, I review literature on the stressors experienced by individuals at undergraduate and graduate level along the faculty pipeline and end with the stressors experienced by faculty of color. I end by supplementing the literature with my own experiences to note areas of need for future research.

First-Generation Students and Mental Health

Stress is a common experience for university students of all backgrounds. For many young adults, it is their first time that they live away from home. University students experience both beneficial stress that can result in improved performance and learning and negative stress (known as distress) due to loss of social support, finances, and academic pressure (Oswalt & Riddock, 2007). About half of university students surveyed (46 percent) report that they feel overwhelmed at least seven times a year (Oswalt & Riddock, 2007).

Students of color experience unique stressors, such as questions regarding their qualifications, that make them feel stressed and unwelcomed on university campuses (Smedley et al., 1993). Also, first-generation undergraduate students experience higher financial pressures and family responsibilities compared with students from middle-class families (Terenzini et al., 1996). Unique sources of stress among first-generation students of color include the pressure of setting an example for younger siblings and feeling that their success can validate parental sacrifices (Ross et al., 1999; Towbes & Cohen, 1996).

Unlike white students, undergraduates of color commonly experience discrimination in university settings (Nora & Cabrera, 1996; Saldaina, 1994). Pieterse and colleagues (2012) argue that the existing research suggests that experiences with racism should be considered a type of trauma. Furthermore, Black adults' experiences with racism and discrimination seem to be associated with poor mental health and negative mental health outcomes such as depression, anxiety, and posttraumatic stress disorder (Pieterse et al., 2012). Similarly, Asian and Latinx undergraduate students' reports of perceived racial discrimination are associated with higher psychological distress, suicidal ideation, states of anxiety, and depression (Hwang & Goto, 2008).

Smedley and colleagues (1993) suggest that the unique stressors experienced by students of color augment the stress that students of color experience from common university challenges, including going to office hours and requesting a grade change. Seeking help, for example, can be particularly challenging for first-generation students of color. Seeking help requires navigating university cultural norms and university bureaucracy, and possibly confirming their worries and other assumptions regarding their academic weaknesses (Smedley et al., 1993).

Students from low-income areas must learn to readjust from classroom practices that emphasize classroom management to white middle-class practices that stress individual initiative while also navigating the cultural expectations of their own communities (Zea et al., 1997). Although it may be difficult to notice the subtle variance in cultural practices in classrooms, these cultural differences may impact how students navigate school settings. For instance, Mexican American students were noted to wait for pauses and appropriate lulls in conversation before requesting help in a classroom activity (Ruvalcaba et al., 2015). U.S. universities also tend to be competitive and focus on individual accomplishments that may heighten perceived or actual academic weaknesses (Smedley et al., 1993). University approaches contrast some Black, Latina/o, and Indigenous approaches to learning that emphasize community, intricate coordination of goals, and a diverse range of nonverbal and verbal forms of communication (Dill & Boykin, 2000; Lee, 2003; Rogoff, 2003).

Graduate Students and Mental Health

The current uncertain career prospects in academia explain high dropout rates among graduate students pursuing academic careers (Hyun et al., 2006). Fear of failure and demands due to exams and completing their thesis are common sources of graduate student stress (Cheshire, 1989; Nature Cell Biology, 2018). In addition to extensive stress, graduate students report experiences of loneliness through graduate school (Beeler, 1991: Kjerulff & Wiggins, 1976; Valdez, 1982).

Underrepresented graduate students experience unique stressors and additional barriers when compared to middle-class white students (Maton et al., 2011; Myers et al., 2012). In addition to unique stressors, students of color and underrepresented students tend to experience higher levels of stress in graduate school than other students (Phinney & Haas, 2003). Distress may impact graduate students' performance inside and outside coursework. For example, high degrees of stress among clinical psychology graduate students impacted academic performance, clinical skills, and personal well-being (Myers et al., 2012). The focus on individual success and competition in U.S. graduate schools, cultural practices prevalent in formalized western schooling (Rogoff, 2003), may help explain the higher stress levels among U.S. graduate students of color compared to international graduate students (Hyun et al., 2007).

In addition to the stress of being a first-generation graduate student of color, it is important to note that women are likely to experience higher levels of stress when compared to men attending graduate school (Cahir & Morris, 1991; Mallinckrodt & Leong, 1992; Toews et al., 1997). Schwarz and colleagues (1987) reported higher levels of stress, depression, daily alcohol use, and personal problems for women in their graduate school transition years (e.g., the first years of residency for medical students). Female graduate students also report less support from their academic departments and families (Mallinckrodt & Leong, 1992). Additionally, Black women experience extreme feelings of isolation and marginalization throughout their graduate programs (Ellis, 2001).

Some of the stressors reported by underrepresented medical students included racial discrimination, racial prejudice, feelings of isolation, and different cultural expectations. Medical students from underrepresented backgrounds who reported these stressors also had higher rates of burnout, depressive symptoms, and reduced quality of life (Dyrbye et al., 2007). Wei and colleagues (2011) found that the unique stressors faced by Asian American, African American, and Latinx graduate students attending predominantly white universities directly related to persistence. Despite the higher rates of mental health issues, research has found that underrepresented groups (such as Asian American and African American) are less likely than white students to seek out counseling services (Hyun et al., 2006).

Faculty Experience with Stress and Anxiety

Faculty of color often have interactions in university settings where their credentials and the rigor of their research are questioned (Aguilar, 2018; Gutiérrez y Muhs et al., 2012). Faculty of color report feeling responsible for addressing difficult conversations around race, privilege, and microaggressions directed at them or students in class (Sue et al., 2011). Faculty report that these microaggressions from students are draining and stressful. In trying to maintain objectivity and a faculty demeanor, faculty must suppress inner emotional turmoil (including feelings of frustration) when personally attacked by their students (Sue et al., 2011).

There is a disproportionate passion and pressure among faculty of color to advocate for students of underrepresented ethnic, gender, and class backgrounds—a service to the campus that seldom counts toward tenure (Ek et al., 2010). In my first years as faculty, I had students from other courses show up to my office door just looking to talk with a faculty of color. Within my first three years at California State University, Northridge (CSUN), I created a summer welcome program for first-generation students, I chaired a department committee on closing the opportunity gap, I joined a university-level educational equity committee, I was a mentor for the psychology honors program, and I was one of three faculty mentors for the multicultural psychology student group.

In addition to classroom resistance, faculty of color often experience questions regarding their competence, academic challenges to the quality and rigor of their work, and experiences that make them feel marginalized based on their appearance (Aguilar, 2018; Gutiérrez y Muhs et al., 2012). Some faculty of color strategically disengage with fellow faculty to avoid emotionally draining and stressful experiences while remaining engaged in their teaching and scholarship (Settles et al., 2019). Faculty of color also experience more critical evaluations than their counterparts. Women of color who display traits valued in men in their teaching, such as assertiveness, often receive biased student evaluations and lack of support from administration (Samuel & Wane, 2005; Sue et al., 2011).

Stress and Mental Health as a First-Generation Latino Psychology Faculty Member

I would like to acknowledge that I bring a specific positionality and experiences influenced by how I am viewed within academia. As a white-skinned Latino, I can pass as a white male in academic contexts unless I have to share my name. As a second-generation Mexican Immigrant with three siblings in STEM careers, I drew on cultural strengths that included unconditional socioemotional support, motivation to give back to my community, and my motivation to validate my parents' decision to leave Mexico.

In graduate school, standard academic practices, such as receiving feedback from my advisor, became sources of extreme stress and anxiety. Despite reassurances from family, peers, and my advisor, I felt like an imposter. I interpreted each mark and suggestion as evidence of my lack of fit, failures, and need to improve. Existing norms and practices within academia led me to question my abilities. For example, writing feedback focuses on pointing out what needed work rather than highlighting the achievements. Ironically, I helped undergraduate students deal with the imposter phenomenon while not being able to shake my own insecurities despite my understanding of the imposter phenomenon (see Langford & Rose Clance, 1993).

In addition to my academic doubts, I spent years questioning my career choice and research focus. As a first-generation student, I naïvely assumed that a PhD guaranteed a good paying job. I was unaware of the scarcity of tenure-track positions and poor part-time lecturer pay. A couple of years into my graduate program, it became common to hear of tenure-track positions that had over a hundred applicants. I was facing a job market where I might not land a tenure-track position and might have to work jobs making less than I could with a master's degree in other fields. The alternative to landing a tenure-track job was sacrificing more of my life to academia by applying to postdoc positions. The culture of doctorate programs promotes seeking academic positions above all other job prospects, postponing life decisions, taking on debt, and investing more time through postdocs were accepted (and expected) sacrifices.

As a psychology graduate student, I also debated whether I had "sold out" by not pursuing a social justice field of study (within social science research, psychology is often seen as the more conservative social science). If I went into industry, I was a sellout; if I stayed in academia, I may not have the necessary income to help my family. Within psychology, I felt unwelcomed due to the marginality of my work. Psychological trends favor large quantitative data sets, but I used small samples and non-flashy (but appropriate) statistics for my work. I also conducted cultural research, which to this day is included superficially by mentioning participants' ethnic background, if included at all, in the majority of psychology research studies. In addition, my rigor as a researcher was often questioned. I am often asked whether my research may be biased considering I am a Latinx research conducting research in Latinx communities. Although it is fair to ask questions regarding scientific rigor, I have never heard these questions at presentations where white researchers presented about white subjects. It is as if who I am already brings skepticism to the research.

Although I did not travel far (from Inglewood to Santa Cruz), I found that this was enough to disconnect from my community of support. It made it difficult to access the social emotional support that supported me through my undergraduate degree. As a graduate student, my work was confined to a single building on campus, so it took more time to find the safe spaces and build community on campus. I was privileged to meet a strong group of Latinas who supported and mentored me throughout my academic career. Several white women in psychology and computer science also played key roles as my mentors. At the end of my first year, two Latinas and I formed a group to help address our need for a Latinx graduate and undergraduate student space in psychology.

When I received the job offer to join the psychology faculty at CSUN, I felt relieved, excited, and blessed. I had been geared to focus on research-focused institutions. I never considered that a job at a teaching-focused institution was the perfect fit for me until I interviewed for the job posting. I was sold on CSUN as soon as I met the students. Like me, the students in my teaching demonstration were primarily first-generation Latinx students. I feel that CSUN is the place where I can do research and positively impact students' lives through my teaching.

In my last year of graduate school, I started noticing signs of anxiety. I was overwhelmed and stressed in everyday interactions, and I felt a heightened sense of social anxiety during group interactions (not just while presenting). I that thought a tenure-track position would magically cure me of the effects of the stress, but I was wrong. In my first year as faculty, I realized that I was still dealing with issues from graduate school. I had to remind myself that each student's question was not a question of my ability. Despite mostly positive evaluations in my first few courses, those few negative evaluations damaged my view of my teaching ability. My last semester evaluations were positive, but one student wrote something along the lines of "he makes homework due on non-class days" as a negative, and I still had to take a moment to remind myself that this was a minor complaint.

I felt (and continue to feel) a constant drive to do more to prove my worth and to help students. In my first year as faculty, I often worked fourteen-hour days and still felt that it was not enough. Admittedly, I agreed to more responsibilities than I should have in that first year. In my first semester I led a grant submission, developed new courses, formed my research lab, and joined several committees focusing on equity and access issues. Despite good advice from my mentors and department chair to avoid committee work by focusing on services related to my passion, I was already a committee chair and leading a summer orientation for our department by the end of my second year. As a member of our university's educational equity committee, I was giving presentations on retaining underrepresented faculty when I was worried about my own retention. I soon found that I had too much on my plate even though I narrowed my service to supporting underrepresented students and faculty.

I think of how both culture and power dynamics made it difficult to turn away service. Given my cultural values as a son from a working-class Mexican family and my drive to give back to my community, I felt compelled to lend myself to helping others (López et al., 2015). This value, coupled with the worry of keeping my job in a limited job market and my own insecurities, made me wonder if turning down a new committee invitation would get me fired. Despite my eagerness and commitment to service, reflecting on this experience exposed the internalized trauma of going through academia.

At the end of my first year, I decided to focus on finding sources of support to work through the social anxiety I developed in graduate school. Despite having a clinical graduate program on campus and the seemingly open discussions regarding mental health, I found it difficult to find help with my anxiety. I was also confused about how to use my health insurance to seek out such support. I finally figured out how to see therapists but found that most were not familiar with the stresses related to academic worlds and were not trained to consider culture in their approaches. Advice was often general and did not seem applicable to my situation. I am better now largely due to support of my support network (family, colleagues, and friends), my increased confidence as a researcher, teacher, and mentor, a more balanced work schedule, and strict health practices (diet, meditation, and exercise).

After seeing other peers and students experience their own health issues, it became apparent that this is an important issue to address when discussing increasing representation of underrepresented faculty. In my second year, I shared in two of my courses that I was dealing with some form of anxiety. Several students of color approached me to share that they felt they were going through similar experiences, and some thanked me for discussing this openly.

Unfortunately, my experiences broaching the mental health concerns among underrepresented faculty has led me to avoid these conversations with fellow faculty. As a pre-tenured professor, I worry that sharing my experience with generalized anxiety influences views of my competence. In my attempts to discuss mental health with other faculty of color, I have received some nods of agreement, made some people uncomfortable, and received some concerned looks. The fear of judgment makes this a difficult topic for faculty of color to discuss. Although stigma against seeking mental health services is common in Black and Latinx communities (Fripp & Carlson, 2017; Turner et al., 2015), perhaps faculty of color hesitate to discuss mental health issues due to the precarious position they hold as faculty in mostly white institutions.

With the goal of understanding how the stress encountered by faculty of color influences mental health, I suggest the following topics as potential research topics:

- How does not receiving a tenure-track job impact first-generation PhD recipients' mental health?
- Would a more realistic understanding of the job market help PhD students prepare for and cope with the market they are entering?
- What are the health consequences of being disproportionally recruited for service as faculty? How can departments protect faculty of color?
- What are common mental health issues among first-generation faculty of color?
- What strategies help first-generation faculty of color to maintain mental health?
- Does a strong connection with their cultural community buffer first-generation faculty of color against negative health outcomes?

Currently, educational and psychological research and interventions programs minimally (if at all) consider mental health in recruiting and retaining faculty of color. A sociocultural approach to understanding the role of mental health among faculty of color may provide important insights to our support of faculty of color. Octavia Butler (1998), a Black sci-fi writer, wrote in one of her novels: "All that you touch, you change. All that you change, changes you. The only lasting truth is change." As faculty of color, our experiences of struggle change us and the fruits of our labor are seen when our work has impact, but we must ask what we are willing to sacrifice as we work toward institutional and societal change.

REFERENCES

Aguilar, S. J. (2018, August 29). On belonging in the academy. *Inside Higher Ed.* https://www.insidehighered.com/advice/2018/08/29/new-tenure-track-scholar-considers-what-it-means-belong-academe-opinion

Beeler, K. D. (1991). Graduate student adjustment to academic life: A four-stage framework. *NASPA Journal, 28*(2), 163–171. doi:10.1080/00220973.1991.11072201

Butler, O. (1993). *Parable of the sower.* Grant Central Publishing.

Cahir, N., & Morris R. D. (1991). The psychology student stress questionnaire. *Journal of Clinical Psychology, 47*(3), 414–417. https://doi.org/10.1002/1097-4679(199105)47:3<414::AID-JCLP2270470314>3.0.CO;2-M

Cheshire, B. W. (1989). Graduate student writing assistance in the counseling center. *Journal of College Student Development, 30*(2), 164–165. https://eric.ed.gov/?id=EJ1000689

Dill, E. M., & Boykin, A. W. (2000). The comparative influence of individual, peer tutoring, and communal learning contexts on the text recall of African American children. *Journal of Black Psychology, 26*(1), 65–78. http://doi.org/10.1177/0095798400026001004

Duckworth, A. L., Peterson, C., Matthews, M. D., & Kelly, D. R. (2007). Grit: Perseverance and passion for long-term goals. *Personality Processes and Individual Differences, 92*(6), 1087–1101. https://doi.org/10.1037/0022-3514.92.6.1087

Dyrbye, L. N., Matthew, T. R., Mashele, H. M., Lawson, L. K., Novotny, P. J., Sloan, J. A., & Shanafelt, T. D. (2007). A multicenter study of burnout, depression, and quality of life in minority and nonminority US medical students. *Mayo Clinic Proceeding, 81*(11), 1435–1442. https://doi.org/10.4065/81.11.1435

Ek, L. D., Cerecer, P.D.Q., Alanís, I., & Rodríguez, M. A. (2010). "I don't belong here": Chicanas/Latinas at a Hispanic serving institution creating community through Muxerista mentoring. *Equity & Excellence in Education, 43*(4), 539–553. https://doi.org/10.1080/10665684.2010.510069

Ellis, E. (2001). The impact of race and gender on graduate school socialization, satisfaction with doctoral study, and commitment to degree completion. *Western Journal of Black Studies, 25*(1), 30–45. https://eric.ed.gov/?id=EJ646531

Fripp, J., & Carlson, R. (2017). Exploring the influence of attitude and stigma on participation of African American and Latino populations in mental health services. *Journal of Multicultural Counseling and Development, 45*(2), 80–94. https://doi.org/10.1002/jmcd.12066

Gutiérrez y Muhs, G., Niemann, Y. F., González, C. G., & Harris, A. P. (Eds.). (2012). *Presumed incompetent: The intersections of race and class for women in academia.* Utah State University Press.

Hwang, W. C., & Goto, S. (2008). The impact of perceived racial discrimination on the mental health of Asian American and Latino college students. *Cultural Diversity and Ethnic Minority Psychology, 14*(4), 326–335. http://dx.doi.org/10.1037/1099-9809.14.4.326

Hyun, J., Quinn, B., Madon, T., & Lustig, S. (2006). Graduate student mental health: Needs assessment and utilization of counseling services. *Journal of College Student Development, 47*(3), 247–266. https://eric.ed.gov/?id=EJ743920

Hyun, J., Quinn, B., Madon, T., & Lustig, S. (2007). Mental health need, awareness, and use of counseling services among international graduate students. *Journal of American College Health, 56*(2), 109–118. https://doi.org/10.3200/JACH.56.2.109-118

Kjerulff, K., & Wiggins, N. H. (1976). Graduate student styles for coping with stressful situations. *Journal of Educational Psychology, 68*(3), 247–254. https://doi.org/10.1037/0022-0663.68.3.247

Langford, J., & Rose Clance, P. (1993). The imposter phenomenon: Recent research findings regarding dynamics, personality and family patterns and their implications for treatment. *Psychotherapy, 30*(3), 495–501. https://doi.org/10.1037/0033-3204.30.3.495

Lee, C. D. (2003). Toward a framework for culturally responsive design in multimedia computer environments: Cultural modeling as a case. *Mind, Culture, and Activity, 10*(1), 42–61. http://doi.org/10.1207/S15327884MCA1001_05

López, A., Ruvalcaba, O., & Rogoff, B. (2015). Attentive helping as a cultural practice of Mexican-heritage families. In C. M. Yvone & E. W. Lindsey (Eds.), *Mexican American children and families: Multidisciplinary perspectives* (pp. 150–161). Taylor & Francis.

Mallinckrodt, B., & Leong, F. (1992). International graduate-students, stress, and social support. *Journal of College Student Development, 33*(1), 71–78. https://eric.ed.gov/?id=EJ444090

Maton, K., Wimms, H., Grant, S., Wittig, M., Rogers, M., Vasquez, M., & Zárate, M. A. (2011). Experiences and perspectives of African American, Latina/o, Asian American, and European American psychology graduate students: A national study. *Cultural Diversity and Ethnic Minority Psychology, 17*(1), 68–78. https://doi.org/10.1037/a0021668

Myers, S., Sweeney, A., Popick, V., Wesley, K., Bordfeld, A., Fingerhut, R., & Rodolfa, E. R. (2012). Self-care practices and perceived stress levels among psychology graduate students. *Training and Education in Professional Psychology, 6*(1), 55–66. https://psycnet.apa.org/doi/10.1037/a0026534

Nature Cell Biology. (2018). A PhD state of mind. *Nature Cell Biology, 20,* 363. https://doi.org/10.1038/s41556-018-0085-4

Nora, A., & Cabrera, A. (1996). The role of perceptions of prejudice and discrimination on the adjustment of minority students to college. *Journal of Higher Education, 67*(2), 119–148. http://doi.org/10.2307/2943977

Oswalt, S. B., & Riddock C. C. (2007). What to do about being overwhelmed: Graduate students, stress and university services. *College Student Affairs Journal, 27*(1), 24–44. https://eric.ed.gov/?id=EJ899402

Phinney, J., & Haas, K. (2003). The process of coping among ethnic minority first-generation college freshmen: A narrative approach. *Journal of Social Psychology, 143*(6), 707–726. https://doi.org/10.1080/00224540309600426

Pieterse, A. L., Todd, N. R., Neville, H. A., & Carter, R. T. (2012). Perceived racism and mental health among Black American adults: A meta-analytic review. *Journal of Counseling Psychology, 59*(1), 1–9. http://doi.org/10.1037/a0026208

Rogoff, B. (2003). *The cultural nature of human development.* Oxford University Press.

Ross, S. E., Nibbling, B. C., & Heckett, T. M. (1999). Sources of stress among college students. *College Student Journal, 33*(2), 312–318. https://eric.ed.gov/?id=EJ872343

Ruvalcaba, O., Rogoff, B., López, A., Correa-Chávez, M., & Gutiérrez, K. D. (2015). Children's avoidance of interrupting others' activities in requesting help: Cultural aspects of considerateness. *Advances in Child Development and Behavior, 49,* 185–205. http://doi.org/10.1016/bs.acdb.2015.10.005

Saldaina, D. H. (1994). Acculturative stress: Minority status and distress. *Hispanic Journal of Behavioral Sciences, 16*(2), 116–128. https://doi.org/10.1177%2F07399863940162002

Samuel, E., & Wane, N. (2005). "Unsettling Relations": Racism and sexism experienced by faculty of color in a predominantly white Canadian university. *Journal of Negro Education, 74*(1), 76–87. https://www.jstor.org/stable/40027232

Schwarz, N., Strack, F., Kommer, D., & Wagner, D. (1987). Soccer, rooms, and the quality of your life: Mood effects on judgments of satisfaction with life in general and with specific domains. *European Journal of Social Psychology, 17*(1), 69–79. https://doi.org/10.1002/ejsp.2420170107

Settles, I. H., Buchanan, N. T., & Dotson, K. (2019). Scrutinized but not recognized: (In)visibility and hypervisibility experiences of faculty of color. *Journal of Vocational Behavior, 113,* 62–74. http://doi.org/10.1016/j.jvb.2018.06.003

Smedley, B., Myers, H., & Harrell, S. (1993). Minority-status stresses and the college adjustment of ethnic minority freshmen. *Journal of Higher Education, 64*(4), 434–452. http://doi.org/10.2307/2960051

Sue, D. W., Rivera, D. P., Watkins, N. L., Kim, R. H., Kim, S., & Williams, C. D. (2011). Racial dialogues: Challenges faculty of color face in the classroom. *Cultural Diversity and Ethnic Minority Psychology, 17*(3), 331–340. http://doi.org/10.1037/a0024190

Terenzini, P. T., Springer, L., Yaeger, P. M., & Pascarella, A. (1996). First-generation college students: Characteristics, experiences, and cognitive development. *Research in Higher Education, 37*(1), 1–22. https://www.jstor.org/stable/40196208

Toews, J. A., Lockyer, J. M., Dobson, D. J., Simpson, E., Brownell, A.K.W., Brenneis, F., MacPherson, K. M., & Cohen, G. S. (1997). Analysis of stress levels among medical students, resident, and graduate students at four Canadian schools of medicine. *Academic Medicine, 72*(22), 997–1002. https://doi.org/10.1097/00001888-199711000-00019

Towbes, L., & Cohen, C. (1996). Chronic stress in the lives of college students: Scale development and prospective prediction of distress. *Journal of Youth and Adolescence, 25*(2), 199–217. https://doi.org/10.1007/BF01537344

Turner, E., Jensen-Doss, A., & Heffer, R. (2015). Ethnicity as a moderator of how parents' attitudes and perceived stigma influence intentions to seek child mental health services. *Cultural Diversity and Ethnic Minority Psychology, 21*(4), 613–618. https://doi.org /10.1037/cdp0000047

Valdez, R. (1982). First-year doctoral students and stress. *College Student Journal, 16*(1), 30–37.

Wei, M., Ku, T., Liao, K., & Zárate, M. A. (2011). Minority stress and college persistence attitudes among African American, Asian American, and Latino students: Perception of university environment as a mediator. *Cultural Diversity and Ethnic Minority Psychology, 17*(2), 195–203. https://doi.org/10.1037/a0023359

Zea, M., Reisen, C., Beil, C., & Caplan, R. (1997). Predicting intention to remain in college among ethnic minority and nonminority students. *Journal of Social Psychology, 137*(2), 149–160. https://doi.org/10.1080/00224549709595426

PART TWO

Teaching

Échale ganas. Credit: Alberto Ledesma.

6

The Classroom as Negotiated Space

A Chinese-Vietnamese American Community College Faculty Experience

CINDY N. PHU

With the backdrop of Donald Trump's anti-Asian rhetoric of the "Chinese Virus" or "Kung Flu" and the rise of anti-Asian hate crimes (Anti-Defamation League, 2020; Rogin & Nawaz, 2020; Wang, 2020), I wrote this chapter with a heavy heart during the beginning of the coronavirus pandemic and civil unrest. Wide-scale protests against racism and state-sanctioned murder have both divided Asian Americans with the anti-Blackness within our communities, yet simultaneously given re-birth to a collective resurgence of an Asian American solidarity of Yellow Peril with Black Power. As today's anti-Asian rhetoric invokes histories of racism against Asians in the United States, what are the experiences of Asian Americans teaching in the classroom, online, and remotely? As an Asian American first-generation faculty of color at the community college, I argue that my positionality and intersectionality is often marginalized. When examining woman-identified Asian American faculty, they are often underrepresented, racially discriminated against, encounter racial microaggressions, occupy junior faculty ranks, and have one of the lowest tenure rates in the academy (Li & Beckett, 2006; Yosso et al., 2009).

Part of my professoriate journey is the adaptation of the American Dream for Asian Americans. Being promised the chance for assimilation, this "opportunity" entails the prospect of owning a single-unit home in the suburbs, with white-picketed fences all around, and 2.5 kids with/without a dog. Asian Americans have been shown this carrot while being expected to uphold the unrealistic expectations of the model minority myth. Furthermore, conservative and neoliberal policymakers have used the model minority myth to tokenize Asian Americans as a one-dimensional, monolithic, and high-achieving group (Buenavista et al., 2009; Poon et al., 2016; Yi et al., 2020). This has divided and stereotyped Asian Americans as hardworking and high-achieving while undermining the efforts of other hardworking, marginalized ethnic groups. Even among Asian Americans, the utilization of the model minority myth has silenced communities that face systems of oppression because it sweeps their experiences under the rug of other successful Asian Americans. Thus, for Asian American faculty, their presence is often used to undermine the systemic racism of other racial and ethnic faculty groups. Personally, the model minority myth has plagued my family for generations.

My ancestors fled China to escape the encroaching communism. As teenagers, my parents left their homes in Vietnam after the war to again escape from communism. In turn, I have inherited the intergenerational trauma of the wars and refugee experiences, and I carry them wherever I go, including the classroom and on campus. I was the first of my family to attend college, acquire a doctoral degree, and teach at the collegiate level. As a first-generation faculty of color in the community college with the intersections of being a daughter of Chinese refugee parents from Vietnam, English as a third language, and a woman-identified Asian American body in the humanities discipline, the classroom and campus climate have always been a hostile environment for me. For a long time, I have held my educational traumas through a deficit lens with a dash of impostor syndrome.

For this chapter, I have two goals. The first goal is to continue the dialogue of breaking down the categories of "Asian," "female," "instructor," and "education," specifically through an autoethnographic examination of my personal teaching narratives to reveal a better understanding of the intersectionality of my racialized identity as Asian American faculty coupled with my sex, gender, and age. To provide a glimpse of my fourteen years of teaching experiences, my second goal is to highlight narratives from my time at various community colleges as a "freeway-flyer" adjunct faculty and in online teaching to showcase specific moments of microaggressions inflicted by students and how those moments continued as I navigated my tenure process. In doing so, I argue that classrooms are negotiated spaces and reveal how transgressions necessarily transform the teaching and pedagogy of first-generation faculty of color.

Graduate Associate Teaching

I started my graduate education with my department advisor laughing at my undergraduate transcripts, noting that my first two years must have been challenging with college partying. Those first two years aligned with the first-generation student literature regarding the struggles associated with navigating a college campus (Cataldi et al., 2018; Chen, 2005; Engle & Tinto, 2012). At that time, I did not correct him because it would have required me to showcase my first-generation vulnerability and educational traumas.

During my graduate program, I spent two years teaching introductory communication courses and coaching the speech and debate team to prepare for nationals. I learned two things during this experience: I loved teaching at the collegiate level, and I was not what the students expected when I walked into the classroom on the first day. During these two years, my biggest struggle was to find my own identity within the social construction of a "professor." I taught my first public speaking class at twenty-two years old. There was no transition from being a first-generation undergraduate student who was on the speech team to a first-generation graduate student, teaching associate, and forensics speech and debate assistant coach. I was learning to be a graduate student, instructor/faculty, and a speech coach all at the same time while struggling with my racialized identity in white-dominant spaces.

In my communication performance theory course, I learned that I was trying to "perform professor" rather than embrace my own racialized teaching identity within the white hegemonic patriarchal system (hooks, 2000). As the only Asian American in the teaching cohort, I always had a blazer for every class session, as well as heavy makeup, heels, and a professional bag—I carried myself like I was walking into an interview. I braced myself emotionally before every class session, hoping for a successful class without any hostile microaggressions or overt aggressions of any kind. This professor performance was exhausting, inauthentic, and wounded me as I fell into impostor syndrome, which was doubting my accomplishments with an internalized fear of being discovered as a fraud. But I still loved teaching. Although my pedagogy was innovative, engaging, and entertaining for students, I was also losing empathy and compassion.

I only realized later in my teaching career that my students presumed that I was incompetent from the beginning of class, which licensed them to openly question, challenge, and push my boundaries. I was the only graduate teaching associate in the cohort who had a student ask publicly if I was a "real teacher" in front of the entire classroom; I felt that students did not have empathy for me. I decided to take it upon myself to "fix" this problem by trying to learn more about my students and my teaching peers. I accepted every opportunity to be a substitute teacher for my peers (unpaid labor) so that I could learn about the different dynamics of their classrooms and students.

Throughout these experiences, I was constantly required to navigate my unique challenges as a result of my intersectional identities. I forgot what it was like as a first-generation student looking for representation, mentors, and empathy, as I was so focused on my own struggles as a first-generation graduate student without a mentor. However, I was able to use my training in speech and debate to win over my students in hostile public engagements while my interpersonal training from the communications discipline helped me to genuinely connect with them. Like that student who asked if I was a real teacher, my reply was, "It is up to you if I am a 'real' teacher, but I will be the person to enter your grades in the system." That statement alone won over that student, *and* I gained the approval of the entire class.

The Community College Adjunct-Faculty Years

An adjunct faculty is a contingent faculty who is given work based on the needs of the institution, provided no job security, and has little hope for a full-time position (Matthiesen et al., 2018). I was a contingent faculty for about three years, traveling an average of one hundred miles each day, which can translate to about two to four hours of driving depending on California freeways. One of those years, I was a full-time faculty at a private university while still teaching at least one class at two other community colleges. Because I knew that I wanted to teach at the community college level, I always had to have at least one class at a community college to keep my foot in the door. At one point I taught nine classes in one semester, at three locations, in order to maintain my job security in case any of the colleges changed my course load. I also had to maintain all the responsibilities of full-time faculty at the private university regarding meetings, shared governance, and conference travel, and I took students to compete at local, regional, and national events. As a new team, we ranked fourteenth in the entire nation that year with a team break, meaning all of our students came home with national titles.

Although I enjoyed varying levels of success with different campuses, the classroom was the most hostile environment in its first week—I would have to win over my students in multiple locations with different course/campus policies. I knew that once I won over my students on the first day, the rest of the semester would be less challenging. Even though I was able to use my previous experiences to navigate these communication encounters, the extra labor was exhausting, in addition to being contingent faculty without institutional support. As my exhaustion grew, so did my racial battle fatigue. To illustrate the burden and rewards with adjunct teaching, I share the following student story— this student became my example of a successful student narrative that I often shared in my interview for teaching positions. I want to note that his actions, behaviors, and attitudes are not uncommon; though he was only one student in one class, he is an example of many of the daily microaggressions in my typical class sessions.

Smoking in the Classroom

At the beginning of a semester, I was going through the emergency procedures with the class as required by this particular community college. While I looked up from the list, I saw a student smoking an e-cigarette casually in a very defiant manner. He was an Asian male student, with a Texas accent and tattooed sleeves. I was completely shocked, and to my dismay no one in the class even pretended to notice. I stopped my lecture to ask him, "Are you smoking in my class, right now?" Taking this transgressive moment and turning it into a teaching moment, I asked him to stop smoking with a series of questions regarding a personal guarantee of the public safety/health of the class. I used the situation later to teach research techniques regarding the informative speech topic of e-cigarettes, as they were new at the time, and taught the class how to research the potential health hazards.

I also informed the department chair of this incident because at this point in my teaching career, I knew and followed all the protocols of reporting students' misconduct because of my prior experiences. Although I was not worried about my safety, my department chair informed me that another instructor teaching a night class at the same time was next door and would check in on me. Although this incident should have ended there, in the next class session, this same student continued smoking in the back of the class. Immediately, I went up to him to verbally nudge him, "I am sure that you promised to stop smoking in this class. Did you accidently forget? If so, please stop smoking." After the third encounter—when I found him smoking with his other friends outside the door of the class—I invited him to see me after class.

Utilizing my experiences as a first-generation faculty of color, I realized his actions were an open challenge to my credibility. With my past experiences of similar situations, I asked about his interests and then used that to empower and focus him on his speeches. That was the last time he smoked inside or near my classroom. His behavior changed completely, and he became one of the most engaged students and completed the semester with one of the highest grades. I wish I could say that over the years he was the only student smoking inside of my classroom, that I did not have to change my syllabus to include a "no e-cigarettes" policy, or that I did not have to actively prevent future smoking incidents by humorously sharing these past experiences on the first day of class. When I recounted these experiences with colleagues in the hope that they could relate and offer advice, though, their reactions made it apparent that these situations did not apply to them.

The Tenured Teaching Years

To continue doing the work I loved, I utilized my previous experience and expertise to turn these transgressions into teaching moments. For many years into my academic career, these struggles lived on as surreptitious experiences I internalized, assuming my experiences were endemic within academic faculty. At my college, the faculty members do not reflect the demographics of the student population. For several years, I was the only female Asian faculty in my department. Over the years I have normalized smokers, mentally unstable students, and aggressive students as part of the community college's open access population. Only when I began sharing my favorite teaching moments did it become clear that my colleagues, especially my male counterparts, were completely untouched by similar teaching tribulations. Their narratives expressed none of the resistances from students in the ways that I experienced.

To not be seen as the "crazy angry Asian Woman" in front of the classroom, I remained calm on the surface while burying my vulnerabilities deeply in the fear that they would be used against me during my first four years of evaluation. After earning tenure, though, I had the job security to speak, challenge, and question. To speed up the process of winning over my students, I often found it necessary to slip in my credentials as the former director of forensics, coordinator of the speech center, or former judge at state and national speech and debate competitions.

Every new space on campus that I stepped foot in required me to present an oral resume to justify my existence there, unless I already had an ally in that space who then would present that resume for me. One of my mentors would actively speak highly about me so that my reputation would precede my encounters, and her labor helped immensely with quickly establishing my creditability. Allies also came in the form of former students. It was always affirming to see a former student take another class with me, and their presence and acknowledgment helped support my credibility to the new students. I am a better faculty today because of my students, allies, and their support. Although this support always felt safe, there were, and are, still many hostile spaces as a first-generation faculty of color.

In the classroom, shared governance committees, and even during observations/evaluations of other faculty, I have faced countless microaggressions. An example of another microaggression occurred at our community college, where we have pathways and cohort classes specifically designed for our veteran students. As a full-time, tenured faculty member, I was assigned to administer the student teaching evaluation of the part-time faculty that was teaching the course. I walked into a room full of men-identified students, and the part-time faculty member introduced me warmly to the class. Upon hearing that I was faculty, the class went from silence to a rapid question-and-answer session about who my favorite speaker was and how long I had been teaching, followed by a series of questions to test my credibility as I stood next to their white male professor. With a knowing smile, I answered all their questions succinctly with a touch of humor and invited them to consider joining the speech and debate team (where I was the former director) and to visit the speech center (where I was the former coordinator/founder).

This was my method of speeding up the credibility-winning process. Even though I was already used to these microaggressions questioning my authority, leadership, and credibility, I was still surprised that I needed to fight these battles when conducting a fifteen-minute student evaluation. This was supposed to be a quick and silent process, but as the students turned in their evaluations, the conversations continued and turned organic as opposed to the initial interrogation. Turning these transgressions to a transformative opportunity, I may have recruited some of them to join the team in those fifteen minutes.

To illustrate just how hostile the classroom could be for me, I provide another example of a student's concern regarding my own life and safety. This happened when I was absent on the same day as an aggressive student in the classroom and I had requested a colleague to take over my class. My white male counterpart told the students as a joke that I could not make it to class because a shark had bitten me. However, later that same evening I ran into a student from that class at an awards ceremony on campus. He was relieved that I was alive, not because of the shark joke, but because he thought the hostile student had killed me. Again, I wish I could say that this was a unique incident but having students express concern that another student may have harmed me is an everyday experience for me.

Online Teaching

I've taught speech courses online for over ten years as both an online teaching assistant at a for-profit online university and adjunct faculty at a community college. This led me to create a model interpersonal communication course for my current community college. I was at the forefront of pushing for distance education to increase access despite the general skepticism of communication courses online. The cyber space offered an illusion of safety, as I did not have to strategize active shooter drills while providing a physical distance in both time and space. While in the online space, I did not have the usual conversations where students shared their concerns about my physical safety. The online environment appeared to provide an opportunity for learning, accessibility, and other means to connect with students beyond the physical classroom, which provided me with a small sense of virtual security. Instances where I did not feel safe in a physical classroom include when a student shared that they were a time traveler that must travel alone since "bad things" happened to others that attempted to travel with them. Another was when a student had a psychological collapse in our classroom, which triggered him to be aggressive, hostile, and threatening. I only found out later that he was transitioning from his schizophrenic medication and that our campus psychological services office and disabilities office were not in communication with each other.

The racial microaggressions were fewer in online discussion boards compared with the physical classroom, but this did not mean they were absent. The racism was packaged differently, and the written comments had more permanence because they often appeared in a class discussion comment, in a teacher questions discussion forum, or in a direct email. For one assignment I had a "hidden bias" discussion board, which required the students to take the Harvard Implicit Association Test from a list of possible topics regarding their attitudes or beliefs. The students had choices of different topics that they could rate their bias on, and some examples were between skin color, age, Native, race, sexuality, Asian, transgender, presidents, weight, disability, gender-science, Arab-Muslim, gender-career, religion, and weapons. Students are allowed to agree or disagree with their results and each other. The students who disagreed with the implication that they may be racist or may see skin color differently reacted aggressively. They started attacking the Harvard research, my teaching, my credibility, and even each other. Seeing as how this assignment resulted in more harm to the other students in the classroom, I had to modify it to be a self-reflective journal assignment so that it would not be a vulnerable public discussion. This assignment showed me how fragile my first-generation faculty of color credibility was in their eyes and how students' problematic perceptions ruined the community dynamic of the classroom.

First-Generation Faculty of Color Mentoring

One way that I have coped with these teaching experiences has been to build a relationship with a femtor/mentor. About seven years ago, when our college divisions merged, I met my mentor, a Chinese American teaching 3D design. In my entire educational experience from kindergarten to my doctoral degree, I probably can name fewer than ten teachers/instructors/professors who identified themselves as Asian or Asian American. As a first-generation faculty of color, I did not realize that I was still craving representation and a mentor who understood my own experiences. We were on the same committees together, and it was so helpful to have her explain the historical context, optics, and campus politics that were the subtext during the committee discussions. She was a supportive mentor who helped me plan my retirement allocations, pushed me to find a better work-life balance, and shared her thirty years of teaching experiences at the college. She was outspoken, tenacious, and brilliant in her navigation of the campus spaces. After teaching more than thirty years, she took an early retirement the same year I earned my tenure status. I am still honored to be in community with her over lunches, text messaging, or following her retirement traveling adventures on social media. In particular, her racial microaffirmations have helped me to heal from my educational traumas as she provided a safe space for me to be vulnerable. Inspired by her impacts on me as a first-generation faculty of color, I actively insert myself as a mentor to our first-generation faculty of color to continue her legacy of mentorship.

The irony is that her replacement was a petite and younger female Japanese American instructor. Even though we look nothing alike, I am constantly approached by the visual arts department faculty member speaking to me as if I were her. I always struggle to determine how far to let the conversations go before I reveal that they made a mistake. There are times when our conversations are so short and fleeting that I don't even have the opportunity to reveal their mistake. Instead, I would send the new instructor a text notifying her of the information, and we would simply find a way to laugh at the persistence of racism inherent in our experiences. It has been affirming to have peer camaraderie about being Asian American faculty and identifying the racist microaggressions that we have both experienced. Together, along with boba and virtual coffee meetings over Zoom, we have often used humor to cope and provide a healing space for each other when the racial battle fatigue becomes too overwhelming.

Femtors and mentors have come in unexpected times and places. When I returned to pursue my doctoral degree after a ten-year gap, I was so excited to meet two amazing Asian American faculty advisors for our cohort who also identified as first-generation. They both have provided a healing, validating, and affirming space for me. Both of these advisors would later become my dissertation chair, committee member, femtors, and friends. As a faculty member with this unique privileged experience, it made me realize the importance of representation regardless of how long I have been teaching in the higher education and this has made me even more intentional in my teaching/advising to provide validation through affirmations and microaffirmations to my fellow first-generation faculty of color and first-generation students.

Recommendations for First-Generation Faculty Mentors

Before the resurfacing of blatant anti-Asian rhetoric during the pandemic, some of the microaggressive statements I received on campus included assertions such as "Is Cindy your real name?" "Your English is great!" and "Hi, [insert another Asian female name], what you said at the meeting was amazing." As an academic community, it is our responsibility to recognize the impacts of racial battle fatigue, microaggressions, intersectionality, first-generational experiences, color-evasiveness, colonization and oppression, and historical and intergenerational traumas, and to recognize the systems in place that uphold white supremacy. Since institutions of higher education can be part of this leadership, more faculty members must reflect their student demographics to increase representation, student success, and student retention. Until the day when systems of oppression, marginalization, and social injustice are addressed and resolved, Asian American faculty will continue to be seen as perpetual foreigners (Yi et al., 2020).

There are many ways to support first-generation faculty of color. Mentorship relationships should be developed by seeking mentors for yourself, being an active mentor to new faculty, and finding peers to help trouble-shoot microaggressions in the classroom, campus, and/or committees. Collectively, we must create communities, seek allies, and create supportive healing spaces for each other. I have multiple group chats with mentors, allies, and colleagues that are affirming and supportive. It is the responsibility for first-generation faculty of color to have wellness check-ins with each other, such as affirming lunch dates or Zoom calls, but there is also an institutional responsibility to help first-generation faculty of color connect with first-generation faculty of color mentors/network on campus.

Higher education institutions should also use a healing-centered engagement (HCE) approach in their training to help with the collective healing and provide a safe space for first-generation faculty of color. HCE acknowledges the intergenerational, family-inherited, contemporary, and educational traumas so that we can be intentional in our institutional responsibilities, course design, classroom/Zoom room, and our interactions with students and each other (Ginwright, 2018). My recommendations for new first-generation faculty of color coping with microaggressions in the classroom are to use an HCE framework in their pedagogy, connect with mentors/peers that you trust, and find microaffirmations/affirmations.

Throughout my years as an educator, I've learned that the Asian American Dream is the illusion of the American Dream promised to Asian Americans and Pacific Islanders with the requirements of internalizing the model minority myth, immigrant bargain, and tokenism. The model minority myth perpetuates the one-dimensional, high-achieving stereotypes of what it means to be Asian American, which undercut claims of systemic racism made by other racial minority groups (Poon et al., 2016; Yi et al., 2020). Ultimately, this results in the tokenism of Asian American bodies in white spaces to represent assimilation under white supremacy instead of acceptance. Being an Asian American faculty member and presumed to be a model minority did not protect me from unsafe classrooms and microaggressions. As first-generation faculty of color, moreover, we are responsible for the development of future generations of first-generation faculty of color as they navigate intergenerational, contemporary, and educational traumas—because we will not "go back to China," especially when our home is here.

REFERENCES

Anti-Defamation League. (2020, June 18). *Reports of anti-Asian assaults, harassment and hate crimes rise as coronavirus spreads.* https://www.adl.org/blog/reports-of-anti-asian-assaults-harassment-and-hate-crimes-rise-as-coronavirus-spreads

Buenavista, T. L., Jayakumar, U. M., & Misa-Escalante, K. (2009). Contextualizing Asian American education through critical race theory: An example of U.S. Pilipino college student experiences. *New Directions for Institutional Research, 142*(2009), 69–81. https://doi.org/10.1002/ir.297

Cataldi, E. F., Bennett, C. T., Chen, X., & Simone, S. A. (February 2018). *First-generation students: College access, persistence, and postbachelor's outcomes.* National Center for Education Statistics. https://nces.ed.gov/pubs2018/2018421.pdf

Chen, X. (2005). *First-generation students in postsecondary education: A look at their college transcripts postsecondary education descriptive analysis report.* National Center for Education Statistics. https://nces.ed.gov/das/epubs/2005171/index.asp

Engle, J., & Tinto, V. (2012). *Moving beyond access: College success for low-income, first-generation students.* The Pell Institute for the Study of Opportunity in Higher Education. https://files.eric.ed.gov/fulltext/ED504448.pdf

Ginwright, S. (2018, May 31). The future of healing: Shifting from trauma informed care to healing centered engagement. *Medium.* https://medium.com/@ginwright/the-future-of-healing-shifting-from-trauma-informed-care-to-healing-centered-engagement-634f557ce69c

hooks, b. (2000). *Feminism is for everybody: Passionate politics.* South End Press.

Li, G., & Beckett, G. H. (Eds.). (2006). *"Strangers" of the academy: Asian women scholars in higher education.* Stylus Publishing.

Matthiesen, S., Perlmutter, D., McGlynn, T., & Ruth, J. (2018, May 30). How to fix the adjunct crisis: Four views from the tenure track. *Chronicle of Higher Education.* https://www.chronicle.com/article/how-to-fix-the-adjunct-crisis/

Poon, O., Squire, D., Kodama, C., Byrd, A., Chan, J., Manzano, L., Furr, S., & Bishundat, D. (2016). A critical review of the model minority myth in selected literature on Asian Americans and Pacific Islanders in higher education. *Review of Educational Research, 86*(2), 469–502. https://doi.org/10.3102/0034654315612205

Rogin, A., & Nawaz, A. (2020, June 25). "We have been through this before:" Why anti-Asian hate crimes are rising amid coronavirus. *PBS NewsHour.* https://www.pbs.org/newshour/nation/we-have-been-through-this-before-why-anti-asian-hate-crimes-are-rising-amid-coronavirus

Wang, C. (2020, September 1). The recent rise in Asian American hate crimes could have impacts beyond the pandemic: Without a reliable database, it's difficult to tackle the aftermath in immigrant communities. *Popular Science.* https://www.popsci.com/story/science/asian-coronavirus-hate-crime/

Yi, V., Mac, J., Na, V. S., Venturanza, R. J., Muscus, S. D., Buenavista, T. L., & Pendakur, S. L. (2020). Towards an anti-imperialistic critical race analysis of the model minority myth. *Review of Education Research, 90*(4), 542–579. https://doi.org/10.3102/0034654320933532

Yosso, T., Smith, W. A., Ceja, M., & Solorzano, D. G. (2009). Critical race theory, racial microaggressions, and campus racial climate for Latina/o undergraduates. *Harvard Education Review, 79*(4), 659–690. doi:10.17763/haer.79.4.m6867014157m7071

7

Taking Up Space

Reflections from a Latina and a Filipino American Faculty Teaching for Racial Justice

NORMA A. MARRUN AND CONSTANCIO R. ARNALDO JR.

As a first-generation Latina and Filipino American, respectively, who were the first in our *familias/pamilyas* to pursue higher education and careers in academia, we have struggled with feelings of ambivalence, self-doubt, and a sense of belonging. However, the presence of faculty of color, as well as transformative and affirming counterspaces—during our academic training and now professionally—helped reduce feelings of isolation, perceived incompetence, and marginalization. Counterspaces are social and academic spaces that "enable Latina/os [and other marginalized groups] to develop skills of critical navigation through multiple worlds (e.g., home and school communities) and ultimately to survive and succeed in the face of racism" (Yosso et al., 2009, p. 678). As first-generation faculty, we realize counterspaces were critical sites through which we made sense of our trajectories and served as spaces of self-preservation (Villalpando, 2003). In these spaces, we were mentored by faculty of color who inspired confidence in our abilities to pursue faculty positions.

In this chapter, we use *testimonio* to argue that it is imperative for institutions of higher education to improve the retention of faculty of color. Our lived experiences are evidence that doing so will only strengthen the retention rates of first-generation and students of color. We write as colleagues who understand that although our identities and lived experiences differ, over the years we have identified points of convergence as first-generation faculty of color. We also acknowledge our intersecting commonalities, differences, and privileges across race, ethnicity, gender, sexuality, language, ability, and immigration status. We both grew up in California and, from an early age, were consciously aware of our internalized oppressive narratives about our identities and especially as first-generation college students. At the same time, we drew from our *familias/pamilyas*, who provided moral support to help us navigate and persist in the unfamiliar terrain of higher education.

Through our *testimonios*, we highlight two themes: the importance of social and academic counterspaces, specifically racial student organizations and ethnic studies courses, and our participation in these counterspaces that led to co-creating a third counterspace in the form of racially conscious mentoring relationships. Our mentors were committed to providing guidance and support to help us contend with the layered challenges of succeeding within the toxicity of white supremacy in academia. Participating in these student organizations and connecting with other students who shared similar racial and classed backgrounds mobilized in us a desire to pursue knowledge of our own lived experiences. Student organizations then facilitated an emerging intellectual groundwork for taking ethnic studies courses. After enrolling in ethnic studies courses, we connected with faculty who were committed to our academic success and personal well-being. As first-generation faculty members, we draw from these experiences to advise and mentor first-generation students. At the same time, we find ourselves lacking racially conscious mentorship and spaces as we navigate the tenure-track process.

In our experiences as first-generation college students, having access to faculty of color and their pedagogical practices created a pathway toward our careers in academia. When students of color see themselves reflected in the makeup of faculty and when their histories and ways of knowing are affirmed and amplified in the curriculum, the university becomes a space where they feel connected to faculty (Marrun, 2018; Villalpando, 2003). As a result, this strengthens their academic confidence to do challenging academic work, which then leads to the retention and graduation of first-generation students. Yet, as first-generation faculty of color, we have observed that while most institutions of higher education claim to value diversity, when we incorporate antiracist mentoring and pedagogical practices into our teaching, we often face rejection from some students and in the process, run the risk of being negatively evaluated on our teaching (Delgado Bernal & Villalpando, 2002). The curricular and pedagogical practices that critical faculty of color bring to academia have always been critical to the advancement of racial justice, but more so in this moment of societal engagement with anti-Black racism and white supremacy. Institutions must create conditions and structures that value our teaching and mentoring practices that move toward racial justice.

There must be an active commitment to institutionally support and racially transform faculty diversity on campuses that move beyond the cosmetic language of diversity on websites and in brochures. Moreover, ethnic studies must be supported by institutions who want to address racial inequities, especially in light of the Black Lives Matter movement and the subsequent murders at the hands of white police officers and white vigilantes. Institutions of higher education continue to allow white supremacy to permeate in their policies (in particular courses and who is teaching) and their actions (notably, the flood of shallow statements of solidarity). Ethnic studies is one of few disciplines that is rooted in teaching the history of white supremacy and connecting the past to the present.

How can students fully comprehend the murder of Black and Latina/o/x folx without having access to academic counterspaces like ethnic studies to engage in critical dialogue? Within ethnic studies, students can openly reflect on the murder of Breonna Taylor, who was shot and killed inside of her home by Louisville, Kentucky police. Or they can refer to the harrowing eight-minute-and-forty-six-second viral video of George Floyd calling for his mother as Derek Chauvin, a white Minneapolis police officer, pressed his knee on Floyd's neck until he suffocated. Ethnic studies links Floyd's subsequent death to the longer history of African American lynchings throughout the nine-teenth and twentieth centuries. Ethnic studies also connects overlooked lynchings like Carlos Ingram-Lopez, a man of Mexican descent who was also murdered by a Tucson police officer by pinning his knee on Ingram-Lopez's back (Carrigan & Webb, 2013). Like Floyd, Ingram-Lopez also cried out for his nana minutes before he was killed. Indeed, there has been a growing racial consciousness about state-sanctioned violence against Black and Brown people.

We must also not forget how Asian/Americans have been targets of verbal and physical racist attacks in the context of the COVID-19 global pandemic. With over 1,200 *reported* attacks, Asian/Americans are dehumanized and seen as "dis-ease carriers" that harken back to Chinese immigrants as "yellow peril" threats to the American national fabric (Tchen & Yeates, 2014). More than ever before, institutions of higher education response to these incidents must move beyond putting out statements and take real action by reallocating resources to ethnic studies and value the pedagogical practices of critically conscious faculty of color who are not afraid to engage and challenge students to examine the roots of a racist, white supremacist society.

Racial Student Organizations as Counterspaces: Finding a Supportive Community of Peers

I (Norma) identify as a Latina/Chicana/Mexicana, cisgender, heterosexual, able-bodied, bicultural, bilingual, immigrant, naturalized U.S. citizen. I am an assistant professor of education and Constancio is an assistant professor in eth-nic studies. We both teach at a public four-year university that is federally des-ignated as a Hispanic Serving Institution (HSI) and Asian American and Native American Pacific Islander-Serving Institution (AANAPISI). I (Constancio) iden-tify as a cisgender, second-generation Filipino American, heterosexual, able-bodied, U.S. citizen.

Norma's Testimonio

Throughout high school, I had good grades and knew I was going to college. I remember my high school counselor encouraging me to start at a community college instead of a four-year college. For many Latina/o/x students, starting at a community college makes sense because it is affordable and accessible (Santiago & Stettner, 2013). However, deficit thinking and low expectations among educators discourages many Latina/o/x students from participating in college-prep courses (e.g., trigonometry) to meet the admission requirements to a four-year college or university (Valencia & Solórzano, 1997). In my case, I was taking the required courses, but my high school counselor held lower expectations by encouraging me to start at a community college, even if I had the grades and courses to apply to a four-year university.

I was fortunate to grow up in the San Francisco Bay Area, surrounded by a variety of college campuses. I was also involved with the Movimiento Estudiantil Chicano de Aztlán (M.E.Ch.A.) and attended youth conferences where I learned about the different college admission requirements. The youth conferences not only provided me with the knowledge about how to apply for college, but I had the opportunity to meet young Chicana/o/x college students whose stories of overcoming academic and personal challenges inspired and invigorated my spirit. I was accepted to both the University of California (UC) and California State University (CSU) systems, but because I did not understand how financial aid worked (i.e., loans, work study), I didn't think I could afford to attend a UC. I decided to attend San José State University because I could save money by living at home.

Navigating the transition from high school to college was an isolating and frustrating experience because I did not know what to expect or who to ask for help. Although my family was supportive, I could not rely on them for advice about college expectations. I felt academically unprepared for the demands of college. Before I could enroll for my first-semester courses, I received a letter from the admissions office informing me about the CSU's system requirement to register for the Entry Level Mathematics examination and the English Placement Test in order to "objectively" assess my math and writing skills. My test scores were then used to place me in the "appropriate" English and math courses, but the subtextual message I received was that I was not college material and needed remediation. After my first year, I tested out. However, none of the credits counted toward graduation. Being placed in developmental courses caused me to question my intelligence and ability to succeed and graduate from college.

It was not until my best friend invited me to attend a M.E.Ch.A. meeting on campus where I found a culturally supportive community of peers. I remember walking into the room and feeling welcomed as folx in the room chatted in

Spanglish and laughed loudly like walking into a family *pachanga* (social gathering). It was in these meetings where I found an affirming space to engage in critical conversations about my identity and while also discussing issues impacting the Latina/o/x community, including anti-immigrant and anti-Latina/o/x policies. I felt comfortable asking my peers why some of them identified as Chicanas/os. Many of them in M.E.Ch.A. were also first in their families to pursue college and came from working-class and mixed-status families, which meant that most of us were working multiple jobs to pay for our college education.

We not only built community but also helped each other access resources, including connecting with caring and supportive faculty. It was in this space where I learned that I could take a course in Asian American studies that could satisfy the U.S. history, U.S. Constitution, and California Government requirement. It was also in this space where I learned about the Ronald E. McNair Scholars program. Professor Marcos Pizarro was my McNair mentor and one of my professors in the Mexican American studies department who taught the importance of working with and producing research that makes a difference in the Latina/o/x community.

Constancio's Testimonio

I was always expected to go to college and never led to believe otherwise. However, throughout high school, I struggled with math and did not feel entirely confident with my math proficiency. My teachers rarely reached out to me to talk about my struggles, and they certainly did not try to help point me in the right direction. Perhaps they thought I could overcome it, or that I simply was not trying hard enough. It is possible that they thought I was the "model minority," the kind of Asian American who should "inherently" be good at solving math problems. The model minority homogenizes Asian Americans and assumes that we are high achievers in the educational and professional realms with "strong cultural values" (June, 2011, p. 128). It assumes that Asian American students do not need resources allocated to them for math subjects (Coloma, 2006). Whereas Norma's high school counselor held low expectations for her college trajectory, my high school counselor, perhaps sensing that I was a "model minority," expected me to apply to college and helped answer any and all questions related to the application process.

Prior to enrolling at California State University, Long Beach, I was unaware of the expectations of being a college student and the time I needed to spend studying for midterms and final exams. Like many first-generation college students, I internalized my struggles (including being placed in developmental math courses) and assumed that I needed to figure things out on my own. To help cope with my lack of a sense of belonging, I joined a student-led organization named the Pilipino American Coalition (PAC); this was my way of building a community. PAC not only served as a social network of support to meet other Filipina/o Americans but also to share in our own strategies of excelling in college. Many of my friends were first-generation college students who were unfamiliar with navigating the corridors of academia. Because of this, we supported each other by pointing to important resources on campus like the Educational Opportunity Program, a program committed to serving the needs of low-income and first-generation college students. Moreover, we formed study groups for our respective classes. My involvement in PAC also served as an important source of self-knowledge that was missing in most of my college courses.

It was not until my cousin (who is also a first-generation college student and PAC member) told me about a course, "The Filipino American Experience," which addressed the different imperialisms (Spain and the United States) that shaped the abject conditions in the Philippines, early Filipina/o immigration to the United States, and the strategies of resistance that equipped early twentieth century Filipinos to survive in a racially hostile America. I enrolled not knowing that the course and the professor would eventually lead me to pursue a PhD. The course was taught by Linda España-Maram, a Filipina American history professor, and I was excited that someone was a scholarly expert on the historical and contemporary experiences of Filipina/o Americans. I excelled in her class and developed a thirst for learning more about my community. She pushed me to become a critical scholar by setting high expectations and providing the kind of rigorous training I needed to perform in graduate school. She helped refine how I read and analyzed texts and equipped me with research tools to conduct preliminary research. Soon after, I enrolled in more of her classes as well as other ethnic studies courses. She continued to mentor me by providing invaluable support to pursue graduate school.

Ethnic Studies Courses as Counterspaces: Taking Pride in Our Racialized Identities and Historical Roots

We realized that throughout our PK–12 experiences, neither of us felt connected or represented in public school educational curriculum. Within our first two years in college, we each took a class in ethnic studies and realized that, even in a state like California, we did not know that our histories or our families' struggles were connected to larger structures of inequalities in the United States. It was only upon learning about Mexican American studies and Asian American studies that we realized that our racial identities could not be divorced from our academic identities. We both share positive memories of being taught and mentored by faculty of color in the social sciences, including Mexican American studies and Asian American studies. These faculty helped us to become politically conscious about how our identities linked to longer histories of systemic racism, linguistic imperialism, occupation, war, and U.S. empire.

Ethnic studies courses served as an academic counterspace where we learned from a culturally rich curriculum. We did not just learn about our respective histories but also were taught how to reflect on multiple and contradictory perspectives. I (Norma) recall how I was introduced to the scholarship of Chicana feminist scholars, including Aída Hurtado's (2003) book *Voicing Chicana Feminisms: Young Women Speak Out on Sexuality and Identity*. My peers and I were encouraged to develop a critical perspective about our gendered experiences and the women in our families through the lens of colonial patriarchal structures. The curriculum was tied to my lived experiences, culture, and generational family experiences. It was also the first class where the classroom layout was arranged in a semicircle, and I felt like I was part of a learning community. My professors in ethnic studies communicated high expectations through rigorous assignments and an emphasis on producing high-quality work. As I took more ethnic studies courses, I felt less socially isolated, became more confident in my ability to contribute to class discussions, and developed skills to apply the knowledge gained from my courses to affect change within my family and community.

Similarly, taking ethnic studies courses served as a critical space for me (Constancio) to be exposed to different kinds of pedagogy beyond Eurocentric forms of learning and without compromising intellectual rigor or critical thinking. My ethnic studies professors implemented a peer review process whereby we exchanged research papers with our peers to garner feedback that was meant to be generative, productive, and critical. The professors stressed the importance of this practice because it allowed us to not only feel empowered but also to learn how to give and receive feedback in order to clarify arguments and substantiate our claims. I felt like I had a stake in the learning community, and that collaboration was key to our growth as emerging scholars.

One other memorable aspect was how one of my professors assigned an oral history project centering on Japanese American incarceration during World War II. We had just read the late Japanese American political activist Yuri Kochiyama's (1991) book chapter, "Then Came the War," and how the U.S. government had forced Kochiyama, along with her family, into an Arkansas incarceration camp. As part of the goal to produce knowledge for and about the Asian American community, I conducted an oral history of a friend whose family had also been incarcerated, but in Manzanar, California. This is one of the hallmarks of ethnic studies: we can find knowledge in our own communities, and we need to center the voices of people of color through oral histories. Because of these experiences, I often incorporate the peer review process into my assignments. I also assign oral histories in the Asian American studies classes I teach in order to broaden the scope of lived experiences along a spectrum of Asian American lives.

Mentoring Relationships as Counterspaces: Creating Supportive Pathways to Diversify Higher Education

Our *testimonios* reveal the importance of having faculty who could not only relate to our racial identities but also help us confront our marginalized experiences in higher education through their pedagogical practices. It was within these ethnic studies courses that our professors provided us with mentorship that responded to our academic and personal identities. When we did not do well on assignments, our mentors took the time to provide critical and productive feedback on our work. They also directed us to resources on campus and to other faculty who might also support us. Beyond this, they were invested in us on a personal level, which allowed us to feel comfortable to seek their advice when we struggled. Our lived experiences and histories are reflected in how our mentors taught us. As faculty, we bring these experiences into the classroom through our critical pedagogies, including spaces that value collaborative dialogue, decolonize knowledge production, center the scholarship of marginalized communities, and value the assets that students bring into our classrooms.

Our mentors took the time to help us prepare and guide us through the graduate school application process, including writing letters of recommendation, offering advice on personal statements, and using their networks to connect us with faculty of color who would support us in our doctoral programs. I (Norma) recall wanting to give up on pursing graduate school because I had been rejected from all the graduate programs in California. I blamed it on my Graduate Record Examinations score and the fact that my prior schooling had not academically prepared me to get into graduate school. But my mentor encouraged me to apply outside the state and drew on his networks to connect me with faculty at other universities. Without my mentor's advice and persistence, I most likely would have given up on my dream of one day becoming faculty.

I (Constancio) recall leaning on my mentor's support during my undergraduate studies and later on, when I applied for PhD programs. She was crucial to my development as a young scholar and guided me throughout my undergraduate degree program. When I decided to go to graduate school, she became the first of many links to my pursuing and completing a PhD. She connected me with scholars of color from various universities in the United States and from a number of disciplines including anthropology, history, and American studies. She also introduced me to her network of colleagues, who then provided guidance on preparing graduate school application materials, gave constructive feedback on my personal statements, and advised me about how to succeed in graduate school.

Faculty of color invested their time by supporting us with formal and informal mentoring and insider knowledge to continue on the path to become faculty members. With the mentorship and transformative counterspaces dedicated to our identities as first-generation students of color, we acquired the skills and knowledge to excel in graduate school. Their commitment to assuring our acceptance into graduate school was also an investment to diversify higher education. At the same time, these lessons set the groundwork to expand the production of knowledge within our classrooms and communities, and through our mentoring relationships.

Lessons We Carry into Our Careers and the Perseverance to Carry Out Racial Justice Teaching

After securing faculty positions, many of the insecurities resurfaced, not because we lacked the confidence but because historical and institutional inequities remain. We routinely face the message by some students, colleagues, staff, and administrators that we are not suited for the academy and that we don't belong. This message is often amplified through student evaluations or acts of erasure, such as being ignored by staff because we "don't look like a professor" (Garcia, 2018). When these incidences occur, we continue to seek out counterspaces of support to not only express our frustrations and challenges but also to collectively address our grievances to the administration.

Although institutions of higher education, including the University of Nevada, Las Vegas (UNLV), have been vocal about their commitment to diversity and inclusion, when conversations shift toward racial justice, the university becomes silent or takes a "neutral" stance. For example, our colleagues of color have been the targets of white supremacy because of their teaching. Moreover, our students of color have also been targeted by Turning Point USA (a conservative student group). Under the guise of "freedom of speech," this student group uses their rhetoric to harass and undermine the activism of students of color. When these incidents occur and when we have turned to university leaders for support, their responses have left us feeling ignored and further silenced. Similar to our experiences in racialized student organizations as counterspaces, we sought out collaborative partnerships and worked in solidarity with a number of on-campus organizations like the Sanctuary Alliance and the Latina/o Faculty Alliance. These partnerships are based on a commitment to speak out against racial injustices like anti-Blackness, anti-immigrant rhetoric, and the anti-Muslim travel ban. For example, police disrupted a Black Lives Matter student event on campus and justified their presence as a "training activity." Soon after, the Sanctuary Alliance and Latina/o Faculty Alliance collectives voiced concerns about the police's lack of transparency and the university's failure to protect students from police harassment. These organizations are crucial ecosystems of support that are not only racial justice–based but are also committed to supporting and retaining critical faculty of color. We have relied on each other by discussing strategies to support first-generation students, some of whom are also undocumented immigrants, process the backlash we confront when teaching about anti-immigrant rhetoric, and balance activism with teaching and research.

Within our first year on campus, we each developed and taught our own courses with a focus on Latina/o/x and Asian American experiences, respectively. We had identified a need for these courses because, as former first-generation college students, courses in ethnic studies had the greatest impact in affirming our identities and validated our academic capabilities to succeed in college (Marrun, 2018; Núñez, 2011). Yet the institution's tenure requirements and process expect us to adhere to a white, cisheteropatriarchal context that does not value our pedagogical and curricular contributions. Because of these hegemonic expectations, we create academic counterspaces that reflect the experiences of and ways of knowing among first-generation college students and students of color.

We were both hired to teach in one of the of nation's most diverse campuses, a narrative that the university celebrates. On the surface level, universities like UNLV have made great strides in diversity efforts, but tenure-track and tenured faculty of color remain underrepresented. Moreover, teaching courses that center critical epistemologies and pedagogy are not as highly valued (Freire, 1970; Vargas et al., 2020). As untenured professors, we took the risk of creating new courses rooted in ethnic studies as part of our ongoing commitment to transform higher education by creating academic counterspaces that validate and affirm students of color.

I (Norma) developed and taught the first course that focused on the various sociopolitical, historical, and cultural factors that have shape the PK–20 schooling experiences of Latina/o/x students. I was confident that students would be excited, but I overlooked the fact that in the state of Nevada, students in education (e.g., pre-service teachers) are required to complete predetermined courses to meet licensure requirements that fail to provide flexibility for students to enroll in courses outside their plan of study. Two weeks before I was scheduled to teach the course, I learned that my course could be canceled because of low enrollments. I grew frustrated that we are preparing teachers to teach in a school district where close to 50 percent of their students are Latina/o/x, but my course was not relevant to their training. With the support of my colleagues and students, I made the minimum enrollment number and was able to teach the first-ever course on Latina/o/x education in the fall of 2017. Later, I found out from one of my students, an African American student, that her advisor had discouraged her from enrolling in my course because it would not count toward her licensure requirements. She refused to take this advice because she was teaching in a district with a large Latina/o/x student population and felt it was important to expand her knowledge about her students.

Through the rigorous efforts of our colleagues writing a Title III grant, our current institution garnered the status as an AANAPISI. Despite this status, the institution did not offer classes that reflected Asian and Pacific Islander American student populations' experiences. To address this need, I (Constancio) created the first-ever "Introduction to Asian American Studies" course. Since its inception in the spring of 2017, the course has consistently drawn high enrollments and is filled with a diverse array of students from across majors. Students have shared how learning about Asian American experiences allowed them to find a connection to their identity. Upon reflecting on some of the course content, one student remarked, "However, after Professor Arnaldo discussed the history of the Chinese poetry written on the walls of Angel Island, I saw the strength and power of my culture."

Teaching these courses is a reminder of why we pursued academia and how they can serve as counterspaces for students who feel disconnected and isolated. These courses have the power to expand upon students' racial literacy in a moment where our country's heightened divisiveness is tied to education's entrenched Eurocentrism and white supremacist beliefs about communities of color.

Conclusion: An Ongoing Commitment to Racial Justice

Over the course of ten years, we have reflected on our individual and collective struggles of producing knowledge grounded in ethnic studies while simultaneously providing a rigorous and affirming education for our students. As first-generation faculty of color, we see these activities as part of our political commitment to ensure that students have access to pedagogical counterspaces that prepare and shape the next generation of critical scholars of color.

As first-generation faculty of color, we carry with us these memories of participating in social and academic counterspaces. We draw from these lessons, tools, and mentorship from ethnic studies to thrive and transform a male-centric and Eurocentric epistemological framework. In this ongoing struggle of anti-Blackness, civil unrest, and the COVID-19 global pandemic that disproportionally affects communities of color (Centers for Disease Control and Prevention, 2020), institutions of higher education must allocate more resources for ethnic studies, especially if universities like UNLV use the language of diversity as its brand recognition.

REFERENCES

Carrigan, W. D., & Webb, C. (2013). *Forgotten dead: Mob violence against Mexicans in the United States, 1848–1928.* Oxford University Press.

Centers for Disease Control and Prevention. (2020, July 24). *Health equity considerations and racial and ethnic minority groups.* https://www.cdc.gov/coronavirus/2019-ncov/community/health-equity/race-ethnicity.html

Coloma, R. S. (2006). Disorienting race and education: Changing paradigms on the schooling of Asian Americans and Pacific Islanders. *Race Ethnicity and Education*, *9*(1), 1–15. https://doi.org/10.1080/13613320500490606

Delgado Bernal, D., & Villalpando, O. (2002). An apartheid of knowledge in academia: The struggle over the "legitimate" knowledge of faculty of color. *Equity & Excellence in Education*, *35*(2), 169–180. https://doi.org/10.1080/713845282

Freire, P. (1970). *Pedagogy of the oppressed* (Myra Bergman Ramos, Trans.). Herder and Herder.

Garcia, N. M. (2018, March 29). You don't look like a professor. *Diverse Issues in Higher Education*. https://diverseeducation.com/article/113239/

Hurtado, A. (2003). *Voicing Chicana feminisms: Young women speak out on sexuality and identity*. New York University Press.

Jun, H. (2011). *Race for citizenship: Black orientalism and Asian uplift from pre-emancipation to neoliberal America*. New York University Press.

Kochiyama, Y. (1991). Then came the war. In P. Rothenberg & C. Accomando (Eds.), *Race, class, and gender in the United States: An integrated study* (11th ed., pp. 460–467). Worth Publishers.

Marrun, N. A. (2018). The power of ethnic studies: Portraits of first-generation Latina/o students carving out *un sitio* and claiming *una lengua*. *International Journal of Qualitative Studies in Education*, *31*(4), 272–292. https://doi.org/10.1080/09518398.2017.1422288

Núñez, A. M. (2011). Counterspaces and connections in college transitions: First-generation Latino students' perspectives on Chicano studies. *Journal of College Student Development*, *52*(6), 639–655. doi:10.1353/csd.2011.0077

Santiago, D. A., & Stettner, A. (2013). *Supporting Latino community college students: An investment in our economic future*. Washington, DC: Excelencia in Education.

Tchen, J., & Yeates, D. (2014) *Yellow peril! An archive of anti-Asian fear*. Verso.

Valencia, R. R., & Solórzano, D. G. (1997). Contemporary deficit thinking. In R. R. Valencia (Ed.), *The evolution of deficit thinking: Educational thought and practice* (pp. 160–210). Falmer.

Vargas, N., Villa-Palomino, J., & Davis, E. (2020). Latinx faculty representation and resource allocation at Hispanic Serving Institutions. *Race Ethnicity and Education*, *23*(1), 39–54. https://doi.org/10.1080/13613324.2019.1679749

Villalpando, O. (2003). Self-segregation or self-preservation? A critical race theory and Latina/o critical theory analysis of a study of Chicana/o college students. *Qualitative Studies in Education*, *16*(5), 619–646. https://doi.org/10.1080/0951839032000142922

Yosso, T. J., Smith, W. A., Ceja, M., & Solórzano, D. G. (2009). Critical race theory, racial microaggressions, and campus racial climate for Latina/o undergraduates. *Harvard Educational Review*, *79*(4), 659–690. doi:10.17763/haer.79.4.m6867014157m707l

8

Ambitions as a Ridah

Using Lived Experience as a Professional Asset Instead of a Liability

PATRICK ROZ CAMANGIAN

A ridah is a term of endearment not ascribed liberally to all people in a neighborhood set or to other street organizations. In both street and gang bang culture, ridahs are respected for their courage and sense of fearlessness. According to Jeff Duncan-Andrade (2007), "Rida[h]s are people who would sooner die than let their people down," and "in schools where students are suffering . . . they are the exception, not the rule" (p. 623). As an educator, a lot of my core identity has come from my experiences as someone who grew up and was groomed in Los Angeles's gang bang culture. Along similar popular cultural lines, Meek Mill (2013) clarified that there are "levels to this shit." While I was gang affiliated as a youth, I was by no means a high-ranking gang member in a notoriously violent or highly organized criminal set. Rather, I was a member of a Filipinx gang formed as a response to other racialized gangs enforcing their threats on individuals in my neighborhood. These individuals would be much more vulnerable to mental and physical harm without an allegiance to a larger body of people able to defend themselves collectively.

Years later, when I was being recruited as a first-year teacher, the Black assistant principal must have recognized a gang-banging background as part of my sensibility. She encouraged me to choose her school: "We think you would be a good role model for the [Black] gang members at our school." Through that sentiment, what I appreciated about her recognizing this was that she saw my disposition as someone with street sensibilities as an asset, as opposed to a deficit. What I found appealing about her recruiting me in that way was the potential of being able to leverage these experiences and insights across ethnic and academic cultures to connect in more positive ways with the students most disengaged in school. In this chapter, I narrate my past experiences being gang-related and the way these experiences are still present for me as a university professor. I am not sharing this narrative to uncritically celebrate the violence that often goes hand-in-hand with gang culture. Far from it, I am taking this opportunity to illuminate the ways my value systems and approach to the profession were, in large part, shaped by my gang-related sensibilities as a youth.

Getting in Where We Fit In

I was pushed out of school in the tenth grade. During the years I was supposed to be attending high school, I spent my time with homies who also did not attend school. Most students in predominantly working-class Black and Brown communities are, generally, at the behest of postcolonial ghetto schooling (Anyon, 1997; Paperson, 2010). Many traditional first-generation college-going students, generally, are thought to be more high-achieving than those in their communities who are pushed out or are not university-eligible upon graduation. Despite having less access to higher education, they, comparatively, spend a lot of their time engaged with school enough to get the type of grades that make them college-going and/or university-eligible. The majority of these students have a strong desire to transform their lives despite the odds against them and, often as a defense mechanism, adapt to the expectations and cultural practices and paradigms of traditional schools in order to do so. Perhaps reifying deficit perspectives of first-generation students of color, the school-aged youths I was close to more openly defied the traditional paradigms and practices of schools. We did not comply—we wanted to defy the social control of schooling and of society at large despite the varying consequences we faced in our families and schools.

While a lot of higher-achieving students attended their classes, did enough of their assignments to score a passing grade, and got along well enough with others to graduate, I was avoiding classes, not doing my assignments, and not getting along with others enough for me to have the privilege of continuing my enrollment in school. Instead, I often used the location of school as a space for my friends and I to meet, but from there we would find less-restrictive places away from school to bond, unify, and build the camaraderie among one another that helped us feel a sense of belonging and connection away from a space that was not providing that for us. At the same time, being able to participate in that space also required a level of commitment that helped me earn membership in that particular gang-related community.

Just to Get a Rep

One of our expectations of each other was to "put in work," which essentially meant advancing the reputation of our gang, whether as rivals or as allies to other gangs. One way to put in work included spray-painting graffiti to mark the territories we were claiming, as well as spray-painting graffiti on the walls in rival gang neighborhoods so as to disrespect their territory—this disrespect was one way for us to establish our sense of importance, communicating our domination of others by writing in their territory. Other ways that members put in work included engaging in various forms of violence: psychological violence through nonphysical forms of intimidation and physical violence where we would enforce harm through fistfights or nonlethal weapons—whether one-on-one or one side outnumbering another—and the occasional rumble when multiple numbers of our members fought multiple numbers of other gangs. Then, of course, there were varying forms of gun violence.

Later in life, Paulo Freire's (2005) *Pedagogy of the Oppressed* helped me to realize that "during the initial stage of the struggle, the oppressed, instead of striving for liberation, tend themselves to become . . . 'sub-oppressors.' . . . Their ideal is to be [important] . . . to be [important] is to be oppressors. This is their model of humanity" (p. 45). One way to feel important was to establish your name—building your reputation as a ridah—by challenging others who are respected in the community, respected in street culture, and respected in gang life, whether in our own gang or others. During moments like those, even though I communicated aggressively to assert my dominance, I was often afraid. I remember my heart beating faster in those seconds that felt like minutes. I remember being nervous that I could not intimidate whoever I was harassing. They would stand up for themselves, and I would have to take my aggression to the next level. If I did not, I believed the targets would then see that the tables were turned and that in that moment, they could be more dominant than me.

The thought of this made me more susceptible to my target's potential counteraggression. In many instances, I have also been on the receiving end of intimidation—I have feared for my safety, sometimes feared for my life, while having to act like I was not afraid. In the instance I described above, however, I was able to walk away from my aggression and intimidation of members of rival gangs with the sense of having won that battle. I knew, too, that they would then tell their members how I had asserted my aggression toward them. This all served the purpose of building up my name and my reputation. I was attempting to create the sense of notoriety that gives gang members social capital among other gangs—I was fulfilling my ambitions as a ridah. Similarly, rival gangs practiced some of the same aggressions toward my homeboys and other members of my gang. In this sense, gang banging was sport. Whenever gang tensions intensified, so too did the violation of one another's supposed territorial lines and violence between sets. There are numerous stories I could tell about these experiences.

The Life-Changing Effects of a Gang Truce

In one of the more heightened stages of intergang tensions between sets in our adjacent neighborhood, physical threats and increasing gun violence began to intensify. After threatening each other back and forth, we decided that we would meet with our rivals to discuss a potential truce. After running the idea by our different camps, we decided on a meeting time and place. Members of both groups initially met at the bottom of a hill on a late Saturday night before making the twenty-minute walk up the hill—there were about twenty-five of them and ten of us. In retrospect, the way I hear them explain the experience was that they thought we were fearless and thus dangerous to have the courage to meet with only ten of our members present while they had over two dozen.

The members of the rival gang thought that, for sure, we were weaponized, and we were. Even though it was not something that we discussed openly on our end, I am pretty sure that the homies I was with were, to varying degrees, intimidated by the quantity of opposing members we faced. And we walked up that hill anyway. Select voices from each side began discussing the roots and evolution of our rivalry. It was not something that we could clearly identify. We began to understand and conclude that our older generations were not rivals. Yet, as each of us in our generation and across our gangs sought to increase our local notoriety and fortify our burgeoning reputations, we found that targeting one another was going to help provide each of us a sense of importance that we did not feel like we had enough of at that time. After talking about our common experiences, common enemies, and common interests, moreover, we collectively concluded that we should experiment with a truce. A gang truce meant that we would not spray paint in one another's neighborhoods, verbally or psychologically intimidate one another, fight, fistfight, or use weapons on each other. In contrast, we were going to unite against our common enemies and work on our common interests.

This truce, eventually, turned into close friendships across our gangs that are present for us almost thirty years later today. Beyond the friendships, the experience showed me how people's worldviews are shaped and how our ways of seeing the world are normalized. It is often not until something devastating, unimaginable, or unforeseeable happens that our entire understanding of the world is shaken. During this time in my life, notions of my world were fixed and rigid. Who I understood my enemies to be was absolute. This understanding of the world provided me a false sense of myself and of my community, and what this meant for life on a day-to-day basis. I believed our rivalry was absolute.

When we transformed this rivalry, the seeds of my future social consciousness were awakened by notions of possibilities that I had not considered previously. My entire understanding of myself and the world around me was disrupted, and the open-mindedness that I experienced at that time provided the basis of possibilities that opened up further when I started studying more critical perspectives of the world. As an educator, this experience helped me teach students that the world, or life, is as fixed as we understand it to be at any moment in time. The more that we are open to multiple and developing perspectives—and if we teach children this while they are young—the less devastated we will be when change occurs in our lives and alternative patterns of thought challenge our ideologies. This truce provided me with an understanding of this in one of the most practical ways I understood life at that time, and this clarity is still present for me.

Critical Reflections from the Streets

Since my time as a gang member, gang culture seems to have become a global phenomenon. For Lam (2019), gang participation among Asian Americans and other communities of color is "a by-product of US imperialism and state violence" (p. 256). Because communities of color find themselves in positions of powerlessness, competing for a limited set of resources, we socially construct notions of power. Rather than submit to the perceived powerlessness that dispossession has placed us in, gangs and gang members are often willing to risk their safety for relative amounts of notoriety. This notoriety compensates for the power we lack in society. Many young people who participate in these spaces have at their core a sensibility that is present for how to navigate much of their adult lives.

When I think of myself as a first-generation U.S. college student turned university professor, I feel that a lot of my professional identity was formed by a local sense of possibility that did not exist in my mind prior to college. This sense of possibility and responsibility is captured by James Baldwin's (1985) *A Talk to Teachers*. Baldwin wrote, "precisely at the point when you begin to develop a conscience, you must find yourself at war with your society" (p. 331). Once I committed to the critically conscious purpose I began to develop as a twenty-three-year-old community college student, I found myself at war with my college and university professors, and my K–12 teaching and university colleagues, as I advocated for the types of pedagogies that would have served my needs more effectively as a youth inspired by gang bang culture.

Unlike a lot of my colleagues of color who formed their professional identities as higher-achieving students who finished their college education in four to five years, my identity was shaped by the willingness to fight, collective accountability, and sense of self I learned during the age I would have been in high school and college. Mainstream society is prone to see people who are gang related and people who have a background participating in gang violence as being people of deficit, as being unworthy of institutional validation and support, and, in many cases, as being second-class citizens. But I see people who have responded to similar material conditions in their lives as having the potential to use those mind-sets and skill sets to benefit and not just destroy the communities that they are from, communities just like theirs, and to benefit society as a whole. To be sure, oppressive society has been responsible for the conditions that shaped our investments in gang culture in the first place. As a university professor, that history is present when I teach and when I interact with my department chair, dean, or colleagues.

As an early career professor of color, when my white colleagues, dean, and department chair communicated to me with an air of condescension, I was reminded of the forms of schooling that I defied.

University Spaces as Enemy Territory

Upon hiring faculty of color in a desire to increase university diversity, the employing of historically marginalized nonwhite professors itself is treated as an award worthy enough of collegiality by the minoritized educators. Many critically conscious faculty of color, while often appreciative, do not share the same sentiment. For example, I was expected to comply with white supremacist paradigms of collegiality, which I detested. While my colleagues might have hoped I would behave much like other colleagues by complying, I did my best to stay true to those aspects of my social identity I was most proud of. I was not going to go along with "business as usual" because business as usual has historically been alienating to my humanity.

Similar to my absence from school as a youth, I spent little of my time at the university, in my office, or walking the halls of the School of Education. In one of the evaluative meetings I had as a first-year, tenure-track assistant professor, I was warned by a high-ranking administrative leader that I should be careful with my poor on-campus visibility because it could negatively affect my tenure process. Typically, early-career university professors are told by many people—and often repeat to themselves—that they should be careful until they get tenure, which is another way to say, "Comply with the white supremacist status quo until your job is secure." For faculty of color, implied in that approach to collegiality is a sense of silencing that we internalize and then embody. Far too often I witnessed people change from being persons who could voice their truth and the truth of the communities they represent to people who reproduce a fear of freedom as they "refuse . . . the appeals of their own conscience" and "prefer the security of conformity" (Freire, 2005, p. 47).

Prior to this advice, other well-respected figures in the school pointed out that my lack of presence in my office or in the hallways as a first-year faculty was glaring. I did not attend faculty association meetings; I missed a few department meetings; I was disengaging. I had decided I would not go to those meetings because when I would spend my time there, they felt incredibly irrelevant to my purpose and needs as a faculty member of color. As a professor, that was just not the type of person I was raised to be. I have faced far more severe forms of intimidation—outsized, outnumbered, and outranked by far more threatening circumstances.

Riding on My Enemies

All of these experiences are present for me as a professor. bell hooks (1995) captures the sentiment I always feel when talking about her own anger, frustration, and righteous indignation as a person and professional of color: "My rage . . . burns in my psyche with an intensity that creates clarity. It is a constructive healing rage . . . self recovery is ultimately about learning to see clearly" (p. 18). When I am told that my poor visibility in the hallways and absence from meetings I found irrelevant would negatively affect my perceived collegiality and qualifications for tenure, my response to this administrative leader was, "Well, then I guess [this university] isn't a place I'm supposed to get tenured." I had sacrificed enough of my life, overcome enough moments of fear, defended the honor of my gang, seen a lot of young people—sometimes very, very close friends—affiliated with our set die in our name, for me to easily unlearn the deep sense of pride and the loyalty I grew up honoring.

I believe that cowering to the expectations of culturally hostile notions of collegiality is disrespectful to the experiences that make me who I am today. As Frantz Fanon (2004) said, "If, in fact, my life is worth as much as the colonist's, his look can no longer strike fear into me or nail me to the spot and his voice can no longer petrify me. I am no longer uneasy in his presence" (p. 10). My participation in gang life was a form of reactionary behavior because it was not based on a critique of social oppression or motivated by social justice.

Further, if I did not have experience transforming spaces in my life that seemed fixed—such as with the gang truce—I would be less likely to believe that I could play a role in helping to transform a historically white-serving, private, Catholic Jesuit university that I experienced as culturally hostile early in my career as a professor. I probably would believe that I was simply an object of history and not a subject, and that there was little that I could do to transform the university conditions I found myself in. Instead, I believe that positive change is possible, having the history that I do. Not only do I believe that positive change is possible because of my past experience, I know that I have a role in making that change happen. Since my time as a first-year faculty member, I can say confidently that I have played a very important role in diversifying the faculty and leadership in the School of Education and shifting the vision and mission in more critically democratic and humanizing ways.

Instead of me driving through my enemy's neighborhood looking for a rival to build my reputation on, I play an important role in changing the writing on the wall, so to speak, at our institution—as a professor, this is my graffiti on the wall. Instead of intimidating someone with my aggression, I am using theory, citing research, and building authentic relationships in order to shift the conversations that we are having as faculty and as a school. Historically, these universities have kept people of color out. A lot of people of color will yield to the alienation of the profession and decide to make their marks in other spaces. When they keep us out, they do not attract teacher candidates of color to teach students of color in local schools.

In essence, then, we have generally been using traditional approaches to prepare teachers to teach. Put plainly, by not foregrounding the needs of communities historically underserved by teachers, we have been indirectly preparing teachers to be hostile to many students' humanities. If we do not want to come to universities and make it safer for students of color, then there will be fewer spaces for students of color to feel safe; universities will continue to be spaces that protect white supremacy by making whiteness the norm, thereby alienating people of color by making them feel like they do not belong. Our presence in the university—positions that we have to fight for, that are not going to ever be given to us—is important because community members of color can look at the university and say to themselves that they might be culturally safer in a university that has been historically hostile to the communities that they come from.

When Infiltration Becomes Transformation

The university is not where I learned to be a teacher. Frankly, when I first got there, my approach to teaching was an ideological threat to the whiteness of the university. Since I was able to help build a program that attracted students that would not normally come to a private university, the institution was able to benefit in multiple ways from what I brought as a professor, teacher educator, and teacher.

While this transformation has taken a struggle to create, my university has been able to see the value of critical community engagement more as a result of collective resistance. Being positioned in the liberal San Francisco Bay Area, I was able to leverage the supposed social justice aim against the very conservative approach the institution was, in fact, reproducing and perpetuating. School of Education leadership and Teacher Education department faculty would resist how I held students, colleagues, and administration accountable to the social justice mission of the university, but the cumulative effect of my advocacy led to a growing acceptance of, and shift toward, a more community-responsive notion of the university's vision for a humanizing education.

Fighting the Good Fight

The departmental transformation I helped to shift began with my own strong sense of self. University professors and teacher educators often come to the university afraid to resist because they do not want to deal with the potential consequences of defying the status quo. In this fear, they conform to the comforts of their ideologically liberal and conservative colleagues. As a university professor, having a strong sense of self—knowing what I stand for and having a strong desire to challenge paradigms that deviate from my commitments as an agent of social transformation—is something that makes me willing to call into question problematic policies and practices of my colleagues and school leadership. My history as a gang member has prepared me to bang on the system—in this case, the hegemony of miseducation in teacher education and in schools of education. The experiences I have joining forces with people I once saw as enemies prior to negotiating a truce have taught me that there is power in numbers, especially when uniting across differences with others who share a common purpose and enemy. I have applied these ways of knowing to my job as a teacher educator.

I understand that however strong I might think I am as an individual, I am much more powerful as part of a collective larger than myself. For these reasons, I used the Urban Education and Social Justice program as an avenue to disrupt a predominantly white profession. To create a more culturally responsive and critical teacher education program, we identify, recruit, and support pre-service teachers who reflect the demographics of the communities we serve. The Urban Education and Social Justice program has had a 74 percent student of color demographic for a profession that is 82 percent white. Without a doubt, the experience of negotiating a gang truce has taught me how to have solidarity for something larger than my own individual interests. My role as a big homie and the leadership role I played in my neighborhood, including my experience recruiting other gang members into our gang, informed how I would recruit preservice teachers of color inside of a profession that has historically kept us out.

Making Teacher Education Our Territory

As I have stated, universities promote themselves as wanting diversity until the so-called diversity shows up. Much of what I saw early on in this process was that a lot of my colleagues would utilize race-evasive pedagogies that protected the whiteness that was so pervasive in our program. These practices were culturally hostile to the students of color that we were beginning to find success at recruiting. This tension eventually became a source of contestation for our department. My colleagues essentially reproduced the white supremacy that the critical diversity had been recruited precisely to disrupt. Students would resist the oppressive ideologies that were normalized as part of their class sessions. Teaching critical students of color in classes where their instructors had not adapted their pedagogies and ideologies to serve a more critical roster often made for intercultural discomfort and ideologically combustible discussions. Instructors for these courses would tend to placate to the comfort levels of those with the most privilege, which compounded the racialized stress that students of color experienced. My colleagues would frame these critical students of color as unprofessional, emotional, and lacking tact.

Many early-career professors silence themselves to the hegemony of these racialized ideologies. While I certainly felt pressure to do so, I knew that silencing myself would only reify the cultural hostility that other faculty of color, our critical students of color, and I myself were experiencing in the predominantly and historically white spaces of my university, its School of Education, and the Teacher Education department. In these recurring moments of clarity, I had decisions to make. Should I temper my tongue to make my colleagues comfortable in their whiteness, or should I wreak institutional havoc on a department that for far too long denied the humanity of communities of color? Rather than succumb to the status quo, I chose to risk how I was received by my colleagues when met with problematic perspectives most protected by the institution.

During these times, I tapped into that same gangbang mind-set of claiming my neighborhood through enemy territory and finding the willingness to fight, despite any fear, in the name of a collective I was supposedly defending. I did my best to stand up and fight for what I believed in, exerting the ideological, political, and pedagogical writing on the wall over a department that protected its institutional hegemony for as long as it could. The influence this had on my colleagues started to shift the ideological culture of the program; we have since increased the cultural and ideological makeup of all the faculty and instructors there. Increasing the critical mass of teacher educators has been a battle in itself, but our collective presence broadened our sphere of influence and protected the critical students of color who experienced much more cultural hostility in the past. This has been a direct result of me banging on the space that was there.

For Life: A Conclusion

I do not communicate this sense of nostalgia to glorify gang violence, nor to romanticize street life or cisheteroaggression in higher education. At the same time, it is important to not conflate street sensibilities as simply cisheteroaggression. Doing so is both ahistorical and deficient, as the conflation does not take into account the context upon which the celebration of street culture operates. Many Black and Brown people across gendered identities from working-class communities celebrate street culture because it is self-determining and represents the people they care about the most. Also, this lifting up of Black and Brown people indicts respectability politics and other aspects of society that make the celebration of their communities necessary. In this sense, street sensibilities are not inherently toxic, despite adherence to respectability politics that might interpret otherwise.

I am simply reflecting on the experiences that made me someone who takes a stance and is willing to defend a position when I believe deeply in something, and in the way I believed in the gang for which I was willing to be a victim or victor. I am definitely not advocating the joining of gangs as a means to gain a sense of self, especially when youth of color have many more pathways today than seemed available to us in the past. I am offended by many people who co-opt and appropriate the performance of street culture to increase their credibility as people who supposedly were a part of those spaces. For many young people of color from working-class, working-poor, and surviving-poor communities during the 1980s, 1990s, and early 2000s, gang life was not altogether a choice.

At that time, participation in gangs was seen as a way to protect yourself from other gang members in Los Angeles. Many other young people of color also had the support systems in place to access safer pathways and assume more socially acceptable identities; they were given passes from the intimidation and vulnerabilities of those choosing to be a part of street gangs. Yet everything that my homeboys and I were experiencing about ourselves in mainstream society and formal institutions of education was telling us that we did *not* belong and that our resistance to the culture of conformity was unacceptable to their realms. The seduction of gangs, on the contrary, was that they accepted our social dissatisfaction as something that could contribute to a larger purpose and could be used to gain access to the sense of belonging for which many of us were yearning.

More broadly, I think it is important for other professors of color to tap into the ways in which they were able to survive racist, sexist, and homophobic worlds prior to being in these university spaces. According to Freire (2005), "It is only when the oppressed find the oppressor out and become involved in the organized struggle for their liberation that they begin to believe in themselves" (p. 65). Finding the oppressor out is more than becoming generally critically conscious of the intersecting systems of oppressions destabilizing the communities we identify with; it also involves identifying the ways hegemonic white supremacy is reproduced in the daily microaggressions and decision-making processes at the institutions we find ourselves in. Rather than feeling like we have to conform to spaces that are hostile to our humanity, we need to figure out ways to assert our experiences and expertise in ways that protect it.

We come into the universities with experiences and expertise that most of our white colleagues will never have. Most of our colleagues are going to conform to a system that despises our humanity: they are not part of networks, collectives, or experiences that they see as larger than themselves and are not willing to take the risks or make the sacrifices that communities we come from need. These colleagues are not willing to stand up for something they believe in if it means potentially compromising their material security or quality of life. What I have found, though, is that my courage—which I have had to tap into in order to stand up to potential threats to me posed by past experiences—has forged the proper perspective to handle the potential and perceived threats of the status quo and of white supremacy at the university. If I have been willing to compromise my safety and overcome fears about standing up for something I believed in and would stand up for then, there is very little that can threaten me in the same way at the university now. As a person and professor, this has been my ambition as a ridah.

REFERENCES

Anyon, J. (1997). *Ghetto schooling: A political economy of urban educational reform*. Teachers College Press.

Baldwin, J. (1985). A talk to teachers. In *The price of the ticket: Collected nonfiction, 1948–1985* (pp. 325–332). St. Martin's Press.

Duncan-Andrade, J. (2007). Gangstas, wankstas, and ridahs: Defining, developing, and supporting effective teachers in urban schools. *International Journal of Qualitative Studies in Education, 20*(6), 617–638. doi:10.1080/09518390701630767

Fanon, F. (2004). *The wretched of the earth* (Constance Farrington, Trans.). Grove Press.

Freire, P. (2005). *Pedagogy of the oppressed* (Myra Bergman Ramos, Trans.; 30th anniversary ed.). Continuum.

hooks, b. (1995). *Killing rage: Ending racism*. Henry Holt.

Lam, K. D. (2019). Asian American youth violence as genocide: A critical appraisal and its pedagogical significance. *Equity & Excellence in Education, 52*(2–3), 255–270. https://doi .org/10.1080/10665684.2019.1672594

Mill, M. (2013). Levels. On *Self made, volume 3* [CD]. Dream Chasers Records.

Paperson, L. (2010). The postcolonial ghetto: Seeing her shape and his hand. *Berkeley Review of Education, 1*(1), 5–34. doi:10.5070/B81110026

9

Sage and Tissue Boxes

Critical Race Feminista Perspectives on Office Hours

JOSÉ M. AGUILAR-HERNÁNDEZ AND ALMA ITZÉ FLORES

This chapter attempts to expand office hours beyond a contractual agreement and to consider the possibility of office hours as a transformative and social justice space. Traditionally, office hours are a teaching requirement in higher education; faculty sit in their office during a set day and time each week so that students can walk in and ask questions related to the course. In this fashion, office hours are what Paulo Freire (1970) describes as a "banking model" exchange, where the professor deposits the "missing" or "unclear" information to students and they successfully regurgitate the information in the course assignments. Further, office hours are often not valued as an important pedagogical practice, and few students and faculty attend them regularly (Newton & Gutman, 1979). Attempting to respond to this challenge, scholars have suggested pedagogical interventions to improve the quality of office hours (Atamian & DeMoville, 1998; Chung & Hsu, 2006). However, there is a gap in scholarship that looks at office hours as pedagogical sites, specifically in relationship to first-generation faculty of color.

We argue that office hours can become a counterspace (Yosso & López, 2010) if we redefine the contractual agreement to a transformative pedagogical practice. Redefined, office hours are sites of resistance, affirmation, and growth, what Delgado Bernal and Aleman (2017) call transformative ruptures, "interactions, experiences, and moments where a disruption of pervasive coloniality, institutional racism, and systemic inequity occurs" (p. 29). Further, we argue that the very presence of first-generation faculty of color in office hours disrupts the historically white male professoriate, thus their presence in academia (and office hours) is significant to students of all backgrounds, including those who are also first generation and of color. One way faculty of color can enact a pedagogy of transformation in office hours is to engage in what Jain and Solórzano (2014) describe as critical race mentoring, an approach where faculty "interact with [their] own students in a way that considers their familial background, how their career intersects with their education, and their raced and gendered experiences in the classroom" (p. 133). In this chapter we ask: How do our experiences as first-generation faculty of color and critical race feminista (CRF) scholars shape how we engage our students during office hours? Further, how can our experiences inform university pedagogical practices and institutional initiatives?

A Critical Race Feminista Praxis

The practices and strategies we apply in our office hours are guided by a CRF praxis (Delgado Bernal & Alemán, 2017), a process of reflection and action that is informed by critical race theory (CRT) (Ladson-Billings, 1998; Solórzano, 1998) and Chicana feminisms (Delgado Bernal & Elenes, 2011). Through a CRF praxis we seek out opportunities for transformative ruptures within and beyond academia. A CRF praxis combines the strengths of CRT and Chicana feminisms. For example, we draw heavily on the CRT tenet that recognizes the experiential knowledge of People of Color as "legitimate, appropriate, and critical to understanding, analyzing, and teaching about racial subordination" (Solórzano, 1998, p. 122). We use Anzaldúa's concept of *nepantla*, the Nahuatl word for "in-between space," to acknowledge the power and privilege that we experience as first-generation faculty of color (Anzaldúa, 1987; Keating, 2006). We hold power and privilege as university professors while we are marginalized in the academy by our other identities, such as being a woman of color and a queer man of color. Individuals who experience nepantla frequently become nepantleras, or "in-betweeners"—people who facilitate passages between worlds. They are able to live within and among multiple worlds and act as intermediaries, or "serve as agents of awakening, inspire and challenge others to deeper awareness, greater conocimiento" (Keating, 2006, p. 9).

The questions guiding this chapter are answered through our own CRF *testimonios*. As a method, *testimonio* emerged in Latin American human rights struggles and has been used to document the experiences of oppressed groups, specifically Women of Color, to denounce injustices (Menchú, 2010). Women of Color have used *testimonio* in their research to document and/or theorize their own experiences of struggle, survival, and resistance, as well as others (Burciaga & Tavares, 2006; Pérez Huber, 2009; Urrieta & Villenas, 2013). In this chapter, we position *testimonio* as a tool of a CRF praxis. Alma writes from the perspective of a first-generation Chicana in a nontenure-track visiting professor position at a private Jesuit university with a majority-white student population; José writes from the perspective of a queer Chicano in a tenure-track faculty position at a public teaching and Hispanic Serving Institution. Yet, despite these very different institutional contexts, we argue that office hours afford a unique pedagogical opportunity to enact a CRF praxis and more holistically engage with students beyond the classroom.

Alma's *Testimonio*

My Relationship with Office Hours

As a first-generation college student, I started my undergraduate career at UCLA with no understanding of what office hours were. My first exposure to office hours was during UCLA's Freshman Summer Program (FSP), a summer bridge program dedicated to preparing first-generation, low-income, and/or historically underrepresented students to successfully transition to UCLA. I remember professors encouraging us to go to their office hours if we needed extra help or support. Unfortunately, it was not until my professor returned my midterm exam back to me with a C+ on it that I decided to attend office hours for the first time. During office hours the professor and I went over my exam, and while I was still disappointed in the grade, I learned from my mistakes. As the final exam approached, I went to office hours more regularly to confirm that I was grasping the material. The effort paid off when I got an A on my final exam. My experience in office hours during FSP became the blueprint for how I used office hours for the rest of my undergraduate career. In other words, I would seek out office hours only when I needed help or support with course material, or when I had questions about graded work.

It was not until I started graduate school and met Dr. Daniel Solórzano—or Danny—that my perspective of office hours shifted. The first time I met with Danny, I walked into his office and was taken aback by all the photographs of students he has proudly on display. Whether in books, art, or photographs, I had never seen so many People of Color represented in one office. Per my undergraduate training, I walked into his office with a list of questions I had prepared ahead of time. When I was ready to get started, I was surprised by Danny's first request: "Tell me about yourself?" No professor had ever asked me this during office hours. This would be one of many meetings with Danny that would inform how I set up my own office hours specifically, but my pedagogy more broadly.

A Nepantlera Professor

Danny pushed me to think about office hours beyond the banking model and instead to create a space of resistance, affirmation, and growth. Now as a first-generation faculty of color, I think a lot about the possibilities of office hours. Soon after I graduated with my doctorate in 2016, I started working as a visiting assistant professor at Loyola Marymount University (LMU) in the Department of Chicana/o Studies. I was very excited to begin my career as a professor in an ethnic studies department and envisioned my classes full of students of color. To my surprise, though, the majority of my students at LMU were white and came from fairly affluent backgrounds.

Being a young Chicana, immigrant, English as a second language learner, and first-generation college student positioned me in direct contrast to my students and the majority of my colleagues. Yet I learned to embrace the in-betweenness, my nepantla identity. As a nepantlera professor, I am committed to helping my students understand systemic oppression. As such, I require all my students to author a racial autobiography, which asks them to reflect, explore, and write about their own racial identification and racialized experiences. After they submit the assignment, they are required to come to my office hours to discuss it. This is one of the practices I use to change my office hours into a site of resistance, affirmation, and growth, and to more deeply engage with my students.

Transformative Ruptures in Office Hours

The racial autobiography appointments begin by asking students to describe the community they grew up in, their families, and their friendship groups. I believe in the power of vulnerability; thus, I model it in my office hours. I discuss my upbringing, my moments of *conocimiento*: I want students to understand that I did not arrive to antiracist work overnight, that it has been a challenging, tedious, and ongoing process. We unpack a lot and I often have to push students in ways that make them feel uncomfortable. I see a range of emotions expressed by students, from anger to sadness to joy. One of the most challenging office hour appointments I had was with John.[1] John was a tall, white cisgender man and transfer student who began class by introducing himself as a "gay Republican." As I read his racial autobiography, it was clear to me that he was carrying a lot of unresolved feelings due to the tension he felt between his gay and Republican identities. He had grown up in a white, upper-middle-class community and had limited interactions with People of Color. His closest relationship with a Person of Color was with his Latina immigrant nanny, who had helped raise him. Before John came to see me, I had noticed a pattern in class where he felt the need to respond to every comment made by my only Black student in class, Malcolm. I was prepared to discuss this with him.

John walked into my office and took a seat. My office is filled with photographs of my family and friends. I have political artwork up with messages like "Brown and Proud," "Que Viva La Mujer," and "Black Lives Matter." I could see his eyes scanning the room as I pulled out his racial autobiography. The session was going well, and he seemed receptive when I explained the ways that systems

---

1. Student names have been changed to protect their identities.

of oppression are intersectional. I described what it meant to be an ally and used myself as an example. I need to use my privilege as a light-skinned, cisgender woman to disrupt cisheteropatriarchy. John agreed and provided examples of how he had used his white privilege to help communities of color.

When I brought up the pattern I had noticed between him and Malcolm, he immediately grew tense. I asked him why he felt the need to always comment after Malcolm spoke. "I just like to play devil's advocate," he responded. I pushed him more, "OK, but I feel like you always do it specifically when Malcolm speaks." He gave me a blank stare until he finally blurted out, "I just don't understand why he has the authority to speak on all things regarding oppression." I explained that as a Black man, Malcolm has experiences that John and I will never experience because we are not members of that community. I described how I do not know what it is like to be queer, just like he does not know what it is like to be Black. He grew angry, defensive, and emotional. "That is unfair for you to say that I do not know what Black people experience. I volunteered for years at an urban school where I tutored mostly Black kids," he said as his voice cracked. I pushed, "John, I can spend my entire life working with queer people, but I will never be able to speak for them." Silence. We both took a deep breath and I decided it was best for us to reflect on what we had shared. I reminded him what we had covered, his upbringing, the idea of intersectionality, white privilege, and how we can be allies. After he left, I lit some sage to clear the air and proceeded to meditate. I was exhausted.

Sage Knowledge

I continuously reflect on ways to create meaningful, affirming, and anticolonial practices in my office hours. I think about the physical space: whose faces and voices are represented? The ways I engage students: how do I center what they already know and avoid the traditional authoritative and banking model of learning/mentoring? I think about my students holistically: who are they beyond being my student? And lastly, how can I use this space to continue to work for justice? You will always find sage in my office, not only because it brings me a sense of relief and peace, but because I often face challenging student appointments such as John's. While I noticed a change in John's behavior after various office hour visits, I am not sure how he feels today. My hope is that this moment of resistance helped him to grow and see the world a little bit differently as a white man. What I have found from doing this work is that transformative ruptures often occur in my office hours where students and I can be vulnerable, disarmed from performing for others in class, and instead focus on building with each other. I share this sage knowledge based on my experiences of navigating academia as a first-generation faculty of color. My hope is that institutions recognize the value and often "invisible" labor that we do.

José's *Testimonio*

My Relationship with Office Hours

My relationship with office hours began at Moorpark Community College. Being a first-generation student, I didn't immediately understand the value of office hours. I met Professor Tomás Sánchez, who taught my first ever Chicana/o studies course. Learning for the first time in a classroom that people of Mexican descent have a history led me to his office hours many times. In those discussions, he radically reframed the way I thought about history. I learned that my ancestors were historical actors, and that the omission of their contributions was a manifestation of power that privileged European history. When I arrived to UCLA as a transfer student I was initially nervous, but I already knew the importance of office hours. Faculty in the Chicana/o studies department (many who were first generation themselves) were supportive of my academic trajectory, and their office hours were critical in developing my thinking, writing, and commitment to social change. In graduate school I was mentored by Professor Daniel Solórzano, who served on my master's committee and was my dissertation advisor. Danny's office hours were transformative. I usually arrived to his office feeling defeated and experiencing imposter syndrome and somehow would always leave feeling like an expert. The many models of office hours I experienced not only formed part of my educational trajectory but also informed my pedagogical approach to office hours with my students.

Physical Space

I knew that as a faculty member, I had to be prepared for office hours with my students, including ensuring that my office space was welcoming. At Cal Poly Pomona, where Latina/o/x students make up 47 percent of the student body, I have been intentional with the way I've decorated my office, specifically because our student body has a large first-generation population. As a first-generation student, I understood the importance of my Chicana/o studies professors' offices, specifically the books on their shelves. Never had I been around so many publications that focused on my history. In a way, those books affirmed my presence in academia, silencing my feelings of culture shock and imposter syndrome that made it difficult to navigate college. So as a first-generation faculty, I display my books to visually show my students that People of Color, women, and queer people have a history too. I also display art, gifts that my students give me, and the tissue box.

I've had conversations with colleagues who teach ethnic studies, and I've found that many of us are purposeful in how we arrange and decorate our office space, specifically where we position the tissue box. Strategically placed at an arm's distance from where students sit, the tissue box is essential because it welcomes vulnerability; it lets them know it's OK to cry. This is something that my students say is unique, in comparison to other professors' office hours. Sometimes we cry because of the pain we feel in learning the historical traumas of genocide of our ancestors; other times we cry because we are inspired to change the world, and it brings forth emotions of passion and love for our communities that re-energize and inspire us. The tissue box, like the other items in my office, creates a counterspace within the university, giving me and my students permission to open up, cry, and return to the academy and the world *desahogados*, or relieved.

Ethnic Studies and Transformative Ruptures

Aside from preparing the space, I see my role in office hours as an active listener: one who asks questions, learns from students, and shares skills they might need to succeed at a four-year institution. I also find that sharing my stories and educational trajectory allows students to engage in transformative actions. For example, during my first year as a tenure-track faculty, Jennifer, a student from El Monte, California, stopped by my office hours to introduce herself and confess that she had never taken a course in Chicana/o studies. I shared my experience taking my first Chicana/o studies course, and we discussed the need for curriculum on People of Color to be introduced to students at a younger age. I asked her if she knew about the El Monte Berry Strike of 1933. After I opened Vicki Ruiz's (2008) text *From Out of the Shadows* and pointed to the pages where it was discussed, Jennifer's eyes grew big. It was the first time she saw her community in a historical text. A few weeks later she returned to my office with another confession: "Profe, I think I'm a Chicana." Jennifer shared how, in taking the course, she began talking with her mother about what she was learning in the class. Jennifer's grandmother had been a part of the strike: "I come from a family of activists, Profe. And I didn't even know it." She reached for the tissue box and she captured her tears as she cried. My eyes swelled up. Together we thanked Ruiz for rupturing the omission of Chicanas' participation in history.

During my third year, Larissa came to my office in shock that I had just delivered a lecture on El Salvador and Salvadorans in the United States. Her family migrated to the United States after escaping the civil war in El Salvador. As she began speaking, she reached for the tissue box. She waved her hands as to dry her tears and said, "I'm here to talk about the project. Not to cry." I assured her that it was fine to cry, and we discussed her research topic. She knew she wanted to write about Salvadorans in the United States, and she said in a determined voice, "But there are no books on Salvadorans." I remembered that feeling as a student. I picked up Leisy Abrego's (2014) book *Sacrificing Families*, handed it to her and said, "read this." That night Larissa emailed me: "To be Salvadoreña AND an academic. That's what I want to be. This book gave me so much life." I emailed Leisy that night, thanking her for inspiring Larissa.

Rituals and Vulnerabilities

Despite being told by dominant society that I shouldn't cry because I am a man, I believe in the importance of creating a space, especially in university settings, where crying is not only allowed but seen as necessary. When I walk into my office today, I turn on the lights and I glance at the air-conditioning unit in my office. "Lo logramos, apa," I tell my dad's photo in my office. Esteban Aguilar Muro, my father, was my first mentor. I am the youngest of nine children and he wanted me to graduate from high school so that I could access an air-conditioned job. After a day of work in the strawberry fields of Oxnard, California, he often arrived home with back pain. He would remind me that he was working that hard for me: he wanted me to graduate high school so that I wouldn't have back pain, so that I could sit in an office job instead of working under the sun. I achieved my father's dream for me—I accessed an air-conditioned job when I landed a tenure-track position. However, I arrived to that position with multiple back problems that began during my academic trajectory in higher education. Air-conditioning didn't save me from back pain. I cried when I realized this: I felt guilty that my back pain was evidence I was betraying my father's immigrant dream for his U.S.-born son.

My father mentored me through his pain because he loved me. This realization informs my approach to mentoring students. Universities often wound those of us who are first generation, queer, and of color while simultaneously shunning us for expressing pain. I am reminded of Professor Sánchez at Moorpark College and Danny at UCLA, who listened, engaged, and centered me holistically (with my pain, curiosities, and questions) during office hours. I remember their intentionality in listening to and learning from me, really wanting to know what I thought about the course material. And I remember them holding space when I cried. Now I sit in their seat, committed to continuing to learn how best to mentor and advise students in a way that allows my students to feel like they belong in my classroom, office, the university, and beyond. At this point in my career I've learned that crying isn't a sign of weakness, but instead a ritual, a manifestation of resistance, a transformational pedagogical practice that values our pain, experiences, and emotions.

Office Hours as CRF Praxis

Our *testimonios* are two examples of how first-generation faculty of color engage their students through a CRF praxis in office hours. They show how our understanding of office hours evolved from not understanding their purpose to seeing their potential to disrupt coloniality in academia. While the context of where we work, specifically the student population we serve, is drastically different, we have shown how this work is possible across institutions. For Alma, being at a majority-white university has pushed her to use her office hours as a space for unearthing privilege and challenging systemic oppression. For José, office hours are a space of challenging the historical omission of minoritized peoples. As nepantleras, we approach mentorship holistically; our focus is not just students' performance in our classes, but their whole beings. We want students to know that we genuinely care about them while nurturing their critical consciousness and affirming their place in higher education. While some faculty may see office hours as a one-way transaction of knowledge where students ask questions and faculty respond, we have experienced them as spaces of transformation and healing. So, whether it is sage to cleanse the air after a difficult session with a student or a tissue box to dry our tears from seeing a student's feeling of validation, we see the transformative potential in office hours.

Based on our *testimonios*, we provide some reflections and recommendations. First, we see the necessity to include office hours as pedagogical spaces within research and teaching trainings. Often, discussions of pedagogy are limited to the classroom, but as discussed here, it extends into the office hour space. As a research topic, we see the necessity for ongoing qualitative and quantitative studies, specifically on first-generation faculty of color, that are funded and supported by research institutions and universities to measure the ways in which office hour spaces can be valued more by faculty and students alike. Second, considering the amount of labor that first-generation faculty of color perform, including teaching and mentoring in office hours, departments and universities need to value the labor done within office hours. Specifically, we see performance evaluations and retention, tenure, and promotion processes as places where that labor is intentionally acknowledged and valued. Last, it is necessary that institutions support faculty with office space. While both of us are fortunate to have our own offices, we know that is not the case for all faculty, especially part-time lecturers. Our *testimonios* show how important office space is for teaching and mentoring students.

REFERENCES

Abrego, L. J. (2014). *Sacrificing families: Navigating laws, labor, and love across borders.* Stanford University Press.

Anzaldúa, G. (1987). *Borderlands/La frontera: The new mestiza.* Aunt Lute Books.

Atamian, R., & Demoville, W. (1998). Office hours—none: An e-mail experiment. *College Teaching, 46*(1), 31–35. https://doi.org/10.1080/87567559809596230

Burciaga, R., & Tavares, A. (2006). Our pedagogy of sisterhood: A *testimonio.* In S. Villenas, D. Delgado Bernal, F. E. Godinez, & C. A. Elenes (Eds.), *Chicana/Latina education in everyday life: Feminista perspectives on pedagogy and epistemology* (pp. 133–142). State University of New York Press.

Chung, C., & Hsu, L. (2006). Encouraging students to seek help: Supplementing office hours with a course center. *College Teaching, 54*(3), 253–258. https://doi.org/10.3200/CTCH.54.3.253-258

Delgado Bernal, D., & Aleman, E. (2017). *Transforming educational pathways for Chicana/o students: A critical race feminista praxis.* Teachers College Press.

Delgado Bernal, D., & Elenes, A. C. (2011). Chicana feminist theorizing: Methodologies, pedagogies, and practices. In R. R. Valencia (Ed.), *Chicano school failure and success: Past, present, future* (pp. 100–119). Routledge.

Freire, P. (1970). *Pedagogy of the oppressed* (Myra Bergman Ramos, Trans.). Herder and Herder.

Jain, D., & Solórzano, D. (2014). A critical race journey of mentoring. In C. S. Viernes Turner & J. C. González (Eds.), *Modeling mentoring across race/ethnicity and gender: Practices to cultivate the next generation of diverse faculty* (pp. 125–142). Stylus Publishing.

Keating, A. (2006). From borderlands and new mestizas to nepantlas and nepantleras: Anzaldúan theories for social change. *Human Architecture: Journal of the Sociology of Self-Knowledge, 4*(3), 5–16.

Ladson-Billings, G. (1998). Just what is critical race theory and what's it doing in a nice field like education? *International Journal of Qualitative Studies in Education, 11*(1), 7–24. doi:10.1080/095183998236863

Menchú, R. (2010). *I, Rigoberta Menchú: An Indian woman in Guatemala.* Verso Books.

Newton, R. R., & Gutmann, G. (1979). The other side of teaching: A student-generated look at faculty commitment to office hours. *Teaching Sociology, 6*(2), 107–120. https://www.jstor.org/stable/1317259

Pérez Huber, L. (2009). Disrupting apartheid of knowledge: *Testimonio* as methodology in Latina/o critical race research in education. *International Journal of Qualitative Studies in Education, 22*(6), 639–654.

Ruiz, V. L. (2008). *From out of the shadows: Mexican women in twentieth-century America.* 10th anniversary ed. Oxford University Press.

Solórzano, D. G. (1998). Critical race theory, race and gender microaggressions, and the experience of Chicana and Chicano scholars. *International Journal of Qualitative Studies in Education, 11*(1), 121–136. https://doi.org/10.1080/095183998236926

Urrieta, L., & Villenas, S. (2013). The legacy of Derrick Bell and Latino/a education: A critical race *testimonio. Race, Ethnicity, and Education, 16*(4), 514–535.

Yosso, T., & Lopez, C. B. (2010). Counterspaces in a hostile place: A critical race theory analysis of campus culture centers. In L. D. Patton (Ed.), *Culture centers in higher education: Perspectives on identity, theory, and practice* (pp. 83–104). Stylus Publishing.

PART THREE

Service

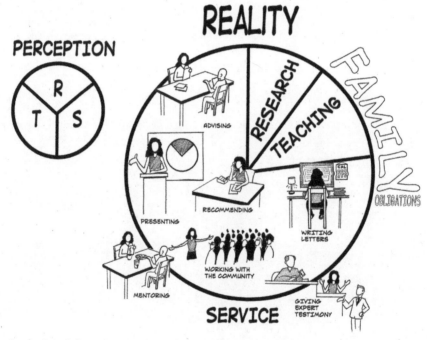

Service Perception versus Service Reality. Credit: Alberto Ledesma.

10

Financial Redistribution as Faculty Service

"The Hustle" and Challenging Racist Classism in the Neoliberal University

TRACY LACHICA BUENAVISTA

The first of the month is for me, like many individuals from socioeconomically insecure families, a day that elicits a myriad of emotions. As a tenured first-generation faculty of color, this day provides material relief in that I receive a consistent salary from which I can afford to pay my rent, my bills, and my school loan, and more recently, to contribute to a retirement account. It is also a day that entails deep frustration in that the majority of my monthly salary is accounted for. The remainder of the month is a practice of maintaining a meager balance in my bank account and a mental exercise of being OK with the fact that a financial emergency can detrimentally impact not only my immediate household but the well-being of my entire family, namely my elderly parents. I acknowledge that to have such bifurcated concerns fundamentally remains an elusive "privilege" for so many scholars from humble backgrounds, but for myself and other first-generation faculty of color, it is indicative of the intersection of racism, poverty, and education generational status that mark our experiences in higher education.

In this chapter, I detail the socioeconomic pressures and financial (il)literacy that shape my first-generation faculty experience. I illustrate my relationship to money through two distinct vignettes as a U.S.-born Pinay from a working-class background and argue that such lived experiences characterize the everyday tensions that are pronounced in the lives of faculty of color from "wealth-impoverished" families and that we have had to negotiate throughout our time in higher education. Among the goals of this chapter is to facilitate an open conversation among first-generation faculty of color centered on financial empowerment in a way that does not promote capitalistic practices and perpetuate shame for the socioeconomic barriers that condition our lives and the dehumanization of our families and communities. Further, this chapter is a call for institutions of higher education to seriously consider financial resources for first-generation faculty as a viable strategy for scholar-of-color recruitment and retention.

Racist Classism in the Academy

My experience in the academy was/is fraught with racist classism. As an undergraduate student and prior to virtual access to books, I often contacted faculty in advance to inquire about required texts to determine if I could borrow them from the library before I spent money on something I would likely use only once. Other students and I would pool our money together to buy one book and make photocopies. When I was a graduate student and eventually a faculty member, I had to be selective about which professional conferences to attend. Participation in such academic exercises are markers of scholarly production, potential contributions, and—less realized—class privilege. My attendance was dependent on sharing rooming costs with colleagues, and on more than one occasion I "crashed" the conference and did not pay registration fees. More obscured is the cost of performativity and public display related to educational attainment. I could never afford the fancy graduation package and photos so many people partake in, despite the desire of my parents for such artifacts to show off their only child who had earned a college degree. In fact, it was not until ten years after I received my PhD that I purchased formal regalia because I could never justify spending hundreds of dollars on something that, at the time of my graduation, was the equivalent of my rent and eventually a monthly loan payment. Even then, I could only make such a purchase because I joined with others in a bulk order of "off-market" regalia. I detail these moments to demonstrate how racist classism in the academy is often subtle: while I am visible as one of a few Pinays in the academy, the socioeconomic barriers I deal/t with are/were invisibilized and treated as an individual deficit and not as a systemic issue. Like many minoritized people, I gained access to the academy, but was/am not able to fully participate.

First-Generation Financial Literacies

There is a body of literature within education that details first-generation college student financial issues. In particular, scholars bring attention to issues of college affordability, money management, and financial aid literacy that shape first-generation college students' access and persistence in higher education (Housel, 2019; Lee & Mueller, 2014; Taylor & Bicak, 2020). More recently, there is growing attention to neoliberalism in higher education, the student debt crisis, and institutional efforts that seek to mediate this issue, including financial literacy education (Boatman & Evans, 2017; Hartlep et al., 2017; Shaffer, 2014). In this section, I detail financial issues affecting first-generation college students and do this as a jumping-off point for my argument that degree attainment is by no means a cure to the socioeconomic concerns of first-generation college students. Rather, these concerns transform and become exacerbated within the lives of first-generation college graduates who go on to pursue faculty careers—a noble, yet not financially commensurate employment option considering the social and economic sacrifices, as well as the high-level educational attainment and skill set, of faculty of color originating from poor and working-class backgrounds.

Scholars have long pointed to the importance of understanding how socioeconomic status and first-generation college student experiences shape not only the access to college for Black, Indigenous, and People of Color (BIPOC) but also the extent to which they are able to fully engage in postsecondary education (Ardoin & martinez, 2019). Among the challenges associated with socioeconomic status are classism within the academy and internalized shame. Thus, it is no surprise that first-generation college students of color are more vulnerable to stress related to college unaffordability and have less access to financial support and material resources that do not require them to disclose their socioeconomic situation (Eitel & Martin, 2009; Housel, 2019).

While these financial issues occur across student populations, the ability to grapple with these issues is particularly challenging for first-generation college students of color, whose race, class, and education generational status coalesce to inform financial literacy practices. Financial literacy is defined as the ability to access, consume, and implement information in order to optimize financial outcomes and security (Boatman & Evans, 2017; Eitel & Martin, 2009). In a capitalistic society such as the United States, financial optimization can be represented through the minimization of costs and maximization of profits. In the context of higher education, financial literacy can entail several scenarios: students having the ability to access grants and scholarships and avoid loans to pay for college; parents capitalizing on equity loans or government subsidies related to their children's college tuition; or faculty supplementing their retirement accounts with tax-deferred income contributions. In every instance, there is a required level of know-how to manage finances in the short term to gain long-term financial security.

More pronounced are the gaps in the financial literacy between BIPOC and white students, particularly among the first-generation college student population. Although there is greater need among first-generation college students of color for financial aid and education around college affordability, they are less likely to exhibit help-seeking behaviors toward financial resources. Such financial "illiteracy" is also related to loan aversion and students often choosing to work over borrowing money as a means to pay for school (Boatman et al., 2017; Eitel & Martin, 2009). This phenomenon is important to highlight because financial stress is an impediment to first-generation college student persistence. However, regardless if one persists in college, such financial barriers are sure to manifest in, or at the very least inform, the meaning of money for both first-generation college student pushouts and graduates.

Multiple Meanings of Money

While it is easy to depict BIPOC first-generation college students as financially illiterate, for me it is important to state that, rather, they experience structural barriers to material capital and have a different relationship to institutionalized forms of capital and money management. As a first-generation college student, I developed a financial literacy that required me to learn about money options that my immigrant parents were unfamiliar with or to which they had no access. Students often develop money behaviors from their families, including how to navigate the credit market (Boatman et al., 2017). I was familiar with the predatory nature of credit cards, and that credit cards with high annual percentage rates are readily available to socioeconomically vulnerable people, while low-interest loans are less accessible. One exception: subsidized—and in some instances, unsubsidized—loans available to low-income students in college. Throughout my undergraduate and graduate school career, I maximized subsidized loans to offset costs that my family would typically incur on a credit card. I understood that I would eventually pay off these loans and trusted that my college degree and eventually my advanced educational attainment would position me to do so with lower financial penalties than would affect my parents.

But how has such a mentality manifested itself in my career as a faculty member? It has done so in two distinct ways: first, I am in debt and will be until I am of retirement age. The first payment I make every month goes toward student loan debt. While such debt is attributed to direct costs associated with higher education, it also represents debt that enabled me to afford indirect costs that lessened any immediate burden that would impact my ability to stay in school. For example, I once used an emergency computer loan to offset the monthly mortgage on my family's home when my parents found themselves behind in payments. While my university granted emergency loans for housing, as a dependent of my parents (versus independent renter) I was not eligible. Further, I was advised by a friend that a computer loan provided the maximum amount ($2,000 at the time) and was easier to justify as a student. While I was not going to purchase a new computer with this loan, the loan would help to save the home in which the desktop and I resided. Some will argue that I was taking advantage of the system, but I understood my actions as maximizing the resources available to me and toward my retention. Besides, I was still responsible for paying the loan back while I was enrolled in school.

It is easy to internalize shame and the negative feelings associated with student loan debt because such a predicament is often depicted as an individual deficit around financial literacy. Yet, absent from such a depiction are the social, political, and economic contexts of the time. My parents' inability to keep up with their mortgage was due to a national housing crisis and a variable interest loan that unpredictably increased their monthly payments at a rate that exceeded their modest monthly budget. Simultaneously, I was an undergraduate and graduate student in higher education during a time that college costs were rising at rates faster than financial aid packages could accommodate. In other words, while my undergraduate and graduate school fees steadily increased over time, the aid I was offered remained the same. I was enrolled in postsecondary education when there were swift shifts to neoliberal treatments of students as consumers and college degrees as commodities, a consequence of the growing structural divestment from and privatization of higher education, which placed the financial responsibility of college on students (Hartlep et al., 2017). Today, we are witness to the worst student debt crisis in the history of the United States; at the time of writing this chapter, the student loan debt loomed at $1.76 trillion (U.S. National Debt Clock, 2022).

The second way that my first-generation college student experience shaped my money practices as a faculty member is that I am a hustler. As a student and before any reliance on loans, I would apply for as many scholarships and fellowships as I was eligible. Completing scholarship and fellowship applications was an integral part of my job as a student. Many first-generation college students and/or working students have time constraints or encounter overcomplicated applications for such monies and, as a result, much of it remains unclaimed each year (Kofoed, 2017). However, I considered the daunting application processes minimal work compared to the manual labor and factory work of my parents. To me, scholarships and fellowships were virtually free monies, and the backbreaking work ethic my parents demonstrated had conditioned me to understand that attempting to access such funds was an expectation I had to fulfill as part of our family collective.

Now as a faculty member, I hustle for every grant or award, knowing that a successful attempt can potentially supplement the incomes of those around me and, in some cases, my time—the latter of which is invaluable. Much of my time is dedicated to pursuing research grants or monetized teaching and service awards. However, truth be told, I consider the acquisition of funds as one responsibility of a mentor to other first-generation college students and colleagues. The vast majority of research monies or other awards I have received are explicit attempts to create employment opportunities. To illustrate, in the past five years I have secured more than $1 million in grants that have provided competitively paid jobs for thirty undergraduates and created three full-time staff positions and service work stipends and course reassignments for colleagues. Whereas most principal investigators set aside monies for themselves, my work is largely uncompensated: I have taken a little over 1 percent of all of my awards. In most of these instances I have bought food for and provided emergency funds to students. I used the federal stimulus monies I received to jump-start a mutual aid fund, and in the past two years (re)distributed $30,000 to undocumented and systems-impacted students and alumni who experienced COVID-related employment, food, and housing insecurity. A colleague with financial planning experience once told me that if I stopped such "expenditures" I would be more financially secure in the future. However, I have not stopped this practice because I personally know the difference that short-term financial relief can have on the wellness of students and their families.

Remittances and Retirement

As a first-generation faculty of color, my priorities have always been to get a job and keep it. In graduate school and when I received my one and only job offer, I was mentored to negotiate a solid salary, as it would be the number on which any subsequent raise would be based. However, at no point in my time as pretenure faculty did I ask myself: how will I sustain myself and my family when I retire from this job? Retirement is as important as—and dependent on—one's income. Yet, I was never conditioned to even fathom retirement as a life goal. Such long-term vision and planning are privileges reserved for individuals whose families had employment with retirement benefits, who do not have to think one day at a time and from paycheck to paycheck. While I technically have the means to contribute to and build my retirement, in reality I have more immediate obligations to which I must tend: remittances.

Remittances are typically understood as money and goods that are sent from a migrant worker in one country to loved ones in their home country. It is a financial strategy grounded in risk-taking and prolonged periods of family separation, particularly among migrants from labor brokerage states. According to sociologist Robyn Rodriguez (2010), a labor brokerage state is a nation-state that promotes policies and practices that send and prepare their citizens to work abroad in order to gain state revenue from remittances sent back. Labor brokerage states such as the Philippines are well-oiled machines in that they develop emigration policies that promote the return of workers and negotiate immigration and recruitment efforts with labor-receiving states, such as the United States. Labor brokerage states will invest in international "professional development" programs and simultaneously divest from domestic employment and economic development programs in such a way that both skilled and unskilled citizens have more income-earning capacity if they leave their home to work abroad.

According to the Philippine Statistics Authority (2020), there are more than 2.2 million overseas Filipino workers. My parents immigrated in the late 1960s and early 1970s, and since then held multiple jobs including but not limited to facilities maintenance, food preparation, factory work, and tax preparation. Their hours were long and the pay was low, yet they were able to support their three children, recently arrived immigrant family members, and those who remained in the Philippines. Like so many Filipinos in the diaspora, my parents regularly sent remittances to various family members in the Philippines. Their remittances funded secure housing and medical care for their parents and siblings, and educational access for countless nieces, nephews, and extended family members.

Due to their own migration experiences from the Philippines and an obligation to send remittances to our family members back home, remittances are an expected/assumed practice in my family, and each month I continue this practice when I send them to my parents. By no means do I seek to minimize the plight of migrant workers by suggesting that the financial contributions I make to my parents, who live hours away from me, are the same as those who are forced to leave their countries of origin. I use remittances as a metaphor to highlight the complex financial understanding I have and the strains I face as a Filipino, first-generation faculty.

Every first of the month, I make a deposit into my parents' bank account. This deposit ranges from 10 to 25 percent of my monthly net income. My contribution is based on three factors: the health of my financial situation that month (ability to pay bills and stay on a budget); whether or not I was able to supplement my income with earnings gained from monetized academic service (paid speaking engagements, academic grants, or stipend work); and unexpected expenses my parents might incur primarily due to their chronic health issues or varying housing costs. Although my parents insist that they can get by without my assistance, I understand that they can do so only by putting themselves into (further) debt, a situation I am unwilling to place them in as they are already in their retirement age on a fixed income and unable to live beyond what they saved while they were working.

My logic, like that of so many first-generation college students, is that the ability to pursue and complete a college degree was precisely to have the ability to help our family members who sacrificed so much to provide us with better opportunities than they had. But at what cost? I am well aware that my decision to ensure the financial stability of my parents now will most likely be to the detriment of my own financial health in the future. Coming from a financially insecure family, there is no material wealth or inheritance that will be passed onto me. More than likely, I will inherit debt. However, I understand how financial stress can shorten the life expectancy of BIPOC communities, so I would rather live a happy and financially safe life with my family for a longer time than accumulate wealth in such a way that no one I love will live long enough to benefit from it. Perhaps this is a poor decision, but it is one that I have negotiated throughout my time in the academy and one that I know many of us struggle with.

Financial Redistribution as Faculty Service

Due to their educational attainment, first-generation faculty of color are incorrectly assumed to know the necessary information and money practices to navigate higher education. We do not inherently possess this knowledge, but we definitely bring and develop a community cultural wealth grounded in our experiences as first-generation college students, as BIPOC, and with proletariat origins. Specifically, my experiential knowledge translates into a logic in which I practice financial redistribution as faculty service. I *take* opportunities to *make* opportunities for others, a decision directly informed by my struggles as a first-generation college student. I learned, as a student, that the money was selectively accessible to people who entered higher education. As a professor, my pursuit of such funds is a modest attempt to redistribute wealth to those of us who do not come from it and to model for others a strategy of maximizing resources available to us so that we can collectively persist in spaces often not of us.

As I previously described, we have an opportunity as higher education practitioners to think about how monies available to us in the form of research and program funds can be used to provide employment and material resources to students, colleagues, and community members. When institutional funds are made available for projects and services on- and off-campus, we are often in positions to leverage our expertise to justify how such finances can support community-based endeavors or to open up access to people often excluded. Further, we are members of an extensive network of individuals and entities who know how to solve problems or get money when it seems that there is none—an effect that is immeasurable.

Beyond the material, first-generation faculty of color from poor and working-class backgrounds have nuanced financial literacy informed by experiential financial struggle. When I have formal and informal service opportunities to reflect on my early experiences as faculty, my mentoring places a heavy emphasis on issues related to money as a means toward collective care. It is important to affirm first-generation faculty of color who might have different relationships with money than the majority of our colleagues. Just as research has established that financial aid jargon serves as a barrier to first-generation college student access and retention (Taylor & Bicak, 2020), so too does language around salary negotiations, loan repayment options, and retirement. I never assume that people on the job market or pre-tenure faculty should know such things, and so my mentoring often starts with an assessment of the financial literacy a colleague might possess, their financial history, and their personal financial health goals. I am not an expert who can provide a detailed financial plan, but I am someone who can lay out basic information, offer my knowledge regarding retirement benefits within my institutional system, plant the seed of future financial security concerns, and provide recommendations as to who they should speak to when their concerns are beyond my capacity.

There are a few caveats of a redistribution-as-service approach. First, advice that prioritizes immediate but collective financial health might appear counter to the ways that colleagues and mentors—who do not share the same socioeconomic conditioning—advise. For example, faculty colleagues I know have chased and received thousands of dollars to fund their research yet prioritize their capital gain over those that work for/with them. I have witnessed these colleagues use research funds to fly first class to academic conferences while their graduate students take a road trip with other graduate students, share four people to a hotel room, and/or attend receptions for the free food. Related, I might recommend to pre-tenure faculty to be selective and to attend one or a local professional meeting so that they do not spend the equivalent of rent or a modest mortgage on conference costs without adequate reimbursement.

When I began my tenure-track position, higher education was hit by a recession that led to my university imposing a faculty furlough and a 10 percent cut in salary. The salary reduction was just enough to influence my decision to opt out of an income-based [loan] repayment plan. Either I would pay more each month in hope of loan forgiveness in the future or remit a portion of my earnings to immediately support my extended family. I chose the latter. More than a decade later and as a result of the COVID-19 pandemic, we are facing an even more precarious situation: an unprecedented decline in enrollment and state and federal support, a worsening of the privatization of higher education that perpetuates an overreliance and exploitation of contingent faculty and the disintegration of the tenure-track faculty model, and the threat of another furlough. As in every context, including the professoriate, BIPOC from more humble beginnings will be disproportionately impacted. Today, more than ever, it is imperative that first-generation faculty of color—whether tenured, on the tenure track, or contingent—are empowered to work toward financial health and security. But I believe we must do this together through open and honest conversation that challenges racist classism and neoliberal practices embedded in the academy, which regularly marginalize and silence first-generation faculty of color.

Recommendations

To reiterate, a redistribution-as-service approach is a strategy to use one's position and professional obligation in the academy to pursue institutional monies and resources for the purposes of (re)allocation to individuals and communities historically and regularly excluded from postsecondary education. To be clear, a redistribution-as-service approach to one's career is an added burden in the context of institutions hostile to minoritized faculty, another level of labor imposed onto faculty of color who do not have the familial capital that enables them to work otherwise. This is part of the invisible labor and value of first-generation faculty of color that institutions refuse to recognize. However, there are some systems that can be put in place to assist, and reduce the racist classism experienced by, first-generation faculty of color.

Financial Planning and Management

In the context of the growing student debt crisis, institutions of higher education have begun to emphasize financial literacy education as a mechanism to ensure that students are equipped with the knowledge to access and manage financial aid. In the same spirit, postsecondary institutions must extend such financial literacy efforts to graduate students and faculty. What happens when human resources begin to talk to you about pensions and retirement plans that were not available in the careers held by your family? Income and retirement-related issues are like a foreign language, and centering "normative" financial literacy education will challenge assumptions of the information first-generation faculty of color are expected to possess already. Institutions can serve first-generation faculty of color by promoting formal and informal relationships to financial institutions, family-based financial management, and an overall paradigm shift toward fostering a culture of retirement.

Graduate student and new faculty orientations should embed open efforts to provide as much education about financial literacy and retirement options as promotion and retention requirements. What retirement and savings incentives exist? What is the meaning behind all of the taxes that significantly reduce one's net pay? How might faculty be able to take advantage of faculty-in-residence or campus-sponsored housing opportunities as a method for engagement and saving on housing costs? What options do faculty have with regard to relocating to different institutional systems—that is, how do you keep your nest eggs when you find another nest? Whereas many human resources entities house such information, I am advocating for more intentional outreach efforts and financial planning programs and services for first-generation faculty of color who are likely from backgrounds where such discussions are not normative.

Eliminate Cost-Prohibitive Retention, Tenure, and Promotion Practices

Aside from technical knowledge, there is a hidden [economic] curriculum on entering a salaried career (versus an hourly wage job) and a very real culture of classism that first-generation faculty of color are expected to engage in as part of their socialization and retention, tenure, and promotion (RTP) practices. These include everyday cost-prohibitive RTP practices, or those direct and indirect activities that promote research, teaching, and service but require some financial investment to achieve. Among cost-prohibitive RTP practices are those not widely supported at non-research institutions, such as professional editing services toward publication or participation in faculty-of-color-centered professional development programs (e.g., the popular National Center for Faculty Development and Diversity). A cost-prohibitive RTP practice hidden in the open includes being expected to pay out of pocket for professional conferences as a mechanism to access institutional funds on a reimbursement basis (if they are available), and even then, reimbursement funds rarely cover every expense incurred. There is not enough word count in this chapter to outline the numerous ways faculty spending are surveilled by reimbursement processes that implicitly communicate an assumption we are irresponsibly spending. Further, upon being hired, first-generation faculty of color are assumed to be able to front expenses related to moving or health insurance during the gap months between their start date and their first paycheck—often unanticipated costs. Postsecondary institutions need to first acknowledge such cost-prohibitive practices as racist and classist, and then establish creative but realistic sources of support, such as signing bonuses for new faculty and professional development grants and institutional payment options that circumvent reimbursement-based processes.

Incentivize a Redistribution-as-Service Approach

In the context of divestment from higher education, academia has embraced grant-seeking behaviors in job announcements and promotions. However, less attention is paid to how these monies are spent—on what and on whom? Postsecondary institutions and external funding agencies should prioritize the awarding of monies to projects that prioritize collective financial health. This might entail supporting projects that serve disenfranchised groups, create new employment opportunities for students and staff, and provide material resources for community partners. Postsecondary institutions should compensate the active pursuit of research and program funding by faculty through stipend and course reassignment for application processes. Further, postsecondary institutions should reward faculty who also actively mentor students and colleagues of color, as often this form of mentorship can be seen as a long-term investment in growing a pipeline of faculty with minoritized experiences and identities. How can we reward first-generation faculty of color for diversifying the academy and growing our community?

We have to seriously consider the documented barriers that shape faculty-of-color well-being and persistence. We must ask ourselves how a lack of access to financial literacy education and implementation for first-generation faculty of color exacerbates the issues they already face in higher education and perpetuates the racist classism that characterizes academia. We also need to imagine faculty hiring and RTP practices that do not disadvantage first-generation faculty of color, especially those from economically insecure backgrounds. These recommendations can promote financial redistribution as faculty service and, in turn, a paradigm shift to meaningfully include these goals and priorities.

First-generation faculty of color are invaluable to higher education, and it is time we are treated as such.

REFERENCES

Ardoin, S., & martinez, b. (2019). *Straddling class in the academy: 26 stories of students, administrators, and faculty from poor and working-class backgrounds and their compelling lessons for higher education policy and practice.* Stylus Publishing.

Boatman, A., & Evans, B. J. (2017). How financial literacy, federal aid knowledge, and credit market experience predict loan aversion for education. *ANNALS of the American Academy of Political and Social Science, 671*(1), 49–68. https://doi.org/10.1177/0002716217 695779

Boatman, A., Evans, B. J., & Soliz, A. (2017, January–March). Understanding loan aversion in education: Evidence from high school seniors, community college students, and adults. *AERA Open, 3*(1) 1–16. https://doi.org/10.1177/2332858416683649

Eitel, S. J., & Martin, J. (2009). First-generation female college students' financial literacy: Real and perceived barriers to degree completion. *College Student Journal, 43*(2), 616–630.

Hartlep, N. D., Eckrich, L.L.T., & Hensley, B. O. (2017). *The neoliberal agenda and the student debt crisis in U.S. higher education.* Routledge.

Housel, T. H. (2019). *First-generation college student experiences of intersecting marginalities.* Peter Lang.

Kofoed, M. S. (2017). To apply or not to apply: FAFSA completion and financial aid gaps. *Research in Higher Education, 58*, 1–39. https://doi.org/10.1007/s11162-016-9418-y

Lee, J., & Mueller, J. A. (2014). Student loan debt literacy: A comparison of first-generation and continuing-generation college students. *Journal of College Student Development, 55*(7), 714–719. doi.10.1353/csd.2014.0074

Philippine Statistics Authority. (2020, June). Total number of OFWs estimated at 2.2 million. https://psa.gov.ph/sites/default/files/attachments/hsd/pressrelease/Press%20Release%20 2019%20SOF%20signed.pdf

Rodriguez, R. M. (2010). *Migrants for export: How the Philippine state brokers labor to the world.* University of Minnesota Press.

Shaffer, L. S. (2014, December). Advising financially at-risk students: Detecting and addressing premature affluence. *NACADA Journal, 34*(2), 32–41. https://doi.org/10.12930/NACADA -13-101

Taylor, Z. W., & Bicak, I. (2020). First-generation college student financial aid: Results from a national financial aid jargon survey. *College Student Affairs Journal, 38*(1), 91–109. doi:10.1353/csj.2020.0006

U.S. National Debt Clock. (2022). Real time. https://usdebtclock.org.

11

Mexicana and Boricua First-Generation Scholars

Serving Our Communities with Alma, Mente y Corazón

JUDITH FLORES CARMONA, IVELISSE TORRES FERNANDEZ,
AND EDIL TORRES RIVERA

As three first-generation academics, dos Puertorriqueños y una Mexicana, we employ *testimonio* (Delgado Bernal et al., 2012) to share our experiences navigating higher education. At the time we wrote this chapter, Ivelisse and I (Judith) were faculty at a Hispanic Serving Institution (HSI) near the U.S.-Mexico borderlands. Edil is a professor at a predominantly white campus in Wichita, Kansas. Drawing from familial, cultural, and communal forms of knowledge, we, the *testimonialistas*, share how we navigate and thrive in academia to disrupt the dominant ideologies that permeate our Brown bodies (Cruz, 2006). However, our distinct educational trajectories also reflect the tensions and disjunctions that we have experienced in academia. None of us fit a traditional academic format and our very presence has been a political act of resistance because, even though two of us are U.S. citizens from Puerto Rico, we have been relegated as second-class citizens in the nation-state. As a former undocumented student, Judith was not even supposed to have entered the doors of the Ivory Tower.

In this chapter, we first situate our voices and experiences as sources of knowledge employing *testimonio*-telling as the tool of our *resistencia*. Doing so allows us to juxtapose the deeply rooted Western, Eurocentric ideologies/values that perpetuate the cycle of oppression for faculty of color in academia (Delgado Bernal & Villalpando, 2002), where we occupy liminal spaces. We share our *testimonios* to shed light on how our values and practices are different from the normative expectations in academia. We conclude by drawing parallels between our *testimonios* and how our *alma, mente, y corazón* (soul, mind, and heart) praxis was shaped.

Judith: Todo Comenzó en México—*Nadie lo Hace Sola*

I was the first in my family to graduate from high school and then from college. Along the way, fem/mentoring has been instrumental and essential to my success. *Nadie lo hace sola* (no one does it alone) and it all started in Mexico. I am one of eight children, the eldest daughter of Josefina and Vicente. My maternal grandfather was murdered in 1978, when I was born, and my family was dispossessed of their land. My father also was murdered when I was three years old. Hence, even though I was born in Veracruz, I was raised in Puebla, Mexico, until the age of ten. My mother had migrated to the United States in 1985, leaving a brother and me with our grandmother, and it was not until 1989 that we were reunited. Strong women—my first example of feministas—raised me.

When we arrived in South Los Angeles, California, the local schools were overcrowded and my sister and I were bused to West Los Angeles. Having crossed to the United States *sin papeles*, as an undocumented student, many resources were denied to students with my status. This is still the case today. Even as an undocumented student, however, I was afforded the opportunity to join a mentoring program in the eighth grade. For high school I returned to South LA, though, where I was placed in a college-track program, one of very few students chosen for this opportunity.

While still in high school, I went to a career day and the keynote address was given by then Executive Assistant to the President of California State University, Monterey Bay (CSUMB), Cecilia Burciaga (QEPD). Her motivational and inspirational speech propelled me to attend CSUMB as an "international" student. Cecilia was instrumental in my admission to CSUMB and in teaching me how to navigate higher education—when I started my academic journey in 1997, fem/mentoring and familial support had made this possible. As an undergraduate student at CSUMB, I learned that my story has value and is worth sharing with others. I learned this by reading the works of Chicanas, Latinas, Latinxs, and scholars of color who shared their lived experiences openly and for others to learn from or connect with—this was affirming and grounding in my educational trajectory. Knowing and claiming my story has continually reminded me of where I come from—a long line of matriarchs who possess immense knowledge, even though my grandmother had no formal schooling and my mother completed only a second-grade education. *Mujeres* in my family have had courage and innate wisdom not learned by or in books but by *lo vivido*, the theory of the flesh (Moraga, 2002).

I was undocumented for my entire undergraduate experience at CSUMB. During this time I worked for a service-learning student leadership program. I worked for one year as a co-teacher in an introductory service-learning course, for one year as a community-based student leader placing students to do their service in the community, and for one year as an upper-division co-teacher within my major—and not one year did I get paid for this exhausting, draining work. Years later I thought about how I couldn't get paid because I was not a "legal" resident in this country, but this experience propelled me to aspire to the professoriate. In 2001, I completed my BA in human communication with an emphasis in American studies; in 2002, I became a legal resident; and in 2003, I continued at CSUMB to earn a master's degree in multicultural education. Overall, my experience was transformative and empowering, and I was finally able to continue dreaming and thriving in school.

Working closely with fem/mentors at the undergraduate and master's level allowed me to feel confident about my aspirations and contributions to academia, and eventually to pursue a PhD in the sociology of education. Again, it was fem/mentors (in my doctoral department) at the University of Utah who demonstrated how essential their guidance is to navigating and thriving in unknown spaces. I learned from them how to treat and work with students, how to collaborate with peers, and how to center my/our epistemologies and pedagogies of the home (Delgado Bernal, 2001). Early on as a doctoral student, I was reminded of the community cultural wealth (Yosso, 2005) that exists in communities of color, and this knowledge led me to design my dissertation research as a five-year-long school-community-university partnership that centered on the pedagogies of the home of Latina/o/x families in Utah. But this is my formal and linear educational trajectory—let me digress and share about how I became a scholar. That is, I will now share all that I learned along the way as the oldest daughter/sister, undocumented person, and cultural broker who was brought to South LA at the age of ten. Specifically, I share how these knowledges have served as pillars in shaping my own pedagogy now that I am a tenured professor at an HSI.

Scholar

For four years, attending schools in West Los Angeles showed me every morning that dividing freeways had accentuated the segregated schooling and very different access to resources that persist in the City of Angels. As the bus drove off from impoverished communities toward the ocean, I recognized that this was a serendipitous opportunity that would literally take me out of the "hood" and show me different worlds. This included differential treatment based on race and class that would teach me from an early age, even before learning English, that some bodies are made to believe that they do not belong in certain spaces.

By the time I was twelve, I had learned enough English to become the official translator for my mom and family. I found myself learning about diabetes, welfare/social assistance, police reports, Child Protective Services, and how to clean a house properly (I helped my mom clean homes on weekends). I often missed school to translate and to learn to navigate El Norte by speaking with people in authority, teachers who held deficit-thinking ideologies about me and my siblings, and doctors who never looked into my mom's eyes when they spoke to her. I learned quickly to defend her, and without me realizing, I was learning to speak back to power, a tool I have used to navigate the bureaucracies of academia.

Fast-forward to my first semester at New Mexico State University (NMSU). As a first-generation tenure-track faculty, I did not know how to negotiate my contract or how to request additional resources, much less how to request to count my postdoctorate years toward tenure. Again, I turned to fem/mentors for guidance. But it was the day-to-day experiences that actually made me realize I was not seen as belonging or as a professor. One example happened during my first official day at NMSU when I was moving into my office. As I unlocked the door, a person across the hall yelled out, "Graduate students are not allowed in faculty offices if the professor is not here." I was perplexed. "I am the professor," I responded. I wondered if it was my age, my height, my skin color, my gender, or all of the above—but I was not seen as a professor. But how could this happen at an HSI? Since then, I have experienced other aggressions, but I always make sure and defend myself, talk back, and remind myself of my femtor Cecilia's words, "*no te dejes*" (don't let yourself be abused).

The "no te dejes" *consejo* also played out when I submitted my dossier for promotion and tenure. When a white male department head saw the list of external reviewers I was suggesting he immediately said, "I see you have all your *comadres* on the list." I quickly replied, "Yes, just like you probably had all your *compadres* on yours!" No te dejes. Indeed, this is a lesson that I impart to students and colleagues, and Ivelisse is one close friend and *colega* with whom I have shared these *consejos*.

Ivelisse: My Journey as a Puerto Rican in Academia—Finding My Voice and My Space

I was born and raised in Puerto Rico. I am the second of three sisters—a middle child. Growing up in a middle-class family, my parents worked very hard to give us everything we needed. For my parents, providing us with an education was of utmost importance. My Grandpa Joaquin and my mother have been my most influential role models. Grandpa Joaquin barely finished elementary school, but he instilled in my mom and Aunt Carmen a love of learning, teaching, and serving. Therefore, it is not surprising that his five grandchildren earned college degrees. Yet, I am the only one with a PhD and a career in academia.

My mom taught me that anything is possible if you merge your alma, mente y corazón. As a former educator and counselor, she was an excellent role model. Through her example, I learned how to treat students respectfully, how to identify their strengths, motivate, support, and femtor them.

The Journey through My Voluntary Exile

My pre-academic career started in Puerto Rico, where I completed a bachelor's degree in psychology with a minor in education. I also completed two master's degrees in school and counseling psychology. However, I always knew that

I wanted to pursue a doctoral degree on the mainland, so in 1997 I embarked on a journey that would change my life forever.

My experiences as a Latina in the doctoral program were similar to that of most students of color (González, 2007; Ramos & Torres Fernandez, 2020). I experienced racism, sexism, and microaggressions related to my accent and perceived ability (Garcia, 2019; Gutiérrez y Muhs et al., 2012). I was constantly reminded of my "minority" status and informed that I got into the program because of affirmative action. When interacting with others, I was referred to as "exotic" and with beautiful "olive skin." Having an accent made me the target of numerous microaggressions, including "Could you say that word again? It sounds so sexy." or "Could you repeat what you said? Your accent is so strong." I also experienced discrimination and oppression related to my perceived legal status and stereotypes related to Puerto Ricans. Many people don't treat us as U.S. citizens.

These experiences have influenced how I have approached my teaching, scholarship, and service. Throughout this process, finding fem/mentors has been instrumental in my ability to overcome barriers, succeed, and thrive. For example, becoming a Holmes Scholar and Diversity Fellow at the University of Iowa's College of Education allowed me the opportunity to access additional support networks that opened pathways to succeed at a predominantly white institution.

Academia

Because my experiences in graduate school reinforced my perception of academia as a very competitive and toxic environment, my academic journey started years later, after I completed my doctoral degree. For five years I focused on helping clients improve their mental health by working as a bilingual school psychologist. At that school I thrived, succeeded, and eventually was promoted to the position of chief psychologist for research and training. I reconnected with my "academic self" by training and femtoring other mental health professionals, developing a research agenda focusing on the importance of fostering resilience and social emotional learning in children and adolescents, and developing staff trainings that focused on multicultural and social justice competencies.

My love/hate relationship with academia is no secret. I am very vocal about my difficulties in finding a space in academia. First, most of my fem/mentors were successful practitioners; thus, research and scholarship were not core components of my professional identity. My struggles with academic writing have been ongoing ever since I wrote my master's thesis. Feelings fueled primarily by bouts of imposter syndrome (Gutiérrez y Muhs et al., 2012) worsened when I entered the doctoral program. I have also found my cultural and personal values at odds with what is expected of an academic. For example, although I worked at a land-grant HSI where faculty are expected to focus primarily on research and scholarship, I have always gravitated toward teaching, femtoring, and doing outreach. Yet, these practices are not valued in promotion and tenure policies. While I also operate from a collectivistic framework, academia values individualism. Last, since becoming an academic and researcher was not my primary career goal, it was not surprising that after landing my first academic job, I found myself lost and confused about how to negotiate my contract and allocation of effort, finding fem/mentors, and learning the overt and covert rules of academia. In other words, I lacked the academic socialization that is so vital to surviving in higher education.

Making the transition from practitioner to academic was difficult. For instance, as a faculty member, time management and organization are critical because we have to take time for teaching, service, and research. One also needs to be strategic in prioritizing our different roles in academia (teaching, research, and service). Setting boundaries is a must—especially for first-generation scholars—so that we are not burdened with service. In addition, there is a socialization process that is critical. Fem/mentoring is essential, particularly in the pre-tenure process. Resilience, resistance, and strength are imperative, particularly when feeling tokenized and invalidated. Finally, I struggled personally and that led to a difficult divorce that pushed me back in many aspects—especially in my ability to publish. Many times I felt lost, confused, and ashamed. I struggled to ask for help and support.

After six years of being recognized with faculty teaching, service, and diversity awards, I was told that my work and efforts were not "good enough" and therefore I was not recommended for promotion. I was devastated, angry, and in disbelief, but above all embarrassed and disappointed in myself. However, I decided to use this experience to better myself in this "HSI" space that is unwelcoming of individuals who look and sound like me. In the process of finding my place in academia, I have been blessed by being involved in the fem/mentoring of students, community outreach, international partnerships, and social justice advocacy. But most importantly, I have focused my energies on building a research agenda rooted in the needs of vulnerable communities and promoting community advocacy and activism. Through my scholarship, I have been able to inform best practices, and these experiences keep me grounded because they all bring me back to my beginnings and remind me of who I am and what is important to me. I remind myself that my work matters and that I am making a significant impact. For that, I am grateful and hopeful that I am where I need to be.

Edil: Finding Balance in a "Hurricane"

This is my *testimonio* of thirty-nine years in the United States after moving here from Puerto Rico, the oldest colony in the Americas (Mullen & Marquez, 2015). This is a *testimonio* of being a first-generation college professor and being in the

U.S. Army. I am the oldest son of a single mother; she attained only a third-grade education. I am the first in my family to earn a bachelor's degree, a master's, and a doctorate. As such, navigating academia has been a lonely and difficult journey. I learned early in life that besides my mother, the only role models that I could follow were in books and/or in *cuentos* and *dichos* (stories and proverbs). Cuentos provided me with an invisible roadmap of life and how to maneuver it, while dichos provided me with a set of instructions on how to navigate the map of life and find meaning and direction. Without role models in academia, I felt that I was creating my own path. However, my mother, grandmother, and ancestors were there with me—spiritually or in person.

My story and professional journey can be condensed by the aftermath of being born and raised in a colonized country. Puerto Rico has suffered under two colonizers—Spain and the United States. While Puerto Rico is a U.S. territory the condition of colonization does not allow Puerto Ricans to have the same benefits as people from Alaska, Hawaii, or the Lower 48. Understanding colonization and the process of personal decolonization, I pride myself as a spiritual person who is compassionate and honest because of my humble beginnings. This is important as these experiences have framed my experiences as a first-generation faculty member.

My journey began in the housing projects where I was raised. My mother understood that in Puerto Rico an education was the only way out of poverty and encouraged me to pursue my education. Eventually, as my curiosity and hunger for knowledge grew, I realized that education was a way to freedom—a way to freedom from oppression and invisibility—and that my teachers were the guides toward consciousness (Freire, 2000; Montero, 2009). My path involved an ongoing struggle for clarity and balance. Professionally and personally, these struggles also have provided me with liberation (Freire, 2000)—liberation from inequality and from systemic oppression. Liberation is also a transformation process that is individual and collective. More importantly, it is a political process that moves the individual and the collective toward a critical sense of citizenship and powerful democracy (Montero, 2009). Being liberated implies an awareness of oppression and the effects of colonialism, which is a complex process that also involves colonizing the psychological and social worlds of the colonial subjects (Tate et al., 2015). This awareness eventually turned into my research agenda of examining how the colonization of the mind affects ethnic minorities' psychological well-being.

Furthermore, growing up in the projects required high levels of resilience, forcing me to become an adult before I understood what being a child meant. I learned quickly to have endurance and persistence to manage the situations I faced. These skills were instrumental in understanding the academic world, specifically by helping me to deal with rejection, particularly in the area of publication. Manuscript reviewers can be brutal, and rejection does not particularly serve those of us who pursue tenure and promotion in academia. As a first-generation student and scholar, I was not mentored on navigating the politics of academia. The endurance and resiliency I learned in the projects have served me well in higher education. I have learned to survive in academia and to overcome its systemic oppressive ways of reinforcing elitism, meritocracy, and competitiveness (Watkins & Schulman, 2008).

My awareness of oppression was heightened when I joined the U.S. Army in 1979. My time in the Army was very much riddled with experiences of racism. I was regularly passed up for promotion and positions of leadership, watching people from the dominant culture (whites, Caucasians) be selected for positions for which I was well qualified. The Army experience helped me to understand structural oppression, something that I teach as we move toward decolonization. These skills also prepared me to access opportunities provided by the Army. While this military experience may seem disconnected from my experience in academia, it is not.

Academic Experience

During my time in the Army, I was able to finish my bachelor's and master's degrees and begin pursuing a doctoral degree in counseling psychology. It was on this journey where I learned that my passion for helping was rooted in and related to undoing colonialism (Memmi, 1957, 2000). I endeavored to work toward decolonization in academia—putting into practice my accumulated tools from lived experience and centering these historically excluded knowledges in my teaching and research. Those tools are resilience, endurance, persistence, patience, flexibility, and having a voice at the table. It is important to mention that as a first-generation scholar, having a voice, though marginally, has come at a cost.

Like many faculty of color, I have been passed up for promotion, been fired, been called a "thug," and have experienced numerous microaggressions and blatant discrimination (Gutiérrez y Muhs et al., 2012). For example, security once escorted me out of my classroom at a private not-for-profit school *while* I was teaching multicultural counseling—two white women students did not feel comfortable with my lecture about privilege and colonization. Professionally, I have experienced rejection in academic circles where more than once I have been told to calm down, to speak slower, and not be aggressive. People seem to take my passion and energy as "violent" rather than as committed to the profession and to my students. The challenge to modify myself from being honest and direct to being more tactful and careful when I relate to others has presented my biggest challenge. This makes me feel stripped of my identity. However, my strength comes from both my experiences in Puerto Rico and my students, research, and writing.

Conclusion: First-Generation Scholars
with Alma, Mente y Corazón

From a young age, we each learned the power of language, the ability to name oppression, marginalization, and discrimination. We served as cultural brokers/translators for our families, and we gained an acute awareness of power relations; we learned from our matriarchs that teaching and learning happen collectively, and that education begins at home. We had an innate reason to survive and thrive—for our mothers, grandmothers, and ancestors. The three of us had continuous familial and communal support, and we had femtors/mentors who helped guide us in this unknown territory, academia. While our schooling often deemed us disposable and academia has presumed us incompetent (Darder, 2012; Gutiérrez y Muhs et al., 2012) because of who we are, our unique positionality has enabled each of us to connect with students who share similar backgrounds as us and who also inhabit liminal spaces in higher education. We are able to serve the whole student because we draw from *lo vivido* (the lived experience); from the enacted resilience we witnessed and learned; from being/living in the margins and surviving and thriving.

Our trajectories and experiences have demonstrated to us that we cannot become fractured beings in academia—disconnected from our genealogies of empowerment (The Latina Feminist Group, 2001). We must remain rooted in our *identidades* and draw from our community cultural wealth (Yosso, 2005). Now as first-generation faculty, we can use the epistemologies and pedagogies of the home (Delgado Bernal, 2001) in our teaching and research, and definitely in our service to our communities and students. We often find ourselves working two or three times harder than other colleagues because students of color seek us for advising, want to take our classes, or simply want to see a friendlier and familiar face in the classroom. Our communal *testimonios* of collective survival in academia demonstrate that we put into practice a holistic approach to education—grounded in the teaching and learning that happened in our upbringing.

Our three *testimonios* create a sort of *trenza de identidades* (braided identities) (Delgado Bernal, 2008)—a braid that captures how our research, teaching, and service are also informed by our first-generation navigational strategies and tools (Solórzano & Villalpando, 1998) that we learned at home and in educational spaces. We demonstrate our commitment to social justice and to produce a change in academia as we challenge Eurocentric, meritocratic, competitive ways of being and doing. This is accomplished through our femtoring/mentoring, by introducing qualitative research methodologies that center our ways of knowing to decolonize academia. We try to balance our teaching, research, and service, but inevitably because of who we are and what we embody, we end up picking heavier loads than our White counterparts. We do this because we are

constantly reminded that for those of us who are first-generation Latinx scholars and activists, we carry *compromisos* that not only impact us but also our *famil-
ias* and *comunidades*, all while enacting a praxis de alma, mente y corazón.

REFERENCES

Cruz, C. (2006). Toward an epistemology of a Brown body. In D. Delgado Bernal, C. A. Elenes, F. E. Godinez, & S. Villenas (Eds.), *Chicana/Latina education in everyday life: Feminista perspectives on pedagogy and epistemology* (pp. 59–75). State University of New York Press.

Darder, A. (2012). *Culture and power in the classroom: Educational foundations for the schooling of bicultural students* (2nd ed.). Paradigm Publishers.

Delgado Bernal, D. (2001). Learning and living pedagogies of the home: The mestiza consciousness of Chicana students. *International Journal of Qualitative Studies in Education*, 14(5), 623–639. https://doi.org/10.1080/09518390110059838

Delgado Bernal, D. (2008). La trenza de identidades: Weaving together my personal, professional, and communal identities. In K. P. Gonzalez & R. V. Padilla (Eds.), *Doing the public good: Latina/o scholars engage civic participation* (pp. 134–148). Stylus Publishing.

Delgado Bernal, D., Burciaga, R., & Flores Carmona, J. (2012). Chicana/Latina *testimonios*: Mapping the methodological, pedagogical, and political. *Equity & Excellence in Education*, 45(3), 363–372. doi:10.1080/10665684.2012.698149

Delgado Bernal, D., & Villalpando, O. (2002). An apartheid of knowledge in the academy: The struggle over "legitimate" knowledge for faculty of color. *Equity and Excellence in Education*, 35(2), 169–180. https://doi.org/10.1080/713845282

Freire, P. (2000). *Pedagogy of the oppressed* (M. Bergman Ramos, Trans.). 30th anniversary ed. Continuum.

Garcia, N. M. (2019, January 17). "But you're not a real doctor!" *Diverse Issues in Higher Education.* https://diverseeducation.com/article/136266/

González, J. C. (2007). Surviving the doctorate and thriving as faculty: Latina junior faculty reflecting on their doctoral studies experiences. *Equity & Excellence in Education*, 40(4), 291–300. doi:10.1080/10665680701578613

Gutiérrez y Muhs, G., Flores Niemann, Y., González, C. G., & Harris, A. P. (Eds.). (2012). *Presumed incompetent: The intersections of race and class for women in academia.* Utah State University Press.

The Latina Feminist Group. (2001). *Telling to live: Latina feminist testimonios.* Duke University Press.

Memmi, A. (1957). *The colonizer and the colonized* (H. Greenfeld, Trans.). Beacon Press.

Memmi, A. (2000). *Racism.* University of Minnesota Press.

Montero, M. (2009). Psychology of liberation revised (A critique of critique). In B. Gough (Ed.), *The Palgrave handbook of critical social psychology* (pp. 147–161). Palgrave Macmillan.

Moraga, C. (2002). Theory in the flesh. In C. Moraga & G. E. Anzaldúa (Eds.), *This bridge called my back: Writings by radical women of color* (2nd ed.). Aunt Lute Press.

Mullen, A. L. (Producer), & Marquez, J. A. (Director). (2015). *The last colony: We need to talk about Puerto Rico* [Documentary]. Last Colony Corporation.

Ramos, S. L., & Torres-Fernandez, I. (2020). Conociendo los Caminos: Testimonios of Latina doctoral students. *Peace and Conflict: Journal of Peace Psychology*, 26(4), 379–389. https://doi.org/10.1037/pac0000450

Solórzano, D., & Villalpando, O. (1998). Critical race theory, marginality, and the experience of minority students in higher education. In C. Torres & T. Mitchell (Eds.),

Emerging issues in the sociology of education: Comparative perspectives (pp. 211–224). State University of New York Press.

Tate, K., Torres-Rivera, E., Edwards, & L. M. (2015). Colonialism and multicultural counseling competence research: A liberatory analysis. In R. D. Goodman & P. Gorski (Eds.), *Decolonizing "multicultural" counseling through social justice* (pp. 41–54). Springer.

Watkins, M., & Shulman, H. (Eds.). (2008). *Toward psychologies of liberation.* Palgrave Macmillan.

Yosso, T. (2005). Whose culture has capital? A critical race theory discussion of community cultural wealth. *Race, Ethnicity and Education, 8*(1), 69–91. https://doi.org/10.1080/1361332052000341006

12

Continuing Cultural Mismatches

Reflections from a First-Generation Latina Faculty Navigating the Academy

REBECCA COVARRUBIAS

My youngest brother and I grew up in a loving, but under-resourced, Mexican American community in South Phoenix, Arizona. I spent my time at [a neighborhood park] connecting with mentors who touted higher education. My brother was pushed out of school by those who held negative ideas about young men of color.

His is one of many stories that illustrate the structural inequity in my community. Take my family as an example. My father is a school janitor and landscaper. He works daily to bring home a paycheck that does not reflect his effort nor commitment. My mother, the backbone of the family, stretches the check in every way.

When I return home from college, I often feel overwhelmed with guilt and confusion. . . . I struggle to reconcile my dual reality of neighborhood poverty and university opportunity.

When I wrote those words as a senior undergraduate in my personal statement for graduate school, I had no idea that I was describing what researchers call a cultural mismatch. In my case, this was a mismatch between the middle-class white norms of university life and the working-class Latino/a/x life of my family and community (Covarrubias, 2021; Stephens et al., 2012; Vasquez-Salgado et al., 2015). The U.S. academy was not designed for students like me—it did not reflect what I looked like, the practices and norms I was used to, the language or ways of speaking I used at home, or how what I was learning applied to my community.

There is a growing evidence base of cultural experiences like mine, highlighting how a mismatch undermines the belonging, motivation, and performance of low-income, Latino/a/x first-generation college students. But what of Latino/a/x college graduates awarded advanced degrees who join college faculties? This is a group who has successfully transcended two critical university transitions to become faculty: both the undergraduate and graduate experience. Do first-generation faculty of color experience a cultural mismatch in their university employment in consequential ways and, if so, how do they navigate this mismatch? To answer these questions, I situate my own experiences as a first-generation Latina faculty from a low-income background within this framework.

First, I introduce cultural mismatch theory to detail the experiences of first-generation students of color as they navigate college. Second, I apply the theory to the experiences of first-generation faculty of color. Given the scare work in this area, I draw on extensive literature on the experiences of faculty of color (Baez, 2000; Fryberg & Martínez, 2014; Padilla, 1994; Pérez-Huber, 2009; Settles et al., 2020; Turner et al., 2008), of Women of Color faculty (Hirshfield & Joseph, 2012; Turner et al., 2011), and of working-class faculty (Ardoin, 2019; Arner, 2016; Case, 2017; Lee, 2017) to examine potential mismatches. I interweave my own experiences to unpack how my multiple intersecting, minoritized identities inform scholarship in this area. Finally, I discuss how I reframe mismatches as sites of social change in university settings and offer specific recommendations for institutions to alleviate ongoing mismatches.

Experiencing the Middle-Class White University as a Low-Income Latina First-Generation College Student

Rooted in whiteness and white supremacy, U.S. postsecondary institutions were established to generate opportunities for middle-class white students and have long reflected their cultural values (Davidson, 2017; Lareau, 2015; Ledesma & Calderón, 2015; Patton, 2016). Among these values are soft independence. The majority of top-level university administrators nationwide (72 percent) surveyed reported that soft independence—being individually motivated, engaging in creative self-expression, working independently, and questioning rules—is the most important skill for students to develop while in college (Stephens et al., 2012). For middle-class white continuing-generation students (i.e., those with at least one college-educated parent), these norms reflect a continuation of the daily practices experienced in natal contexts, such as schooling, neighborhoods, and home life (Lareau, 2003). Indeed, there is a tendency in middle-class white neighborhoods to socialize children to express their unique preferences and talents and to ask questions with curiosity (Kusserow, 2012). Yet, in working-class communities, children might navigate hard and unpredictable environments, limiting access to the same privileges and luxuries of their middle-class counterparts (Kusserow, 2012). The environmental, financial, and safety constraints of

the low-income setting require families to work together for support and survival, thus fostering a sense of resourcefulness and collaboration.

According to cultural mismatch theory, university norms of independence
foster performance and well-being for middle-class white students and weaken
outcomes for low-income first-generation students of color (Covarrubias, 2021;
Jehangir, 2010; Phillips et al., 2020; Stephens et al., 2012). The privileging of independence ignores the communal commitments of these students—commitments
that include taking care of family members who might be struggling financially,
emotionally, or in other ways propelled by poverty (e.g., food and housing insecurity) (Covarrubias et al., 2019) or earning a degree to improve one's community
and life circumstances (Jackson et al., 2016). In not recognizing these commitments, the university renders invisible the extensive assets, including collaboration, resourcefulness, and tenacity, that first-generation students of color
bring (Rios-Aguilar et al., 2011; Yosso, 2005).

The university also ignores the immense stress associated with balancing
the important need at home with university privilege and demand. To overlook
our assets and our emotional health means to jeopardize our retention in the
university and our eventual contributions to building a diverse workforce.
My students and I have felt what we call "family achievement guilt"—a socioemotional tension related to "leaving family obligations" to focus on individual
scholarship and activities in college (Covarrubias et al., 2021; Covarrubias & Fryberg, 2015). Even though my college was only two hours from home, the worlds
felt vastly different. I lived in an expensive dorm room; the idea of having a personal, quiet space was a noticeable difference for me. I concurrently felt guilt
when I recognized that school expenses and activities took away from contributions I could make at home. For many students, buying new bedding afforded
an exciting opportunity to express uniqueness in the dorm space; for me, it was
a reminder of the expense of college and of the money I was not sending home.
It took me a year to save my financial aid to buy a laptop because I was simultaneously sending money to family. There was also the guilt of feeling like my
worldview was changing, making me different from loved ones at home.

This guilt worsened when I became a graduate student, where school and
home felt farther apart. The stakes were higher in that you were evaluated by
even more extreme measures of soft independence; you were assessed on your
abilities to express your thoughts and ask critical questions, to defend the novel
contributions of your ideas, and to develop into an independent scholar. The
expectation was to dedicate significant time to your individual work. As the only
Latina student in my graduate program, I carried the weight of the responsibility in meeting these expectations to set a pathway for my community and for
students like me. Yet, what was not evident to others was that these expectations had to be balanced with persisting home responsibilities. My guilt was
most apparent during graduate seminars; as we sat in a classroom discussing

theory, I remembered that people back home continued to struggle in real ways. That is, I was dedicating time to studying what felt like a "passion" rather than to pursuing full-time work to help support family.

I completed, and even excelled, in program requirements with these larger concerns in mind. As cultural mismatch theory suggests, these conflicts impacted my productivity, well-being, and belonging. I continually questioned whether the sacrifices—being away from family, slowly becoming different from family, not providing essential support to loved ones, doubting myself and my ability, wondering if I would ever make the change I wanted to see in society, feeling isolated—were worth this elite degree. It was the assets of my working-class home—resourcefulness, resilience, good humor, and collaborating with trusted mentors—that helped me survive the mismatch in both the undergraduate and graduate contexts. My orientation toward and grounding in community anchored me. It sustained me.

Experiencing the Middle-Class White University as a First-Generation Latina Faculty

The middle-class white cultural norms of the university permeate all academic processes and expectations, which impact me as a first-generation Latina faculty. For example, the metrics used in the tenure process, which have been normed by and for middle-class white faculty, also preference individualism. These metrics do not reflect the wealth of knowledge and traditions of working-class first-generation People of Color (Pérez-Huber, 2009; Settles et al., 2020). Many faculty of color, especially those from first-generation backgrounds, commit themselves to careers and disciplines where they serve the betterment and fight against the marginalization of their communities (Fryberg & Martinez, 2014). For example, faculty of color spend more time engaged in community service, teaching, advising tasks, and diversity-related initiatives compared with white faculty (Antonio et al., 2000; Casado Pérez et al., 2021; Duncan, 2014; Hirshfield & Joseph, 2012).

Yet, tenure reward systems are predicated on several markers of individual achievement that run contrary to our communal approaches (Fryberg, 2010). Faculty are rewarded for scholarship, such as sole- or first-authored work, that easily indicates contributions of individual merit (Delgado Bernal & Villalpando, 2002; Fryberg & Martinez, 2014). Tenure decisions weigh independent scholarship more heavily than teaching, service, and diversity work (Baez, 2000; Tippeconnic Fox, 2008), and service commitments are seen as the least important criterion (Baez, 2000). The individual culture of academia makes it so faculty of color describe engaging in service activities as detracting from producing scholarship (Baez, 2000). Common advice for early-career faculty is to not engage in "too much service" or to limit the time spent with students in teaching or mentoring contexts—the exact communal commitments that anchor and sustain us.

This advice disregards the value placed on serving our communities in comprehensive ways. As a first-generation Latina faculty, I consciously participate in service, mentoring, consulting, and advocacy-related activities designed to serve minoritized students and to improve the climate of the university. *Transformative resistance* is a conscious process where minoritized people engage with institutional norms while also deliberately critiquing how these institutional systems are oppressive (Solórzano & Delgado Bernal, 2001). For example, because minoritized students have limited models of success within the university, as Latina faculty I am flooded with student requests for meetings and conversations. My exchanges with students are often emotional as we both engage in sharing our journeys and challenges navigating institutions that feel foreign and hostile. These are vital conversations; they give students strategies and support for confronting their challenges and signal that someone understands them. My time with students is the best part of my day, and the main reason I became faculty, yet how does one translate this work for tenure review? As Bryan McKinley Jones Brayboy (2003) noted: "One has to wonder where on a curriculum vitae faculty of color are supposed to place 'being a role model'" (p. 81). The mismatch is in the underlying assumption that independent scholarship is more valuable than time spent shaping the academic, professional, and personal trajectories of students.

These communal commitments also extend to family support (Collay, 2002). As in college and in graduate school, I continue to support my family and witness the ways in which poverty steals opportunities for financial well-being and health. As faculty, I am better able to support my family financially, but I still feel concerned about our precarity and health as we continue to confront the real effects of poverty. The life of a faculty member is inherently privileged; daily I engage in creative thinking, pursue what interests me, and demonstrate control over my schedule. These are luxuries not afforded in working-class contexts. Yet having to switch between the demands of the job and the commitments to our communities and families is taxing, an experience not accounted for in fast-paced, independent-oriented tenure metrics.

Transforming Cultural Mismatches
into Sites of Social Change

Cultural mismatch allows us to explain the disparate impact of mainstream academic cultural values and norms on first-generation faculty of color and to consider how faculty transform mismatches into sites of social change. The communal and social justice commitments of first-generation faculty of color across research, teaching, and service sustain us in the university and change the climate for us and for similar others. We leverage our diverse home knowledge, lived experience, and cultural strengths—known "pedagogies of the home"—to function in and transform mainstream spaces (Delgado Bernal, 2001; Delgado Bernal & Villalpando, 2002; on cultural intuition, see Delgado Bernal, 1998).

As a first-generation Latina faculty, I leverage my pedagogies of the home to bridge cultural mismatches for students through research, teaching, and service. In my first years as new faculty, I was overwhelmed by the interest and commitment from students like me to engage in the classroom and in research. My institution, the University of California Santa Cruz (UCSC) is a public Hispanic Serving Institution where 31 percent of our students are of Latino/a/x backgrounds and 42 percent are first generation. My research group is the Collaborative Research for Equity in Action, what we call the "Collab," which includes a group of ten to thirteen undergraduate and three to five graduate first-generation, low-income, and/or students of color. The word "Collab" symbolizes for us the combination of community and research. The lab has transformed into a "counterspace" in which we challenge deficit narratives of our minoritized identities and affirm these identities (Case & Hunter, 2012). Our team engages in social justice research aimed at legitimizing the voices of minoritized students and developing strategies for reshaping institutions. The Women of Color doctoral graduate students provide holistic support as they lead and mentor students through the research process. We ground our research questions in our lived experiences and, as such, our research becomes a tool for transformation in the ideas produced and in the lives of the student researchers. Our work empowers students to see themselves in the research process, as research scientists and as social change makers.

Our research on educational equity informs my pedagogy and the content of my teaching. Like many faculty of color in the social sciences and humanities, my courses invite students to examine the structural inequities that perpetuate the marginalization of first-generation, low-income and/or People of Color. When teaching research methods in psychology, for example, the conversations necessarily involve how research is used as a tool for social justice. Students engage in activities and questions that reveal structural inequity and how critical scholarship can address these systemic barriers. Moreover, the elements of the course consider different ways of knowing, including inviting student to apply their own expertise. There are active conversations about the experience of being first generation, including feelings of imposter syndrome, of pressure to succeed, of guilt for leaving family, and of resiliency, to name a few. There are personal one-on-one conversations that consider the whole student, including their experiences with family and community. Through personalized encounters, students recognize my home pedagogy.

Finally, first-generation faculty of color also engage in service work that is a tool for social change (Urrieta & Méndez Benavídez, 2007). These service commitments are intentional acts of transformative resistance designed to reshape the university culture in ways that reduce mismatches and, instead, reflect the strengths of an increasingly diverse student body. I offer only one example of such service work, although like many other women faculty of color, my list of service work is extensive. I was faculty cofounder and codirector of the UCSC First Generation Initiative, which is designed to support the first-generation community on campus. The Initiative is a grassroots effort pioneered by other first-generation faculty of color at UC Irvine. Our first step was to highlight stories of first-generation graduates to create pathways of success and points of contact for first-generation students and to foster belonging. With first-generation student leaders and staff, we hosted a dinner conversation with over 200 first-generation students about the challenges and strengths of being first generation at UCSC. Finally, with a committed team of staff and faculty, I co-organized the 2018 First-Generation Students at UC Conference, which engaged over 250 staff, administrators, and faculty for two days about how to support first-generation students.

These are just a few examples of how minoritized leaders leverage their power to offer distinctive classroom and research experiences to diverse students and to change the climate of the university. The work is especially critical given the slow response of universities to change. Instead, we are left to create our own counterspaces as we navigate a system that treats us as "guests in someone else's home" (Case, 2017; Turner, 1994). The responsibility is on us to claim a space of belonging for ourselves and for our students all while fulfilling the same requirements as our white middle-class colleagues. For some, this resistance is a conscious effort reflecting years of skillfully navigating hostile, unwelcoming, and discriminatory schooling systems; for others, resistance is not always a conscious, deliberate act, but an everyday yearning to be seen and heard and to undermine power (Casado Pérez et al., 2021; Rosales & Langhout, 2020). The work to claim space while navigating the rules of the game is heavy and exerts a large physical and emotional toll (Hirshfield & Joseph, 2012; Padilla, 1994). Without more deliberate support, institutions will continue to promote normative experiences while undermining the efforts, well-being, and retention of their first-generation constituencies. These constituents are critical leaders, necessary for building a climate that sustains and supports students, and prepares them to thrive in a diverse world.

Recommendations for Institutional Support
for First-Generation Faculty of Color

Although there are various ways that first-generation faculty of color can experience a cultural mismatch, I reflect on the disconnect between the communal values fostered by my background and the middle-class white individualism in the academy. In this section, I offer recommendations for universities to practice in order to eliminate points of disconnect for first-generation faculty of color and to ensure they are valued and supported holistically.

First, universities must recognize mentoring and service as critical contributions. One reason I accepted a position in social psychology at UCSC was because of the commitment to social justice. Although there are high research expectations, the understanding that excellent teaching and service take considerable time facilitates thoughtful discussions around research productivity. Our area encourages faculty to publish in journal outlets in which the audience is most important for the work. There is also an understanding of how much time different methodological approaches take (i.e., community-engaged research with minoritized populations can be more involved than laboratory studies) and the likelihood of the research being funded (i.e., national funding agencies fund quantitative work more frequently than qualitative work). The area acknowledges how these features of the research process impact productivity. This is one step toward acknowledging the assets of diverse faculty. Yet, university-wide policies should detail how to fairly evaluate and acknowledge extensive communal activities of faculty, activities that contribute to the success of universities.

Institutions should also reward the collaborative process of research (Fryberg, 2010). The image of the scientist working alone in the lab is a persisting one (Cheryan et al., 2013). Yet, it undervalues the richness that collaboration and diverse perspectives offer in scientific inquiry. In fact, as I wrote this sole-authored paper, I experienced discomfort and frustration, including the pressure to express my opinions confidently and the difficulty in balancing personal narrative with academic writing. To strengthen this work, it was necessary to engage in several discussions and revisions with the editors of this book, trusted colleagues, and students to think about the framing of this work. As with all of my work, this chapter is a community effort. Evaluation metrics need to develop processes for assessing collaboration as an important part of scholarship.

To holistically support first-generation faculty of color, institutions must also consider their extensive commitments. As one example, housing and living concerns, particularly in expensive-to-live cities, are a reality for many faculty. This is especially the case for first-generation faculty of color who might be supporting families back home and/or minoritized graduate and undergraduate students in research work. Salary inequities not only devalue the contributions of minoritized faculty, but they also force early-career faculty to leave institutions early (Renzulli et al., 2006). These inequities can also exist in research funds meant to support student researchers, conference travel, and research space. When considering the potential financial, emotional, and physical commitments of first-generation faculty of color in supporting others, one critical area of institutional support is to offer funding and pay opportunities that promote equity and sustainable living.

Finally, institutions must move from privileging middle-class white ways of being in the academy to recognizing other ways of knowing. This is particularly important given the changing demographic of our classrooms. To value other ways of knowing, institutions must aggressively hire diverse faculty. Representation matters; the more I can see people like me reflected in faculty positions and the more I can interact with people who understand my journey, the more connected I feel in this space. The same is true for our students. Institutions must also acknowledge the effort it takes to develop the assets we offer the university. I have years of experience surviving a hostile, foreign university environment, including proving my expertise in the classroom and in research and balancing intensive support for my community. I am well equipped to support our diverse students in holistic ways because I have had to learn these skills (Yosso, 2005). Institutions need to value the skills we have acquired by reshaping mainstream metrics (e.g., teaching evaluations and number of publications) so that they are inclusive of our assets and so that they reduce inherent biases that exist within them.

Careful consideration of the cultural mismatches for minoritized people across all university positions—undergraduate and graduate students, postdoctoral scholars, faculty, staff, and administrators—is critical for their well-being, retention, and productivity and for the success of the university. As diverse leaders, our home pedagogies not only mirror the needs, strengths, and commitments of our changing student demographic, but they also prepare all students better for a multicultural workforce and society. Although the mismatch is distinctive in each situation, it is a constant, ongoing experience for us all. For me, these mismatches emerged in high school—the first predominantly white space I navigated—and have manifested in similar and different ways throughout my academic journey. I am one of the few first-generation Women of Color to survive these mismatches because I was fortunate enough to have the love and care of my family, friends, mentors, and students. Yet, we sacrifice endlessly to create a place of belonging in a setting that scarcely acknowledges us. Why do we fight these cultural mismatches? Because we enter the academy with a deep, unwavering commitment to eliminating inequities for our communities at home, on campus, and in society. Universities must honor these commitments and our home pedagogies in intentional, transformative ways if they intend to equitably serve and reflect all members of the academy.

REFERENCES

Antonio, A. L., Astin, H. S., & Cress, C. M. (2000). Community service in higher education: A look at the nation's faculty. *Review of Higher Education, 23*(4), 373–397. doi:10.1353/rhe.2000.0015

Ardoin, S. (2019). *Straddling class in the academy: 26 stories of students, administrators, and faculty from poor and working-class backgrounds and their compelling lessons for higher education policy and practice.* Stylus Publishing.

Arner, L. (2016). Survival strategies for working-class women as junior faculty. In A. L. Hurst & S. K. Nenga (Eds.), *Working in class: Recognizing how social class shapes our academic work* (pp. 49–64). Rowman and Littlefield.

Baez, B. (2000). Race-related service and faculty of color: Conceptualizing critical agency in academe. *Higher Education, 39,* 363–391. https://doi.org/10.1023/A:1003972214943

Brayboy, B.M.J. (2003). The implementation of diversity in predominantly white colleges and universities. *Journal of Black Studies, 34*(1), 72–86. http://www.jstor.org/stable/3180858

Casado Pérez, J. F., Roundtree, S. M., & Pérez, D. C. (2021). Motivation and meaning in everyday resistance by minoritized faculty. *Journal of Diversity in Higher Education.* Advance online publication. http://dx.doi.org/10.1037/dhe0000269

Case, A. D., & Hunter, C. D. (2012). Counterspaces: A unit of analysis for understanding the role of settings in marginalized individuals' adaptive responses to oppression. *American Journal of Community Psychology, 50*(1–2), 257–270. doi:10.1007/s10464-012-9497-7

Case, K. A. (2017). Insider without: Journey across the working-class academic arc. *Journal of Working-Class Studies, 2*(2), 16–35.

Cheryan, S., Plaut, V. C., Handron, C., & Hudson, L. (2013). The stereotypical computer scientist: Gendered media representations as a barrier to inclusion for women. *Sex Roles, 69,* 58–71. https://doi.org/10.1007/s11199-013-0296-x

Collay, M. (2002). Balancing work and family. In J. E. Cooper & D. D. Stevens (Eds.), *Tenure in the sacred grove: Issues and strategies for women and minority faculty* (89–106). State University of New York Press.

Covarrubias, R. (2021). What we bring with us: Investing in Latinx students means investing in families. *Policy Insights from the Behavioral and Brain Sciences, 8*(1), 3–10. https://doi.org/10.1177/2372732220983855

Covarrubias, R., De Lima, F., Landa, I., Valle, I., & Hernandez-Flores, W. (2021). Facets of family achievement guilt for low-income, Latinx and Asian first-generation students. *Cultural Diversity and Ethnic Minority Psychology, 27*(4), 696–704. https://doi.org/10.1037/cdp0000418

Covarrubias, R., & Fryberg, S. A. (2015). Movin' on up (to college): First-generation college students' experiences with family achievement guilt. *Cultural Diversity and Ethnic Minority Psychology, 21*(3), 420–429. doi:10.1037/a0037844

Covarrubias, R., Valle, I., Laiduc, G., & Azmitia, M. (2019). "You never become fully independent": Family roles and independence in first-generation college students. *Journal of Adolescent Research, 34*(4), 381–410. https://doi.org/10.1177/0743558418788402

Davidson, C. N. (2017). *The new education: How to revolutionize the university to prepare students for a world in flux.* Basic Books.

Delgado Bernal, D. (1998). Using a Chicana feminist epistemology in educational research. *Harvard Educational Review, 68*(4), 555–582. https://doi.org/10.17763/haer.68.4.5wv1034973g22q48

Delgado Bernal, D. (2001). Learning and living pedagogies of the home: The mestiza consciousness of Chicana students. *International Journal of Qualitative Studies in Education, 14*(5), 623–639. https://doi.org/10.1080/09518390110059838

Delgado Bernal, D., & Villalpando, O. (2002). An apartheid of knowledge in academia: the struggle over the "legitimate" knowledge of faculty of color. *Equity & Excellence in Education, 35*(2), 169–180. https://doi.org/10.1080/713845282

Duncan, P. (2014). Hot commodities, cheap labor: Women of color in the academy. *Frontiers: A Journal of Women Studies, 35*(3), 39–63. doi:10.5250/fronjwomenstud.35.3.0039

Fryberg, S. A. (2010). Constructing junior faculty of color as strugglers: The implications for tenure and promotion. In D. Little & S. P. Mohanty (Eds.), *The future of diversity: The future of minority studies* (pp. 181–218). Palgrave Macmillan.

Fryberg S. A., & Martínez, E. J. (2014). Constructed strugglers: The impact of diversity narratives on junior faculty of color. In S. A. Fryberg & E. J. Martínez (Eds.), *The truly diverse faculty: The future of minority studies* (pp. 3–25). Palgrave Macmillan.

Hirshfield, L. E., & Joseph, T. D. (2012). "We need a woman, we need a Black woman": Gender, race, and identity taxation in the academy. *Gender and Education, 24*(2), 213–227. https://doi.org/10.1080/09540253.2011.606208

Jackson, M. C., Galvez, G., Landa, I., Buonora, P., & Thoman, D. B. (2016). Science that matters: The importance of a cultural connection in underrepresented students' science pursuit. *CBE—Life Sciences Education, 15*(3), Article 42. https://doi.org/10.1187/cbe.16-01-0067

Jehangir, R. (2010). Stories as knowledge: Bringing the lived experience of first-generation college students into the academy. *Urban Education, 45*(4), 533–553. https://doi.org/10.1177/0042085910372352

Kusserow, A. (2012). *In facing social class: How societal rank influences interaction.* Russell Sage Foundation.

Lareau, A. (2003). *Unequal childhoods: Race, class and family life.* University of California Press.

Lareau, A. (2015). Cultural knowledge and social inequality. *American Sociological Review, 80*(1), 1–27. https://doi.org/10.1177/0003122414565814

Ledesma, M. C., & Calderón, D. (2015). Critical race theory in education: A review of past literature and a look to the future. *Qualitative Inquiry, 21*(3), 206-222. https://doi.org/10.1177/1077800414557825

Lee, E. (2017). Where people like me don't belong: Faculty members from low-socioeconomic-status backgrounds. *Sociology of Education, 90*(3), 197–212. https://doi.org/10.1177/0038040717710495

Padilla, A. M. (1994). Ethnic minority scholars, research, and mentoring: Current and future issues. *Educational Researcher, 23*(4), 24–27. doi:10.2307/1176259

Patton, L. D. (2016). Disrupting postsecondary prose: Toward a critical race theory of higher education. *Urban Education, 51*(3), 315–342. https://doi.org/10.1177/0042085915602542

Pérez-Huber, L. (2009). Disrupting apartheid of knowledge: *Testimonio* as methodology in Latina/o critical race research in education. *International Journal of Qualitative Studies in Education, 22*(6), 639–654. https://doi.org/10.1080/09518390903333863

Phillips, L. T., Stephens, N. M., Townsend, S. S., & Goudeau, S. (2020). Access is not enough: Cultural mismatch persists to limit first-generation students' opportunities for achievement throughout college. *Journal of Personality and Social Psychology, 119*(5), 1121–1131. https://doi.org/10.1037/pspi0000234

Renzulli, L. A., Grant, L., & Kathuria, S. (2006). Race, gender, and the wage gap: Comparing faculty salaries in predominately white and historically Black colleges and universities. *Gender & Society, 20*(4), 491–510. https://doi.org/10.1177/0891243206287130

Rios-Aguilar, C., Kiyama, J. M., Gravitt, M., & Moll, L. C. (2011). Funds of knowledge for the poor and forms of capital for the rich? A capital approach to examining funds of knowledge. *Theory and Research in Education, 9*(2), 163–184. https://doi.org/10.1177/1477878511409776

Rosales, C., & Langhout, R. D. (2020). Just because we don't see it, doesn't mean it's not there: Everyday resistance in psychology. *Social and Personality Psychology Compass, 14*(1), e12508. https://doi.org/10.1111/spc3.12508

Settles, I. H., Jones, M. K., Buchanan, N. T., & Dotson, K. (2020). Epistemic exclusion: scholar(ly) devaluation that marginalizes faculty of color. *Journal of Diversity in Higher Education*. http://dx.doi.org/10.1037/dhe0000174

Solórzano, D. G., & Delgado-Bernal, D. (2001). Examining transformational resistance through a critical race and LatCrit theory framework: Chicana and Chicano students in an urban context. *Urban Education, 36*(3), 308–342. https://doi.org/10.1177/00420 85901363002

Stephens, N. M., Fryberg, S. A., Markus, H. R., Johnson, C. S., & Covarrubias, R. (2012). Unseen disadvantage: How American universities' focus on independence undermines the academic performance of first-generation college students. *Journal of Personality and Social Psychology, 102*(6), 1178–1197. https://doi.org/10.1037/a0027143

Tippeconnic Fox, M. J. (2008). American Indian women in academia: The joys and challenges. *NASPA Journal about Women in Higher Education, 1*(1), 204–223. doi:10.2202 /1940-7890.1011

Turner, C.S.V. (1994). Guests in someone else's house: Students of color. *Review of Higher Education, 17*(4), 355–370. doi:10.1353/rhe.1994.0008

Turner, C.S.V., González, J. C., & Wong (Lau), K. (2011). Faculty women of color: The critical nexus of race and gender. *Journal of Diversity in Higher Education, 4*(4), 199–211. https:// doi.org/10.1037/a0024630

Turner, C.S.V., González, J. C., & Wood, J. L. (2008). Faculty of color in academe: What 20 years of literature tells us. *Journal of Diversity in Higher Education, 1*(3), 139–168. https://doi .org/10.1037/a0012837

Urrieta, L., Jr., & Méndez Benavídez, L. R. (2007). Community commitment and activist scholarship: Chicana/o professors and the practice of consciousness. *Journal of Hispanic Higher Education, 6*(3), 222–236. https://doi.org/10.1177/1538192707302535

Vasquez-Salgado, Y., Greenfield, P. M., & Burgos-Cienfuegos, R. (2015). Exploring home school value conflicts: Implications for academic achievement and well-being among Latino first-generation college students. *Journal of Adolescent Research, 30*(3), 271–305. https:// doi.org/10.1177/0743558414561297

Yosso, T. J. (2005). Whose culture has capital? A critical race theory discussion of community cultural wealth. *Race Ethnicity and Education, 8*(1), 69–91. https://doi.org/10.1080 /1361332052000341006

13

Fugitivity within the University as First-Generation Black-Pinay, Indigenous, and Chicanx Faculty

Cultivating an Undercommons

NINI HAYES, DOLORES CALDERÓN, AND VERÓNICA NELLY VÉLEZ

As first-generation faculty who identify as Black-Pinay, Indigenous, and Chicanx, we have intimate knowledge of what Harney and Moten (2013) theorize as the *undercommons*—those fugitive spaces outside sanctioned university spaces where we come together to radically engage in collective study, support, and research. We recognize that we are "first" not because of our exceptionality, but because of our respective communities' positions to power and not being allowed "in." We reflect the generations of those denied entry into these institutions. However, our argument is not about being allowed entrance; instead we assert that as first-generation Black, Indigenous, People of Color (BIPOC) faculty in the academy, our fight is against the very nature of the university and for liberatory research approaches that counter the problematic narratives inherent in white racial knowledge. We use notions of fugitivity and enclosure to elaborate a position that allows imagining a future beyond capitalist institutionalization and corporatization of knowledge. Through our own individual narratives, we say that resistance is not futile! We document our unique relationship to the academy and how this informs the methods and aims of our research.

As we write this, we are in the midst of local, national, and international uprisings spurred by the police murders of George Floyd and Breonna Taylor, two of many state-sanctioned murders of BIPOC in this country, while in the thick of a global pandemic. Floyd and Taylor's murders have amplified the movement against police violence and racial injustice that has been ongoing since the inception of this country. Weeks of sustained protests have prompted us to support in various ways and reflect on our roles in the social change ecosystem as educators and researchers in the pursuit of justice. Calhoun (2008) asserts: "Commitment to social action in pursuit of social change is one of the sources for a commitment to social science" (xxi). Thus, as educational scholars, we heed the call now more than ever, the importance of activist scholarship and that our research is a political act in which knowledge creation and dissemination are deemed necessary for human liberation (Young et al., 2010). In conclusion, our experiences with the majoritarian approach to research have been significant in the trajectory of our own research; such that we center critical social science approaches that aim to abolish the institutional forces of white supremacy and anti-Blackness, which the damned of the earth are revolting against (Fanon, 1963).

The Enclosure

> Our task is the self-defense of the surround in the face of repeated, targeted dispossessions through the settler's armed incursion. And while acquisitive violence occasions this self-defense, it is recourse to self-possession in the face of dispossession (recourse, in other words, to politics) that represents the real danger. Politics is an ongoing attack on the common—the general and generative antagonism—from within the surround. (Harney & Moten, 2013, p. 17)

Harney and Moten's (2013) understanding of fugitivity guides our work here. As first-generation BIPOC faculty, we have had to create spaces, find the fissures, the interstices, the spaces in the basement and seats at the dining table to come together, a feat that we are intimate with since our time as undergraduates. The spaces we create are both within and without the university. Guided by theorizations of the university as an enclosure (Grande, 2018; Harney & Moten, 2013; Kamola & Meyeroff, 2009; Kelley, 2016; la paperson, 2017), we examine what it means to come into the university as outlaws from the surround and to then document the work we do once inside—undertaking fugitive planning all the while—in which we center relationships with community, land, and water rather than with the university. Here, we depart from the argument of Kamola and Meyeroff (2009) that we can reclaim the commons within the university, instead agreeing with Harney and Moten's (2013) claim that the commons has always been exclusionary and that the university is invested in maintaining this exclusion through what la paperson (2017) names "its desire to settle, to self-sustain, to seduce, and to school" (xxii).

   The university acts as the enclosure similar to the military forts that accompany colonial expansion. Harney and Moten (2013) offer a provocative image, pointing out that the representation of colonial settlement in films "like *Drums along the Mohawk* (1939) or *Shaka Zulu* (1987)" always portray "the settler . . . as surrounded by 'natives,' inverting . . . the role of aggressor so that colonialism is made to look like self-defense" (p. 17). The settlers within the forts are not portrayed as the invaders; rather, what exists outside the fort—*the surround*—is constructed as the problem. Universities do the same. This is why we often encounter researchers framing BIPOC communities as the problem, especially in the field of education.

Critiques of academic disciplines offer similar views. In anthropology, Audra Simpson (2007) points out in agreement with Linda Tuhiwai Smith's (2012) seminal text *Decolonizing Methodologies*—research traditionally emanates from within structural mechanisms of empire with the goal of knowing and ordering the spaces empire absorbs. The university and its disciplines act to name, order, catalog, and offer solutions for the surround (Grande, 2018; Willinsky, 1998). Following Harney and Moten (2013), the university as the fort is symbolic of settler society's ideological and spatial organization. Those people and places that exist outside the fort and the enclosure unsettle what is inside. Thus, we ask, "What happens when people are invited/coerced/tricked into the university from the surround through liberal multicultural policies of inclusion and diversity?"

If we understand the university as an enclosure as many before us have (Piper et al., 2019; Richardson, 2011; Simpson, 2007; Smith, 2012; Willinsky, 1998), then we also know that as first-generation BIPOC scholars, we smuggle in knowledge from the surround that potentially allows us to refuse certain terms (Calderón, 2016; la paperson, 2017; Patel, 2015; Simpson, 2007, 2014; Tuck & Yang, 2012). Our unfamiliarity with the pitfalls of enclosure as first-generation scholars provides opportunities for subversive navigation, since we rely primarily on the outlaw wisdom to maneuver. We have also been intrigued about these questions in our research, as an extension of our every day. For example, we have engaged in an intimate dialogue about how our bodies mediate the enclosure of the university (Fanon, 1963; Ferreira da Silva, 2007; Matias, 2016); curricular work or what Patel (2016) describes as learning as marronage; and the informal of everyday talk (Collins, 2009; Combahee River Collective, 1986; Lorde, 1984; Martínez, 1998; Moraga & Anzaldúa, 1983).

Indeed, as the collective work of the Black radical tradition (Combahee River Collective, 1986; Kelley, 2016; Robinson, 2000), critical Indigenous thought, and certain iterations of Latinx studies demonstrate (Blackwell et al., 2017), settler colonialism has never created spaces for Black and Indigenous presence, much less imagined it. For these reasons, coupled with our own experiences, we seek to engage the notion of the undercommons as a site of both resistance and sustenance for first-generation BIPOC faculty, acknowledging that the work is not easy, nor does it require us to stay in a place that does not want us. Thus, we hope to offer an initial exploration of what it means to commit and maintain an undercommons that is more than refusal, but also possible by our first-generation status that we reframe as *outlaw*.

Toward Fugitivity

Borrowing from Tuck and colleagues (2014), we understand ourselves as collaborators, not only in the place we work, but as friends, as comrades, and as scholars who locate our work in various traditions. Much like research that demonstrates that spaces for BIPOC students are vital for retention (Graham et al., 1998; Hurtado et al., 1999; Nieto, 2010; Tatum, 2017; Youngbull & Mintorn, 2018), first-generation BIPOC faculty also require such spaces (Diggs et al., 2009; Henry & Glenn, 2009; Muñoz et al., 2017). While research shows cluster hires of BIPOC faculty are key to retention (Severin, 2013; Smith et al., 2004; Turner et al., 2008), that mentoring for BIPOC faculty is important for success (Stanley, 2006a, 2006b; Turner et al., 2008), and that incorporating the unique knowledge that BIPOC faculty bring into the academy is important for faculty health (Delgado Bernal & Villalpando, 2002; Salazar et al., 2017; Turner & Myers, 2000; Umbach, 2006), we believe that as first-generation BIPOC faculty we are also uniquely suited to say that *even this is not enough*. We argue that we must rely on what has made us first-generation—our position as outlaws—to resist the disciplining and co-opting mechanisms of the university.

Although our work must unsettle (Rosa & Bonilla, 2017; Rosas, 2018; Tuck & Yang, 2012), this does not come without a cost. Teetering on the tightrope requires certain labor we never imagined we had to expend, yet we do so in an effort to "wreck, scavenge, retool, and reassemble the colonizing university into decolonizing contraptions" (la paperson, 2017, xiii).

Our Relationship to Institutional Enclosure

We share our stories, to be both in solidarity about our collective experiences as first-generation BIPOC faculty and also to illuminate the ways in which being outlaws has shaped our experiences in and out of institutional enclosures and our approaches to collective study. Through our stories, we are reminded precisely that there is knowing and wisdom in embodied experiences.

Nini

As a Black-Pinay womxn in graduate school, I endured "spirit-murdering," a phrase coined by Patricia Williams (1987) describing "racism as a crime, an offense so deeply painful and assaultive" (p. 129). It was the constant skepticism of whether I belonged and deserved to be there, problematizing my need and use of resources automatically afforded to others, gaslighting, navigating Eurocentric curriculum, knowledge production, ways of being, expectations, and the mental and emotional burnout of addressing my second-class status in the academy. I survived by smuggling in generational wisdom, consistent practices of well-being, righteous anger, perseverance, and an unwillingness to hold my tongue. Audre Lorde's (1995) wise words from her poem, "A Litany for Survival," resonated with my experience:

> So it is better to speak
> remembering
> we were never meant to survive (p. 32)

My graduate school years were marked by a duality and double consciousness that I was simultaneously at the university and fleeing the university and even now, as a tenure-track assistant professor, that has not changed. As Harney and Moten (2013) state, "it cannot be denied that the university is a place of refuge, and it cannot be accepted that the university is a place of enlightenment" (p. 26). Without romanticizing higher education, tenure-track work has some appeal; professional status, pursuing intellectual endeavors of your own interest, financial stability, teaching, autonomy, femtoring students, and collaborative work with like-minded colleagues, to list a few. I think for many first-generation minoritized faculty, being able to have access to some of the aforementioned benefits is compelling enough to pursue admittance into a notoriously exclusionary and discriminatory enterprise. And for most, we were/are lied to. The university espouses to welcome underrepresented faculty in their performative rhetoric but then undermines our very presence and work in practice.

In my current position, the duality and double consciousness of being first-generation minoritized faculty is to witness a dignity and reciprocity of work that is rewarding for able-bodied cisheterosexual white middle- and upper-class men. Meanwhile, I am simultaneously navigating a toxic academic-industrial complex, trying to bring and hold onto my own knowledge and culture, and build a more inclusive space. Currently I am the only Black-Pinay faculty in my college, and my scholarship is focused on identifying processes through which structural and systemic inequities are reproduced, maintained, challenged, and transformed in education. I aim to accomplish this specifically through my work preparing critical anti-oppressive environmental educators for all people, all living beings, and the planet. Unsurprisingly, doing this work using critical research, BIPOC epistemologies, intersectionality, discourses of power, oppression, resistance, and liberation from a Black-Pinay female body has been met with resistance, essentialism, tone policing, and marginalization. I have been treated with disdain for refusing the politics of assimilation and tokenism and contend daily with the animus that BIPOC womxn are too vocal, cause trouble, and do not go about things the right/white way. This makes clear to me that my only possible relationship to the university is a criminal one, which is a notion that Harney and Moten (2013) elaborate upon:

In the face of these conditions one can only sneak into the university and steal what one can. To abuse its hospitality, to spite its mission, to join its refugee colony, its . . . encampment, to be in but not of—this is the path of the subversive intellectual in the modern university. (p. 26)

To be bold, brave, and foolish enough to labor in the academy, I am acutely aware of the importance of continuing collective scholarship that is intergenerational, interdisciplinary, interrogates power structures, is liberatory, and centers on an intersectional feminist ethic of care. In my research and teaching in critical environmental education, I implement these values grounded in BIPOC futures and epistemologies, land/air/water education, and place-based approaches. This applied research is the difference between neoliberal accountability and Indigenous concepts of relational accountability (Wilson, 2008).

Although I feel weary—physically, psychologically, emotionally, and spiritually—I am inspired to move forward, to center rest and healing and continue to cultivate love for a community that is committed to building a world where BIPOC life is joyful and love is abundant. I am moved by the work of Tricia Hersey (2020), an offering that our bodies are a site of liberation, that rest is a form of resistance and that rest is a portal such that we can reclaim our imaginative power through sleep: "The revolution will be led by well rested people, people who are connected, people who are inventive, who are tapped into the spiritual component of rest and what it can do for us." As challenging as this will be in practice, it is time to prioritize rest and self-care: we need it in "the downlow lowdown maroon community of the university, in the *undercommons of enlightenment*, where the work gets done, where the work gets subverted, where the revolution is still black, still strong" (Harney & Moten, 2013, p. 26; emphasis in original).

Lola

My journey started as the typical story of a first-generation student of color who "succeeded," though success is not truly what it is; rather, I was one of the few they allowed in. I refuse the narrative of success. I also understand that my journey is not simply my own, that it belongs to others. While I complicate success above, after graduating high school I was driven by a need to show that we (in the surround) are not who the world around us thinks we are. I graduated from high school and attended a prestigious liberal arts college in New York, then went to law school in West Texas. The law, I realized, was not what I wanted, and that path of success was actually another kind of harm. While in law school I did the best I could to survive in a racist context: I immersed myself in the literatures of critical race theory in the law, liberation theology (especially the work of James Cone), and Vine Deloria's work, which together pushed me to question my Black letter legal training.

To be sure, my work as a public defender further cemented my critique of criminal law, and I shifted careers to education. I found my route to the PhD was more in line with my political activism and idealism, fighting for equity, and the belief that there has been and should be another way to be in the world. Yet the academy almost killed me. The stress from academic work caused me to suffer a serious medical crisis. I collapsed in class, in front of students; and even when struggling to stand up I could not, as the headache and dizziness I was experiencing was overwhelming. I was angry at myself for collapsing in front of students, for showing weakness and terrified that perhaps I was dying. Perhaps I could have; I still struggle thinking about this, much less writing about it. This medical issue is now chronic, resulting in cascading medical issues. And yet my story is not unusual. I ask myself, "How can I encourage others to walk in my steps?" Yet this refusal for me needs to be grounded in something.

As a first-generation scholar of color, there have been obvious disciplinary mechanisms that motivated me, but more powerfully, there are community histories that give me a different way to think about the enclosures we theorize here. For me, it's a deep understanding that the surround is actually the deep center and place of origin for the community I come from. I draw strength from this. Indigenous scholar Audra Simpson (2007, 2014) names this as "refusal," built from her own communities' refusal of the mechanisms of control by the state, which informs her approach to research. Tuck and Yang (2014) describe this refusal in educational work and I follow this, examining my own community's educational story of access (Calderón, 2016). In my current research, the local Indigenous community guides the work I support. It is their dreams and desires of futurity that allow me to build work with others that rejects productivity and demands a relationality that institutionalized academic work does not hold space for: a refusal of the terms of the academy. Relatedly, it is the labor organizing and strong union of my university that allows for this different orientation. Thus, we must organize our labor as faculty to account for refusal.

Certainly, refusal has informed how I engage *being* a first-generation faculty of color, though it was not always apparent to me. I received tenure at a research-intensive university but refused the mounting politics of accountability and productivity and moved to a teaching institution that has not fully succumbed to such measures, though the future of budgetary crisis after COVID will likely shift this terrain. In doing so, I gave up tenure. Getting tenure the second time caused my medical emergency described above, which has radically altered my being. I am much more firm in both my refusal and my desire to be an outlaw/fugitive. I often think of my father, who told me to "come home" when I called him crying about my graduate school experience many years ago. My father lived a life of gentle refusal and embodied what it meant to be fully alive. Through my father's memory, I see what refusal should look like. Refusal means not only saving myself but also returning to the work that is needed and being honest about why I stay in academia, not because it has granted me what I dreamed of but because it is a job that provides for me and my family. I dream of exits (Harney & Moten, 2013) out of the enclosure and the possibility of returning home, and at the same time I am terrified of precarity, understanding it too intimately. This is the dilemma that haunts me, and this is the contradiction of capital we all live with. This is what refusal allows me to bear witness to, and yet, in the present moment I am also hopeful because the youth of the oppressed world are inspiring and conspiring to imagine an otherwise in the face of a retaliatory white supremacy. Indeed, I dream of something different for my daughter, the children I claim and those that claim me. The university is not part of these dreams.

Vero

I have a vivid memory as a doctoral student when my father decided he wanted to accompany me to one of my classes. As a child, my father was very present in my schooling. He worked graveyard shifts in order to pick me up from school each day, sit down and help me with homework, and attend every one of my basketball games. Thus, his request that day was nothing unusual. On our way to UCLA, I could feel his excitement. He always wanted to go to college, periodically enrolling in our local community college in the hope that he could finish his transfer degree and pursue a bachelor's. His dream was to become a lawyer. As we approached the classroom, he paused. He turned to me and said, "*Mija*, I can't go in. I'm just not smart enough to be here." Despite my many attempts to get him to see otherwise, to acknowledge his brilliance, I couldn't convince him to enter the room. Instead, he waited four hours until my class ended. I checked on him periodically during my breaks to find him staring at passing students, wondering what his life might have been. Fast forward ten years. I often share this memory when my students stop by my office to ask a quick question. Rather than respond equally hastily, I invite them in, tempting them with snacks, tea, and, on occasion, sugary drinks in my office fridge. I remind them that they deserve mentors and an education that sees them as a whole person, which recognizes their brilliance, the way I wished my father would have been recognized for his. I relay to them that how I mentor and, by extension, what motivates my research is often less about what they need and more about what my father was denied. I want to make sure they have an education that I struggled to access as a first-generation student. Grateful for the extra advising time, they exit my office, lovingly reminding me to take care of myself as they witness the visible exhaustion that I, and other women BIPOC faculty on our campus, clearly show, despite our attempts to mask it.

My experience as both faculty and director of an academic program in social justice education is not unique. Reflecting on their early experiences in university classrooms, Johnson-Bailey and Lee (2005) highlight the complexities

and tensions faced by women BIPOC faculty in designing programs and conducting research that questions traditionally accepted knowledge about race
and gender in predominantly white institutions. Their insights add to a growing body of scholarship exposing hostile academic environments wherein BIPOC
faculty, women and femmes in particular, must navigate and work against pre-
sumptions of incompetence to generate knowledge in the classroom and in
scholarship (Agathangelou & Ling, 2002; Gutiérrez y Muhs et al., 2012; Johnson-
Bailey & Lee, 2005). My own experience attests to this reality, further exacerbated by the invisible labor of supporting hundreds of BIPOC students on my
campus. My first-generation identity amplifies these practices, insisting on
everyday acts of resistance in my teaching, mentoring, and research, regardless
of the consequences. The memory of my father at UCLA generates the imperative for these acts.

To be specific, I took on roles as a new faculty member to advise student
groups like Movimiento Estudiantil Chicana/o de Aztlán (M.E.Ch.A.) and Students for Ethnic Studies, and partnered strategically with other faculty and centers on campus to (re)claim space for learning communities that fostered
student-centered pedagogies and furthered liberatory multigenerational scholarship. We met in basements, in homes, and in local community spaces to think,
read, learn, research, and write about social movements, structural oppression,
and the neoliberal university, and to unpack our desires for the future(s) we do
not yet know. We drew from the most radical traditions, and especially from the
writings of BIPOC women, to tell our stories—*counterstories*—to make sense of
the political moment on our campus (and the world).

These experiences profoundly shaped me as new faculty. Though imperfect,
I felt I had made my father proud in my attempts to destabilize neoliberal co-
optations of social justice from *within* the university while working to establish
"fugitive schools" *outside* of such programs. At the same time, I found myself
wrestling with the tension of needing these spaces to fully embody my political
commitments while simultaneously refusing untenable working conditions that
were literally making me sick: I experienced three miscarriages as a junior faculty working toward tenure but never missed a day of work. Despite close colleagues and family imploring me to refuse the physiological, psychological, and
spiritual assaults of the enclosure, I couldn't stop working. Determined to figure out how to nurture a political practice aimed at ending repression away from
the gaze of the university while still "making it count" for tenure, I found myself
in the most impossible of contradictions. I could feel my father's heartache
weighing on my decision to refuse the university. Recently I resigned from the
director's position, and I am leaning on my co-authors to refine my analysis of
the enclosure in order to embark on a path of healing—for me, for my father,
and for the generations that follow.

Concluding Thoughts

As first-generation BIPOC faculty, the white supremacist, heterosexist, ableist, settler-colonial, and capitalist enclosure does not want us, and therein lies a blessing and way forward. Our narratives highlight ways in which we refuse what the university offers us and how our refusal from the surround helps us to create possibilities of what the academy can be, or if it should even exist. bell hooks (1989) reminds us that it is in the margins, in effect, the surround that is a "site of radical possibility, a space of resistance" (p. 20). And so, we labor here and bear witness together. We help each other to live in line with our values, values that lead us to choices of refusal that make it easy for us to choose ourselves, each other, and our communities. We want to bring radical love to a loveless place. "After all, the subversive intellectual came under false pretenses, with bad documents, out of love. Her labor is as necessary as it is unwelcome. The university needs what she bears but cannot bear what she brings" (Harney & Moten, 2013, p. 26). And while what the university offers is not enough, as fugitives we push into the wild beyond where we do not accept nor are placated by the lies of the academy. Instead, we urge, "We want to take apart, dismantle, tear down the structure that, right now, limits our ability to find each other, to see beyond it and to access the places that we know lie outside its walls" (Halberstam, 2013, p. 6).

REFERENCES

Agathangelou, A. M., & Ling, L.H.M. (2002). An unten(ur)able position: The politics of teaching for women of color in the US. *International Feminist Journal of Politics, 4*(3), 368–398. https://doi.org/10.1080/1461674022000031562

Blackwell, M., Lopez, F. B., & Urrieta, L. (2017). Critical Latinx indigeneities. *Latino Studies, 15*(2), 126–137. doi:10.1057/S41276-017-0064-0

Calderón, D. (2016). Moving from damage-centered research through unsettling reflexivity. *Anthropology & Education Quarterly, 47*(1), 5–24. https://doi.org/10.1111/aeq.12132

Calhoun, C. C. (2008). Foreword. In C. R. Hale (Ed.), *Engaging contradictions: Theory, politics, and methods of activist scholarship* (pp. xiii–xxvi). University of California Press.

Collins, P. H. (2009). *Black feminist thought: Knowledge, consciousness, and the politics of empowerment* (2nd ed.). Routledge.

Combahee River Collective. (1986). *The Combahee River Collective statement: Black feminist organizing in the seventies and eighties.* Kitchen Table, Women of Color Press.

Delgado Bernal, D., & Villalpando, O. (2002). An apartheid of knowledge in academia: The struggle over the "legitimate" knowledge of Faculty of Color. *Equity & Excellence in Education, 35*(2), 169–80. https://doi.org/10.1080/713845282

Diggs, G. A., Garrison-Wade, D. F., Estrada, D., & Galindo, R. (2009). Smiling faces and colored spaces: The experiences of faculty of color pursuing tenure in the academy. *Urban Review, 41*(4), 312–333. doi:10.1007/s11256-008-0113-y

Fanon, F. (1963). *The wretched of the earth* (Constance Farrington, Trans.). Grove Press.

Ferreira da Silva, D. (2007). *Toward a global idea of race.* University of Minnesota Press.

Graham, J. A., Cohen, R., Zbikowski, S. M., & Secrist, M. E. (1998). A longitudinal investigation of race and sex as factors in children's classroom friendship choices. *Child Study Journal, 28*(4), 245–245.

Grande, S. (2018). Refusing the university. In E. Tuck & K. W. Yang (Eds.), *Toward what justice? Describing diverse dreams of justice in education* (pp. 47–65). Routledge.

Gutiérrez y Muhs, G., Niemann, Y. F., Gonzalez, C. G., & Harris, A. P. (2012). *Presumed incompetent: The intersections of race and class for women in academia.* Utah State University Press.

Harney, S., & Moten, F. (2013). *The undercommons: Fugitive planning & Black study.* Minor Compositions.

Henry, W. J., & Glenn, N. M. (2009). Black women employed in the ivory tower: Connecting for success. *Advancing Women in Leadership Journal, 29*(2), 1–18. https://doi.org/10.18738/awl.v29i0.271

Hersey, T. (2020, June 8). *Tricia Hersey on rest as resistance* [Audio podcast]. https://forthewild.world/listen/tricia-hersey-on-rest-as-resistance-185

hooks, b. (1989). Choosing the margin as a space of radical openness. *Journal of Cinema and Media, 36*, 15–23. https://www.jstor.org/stable/44111660

Hurtado, S., Milem, J., Clayton-Pederson, A., & Allen, W. (1999). *Enacting diverse learning environments: Improving the climate of racial/ethnic diversity in higher education.* Jossey-Bass.

Johnson-Bailey, J., & Lee, M. Y. (2005). Women of color in the academy: Where's our authority in the classroom? *Feminist Teacher, 15*(2), 111–112. http://www.jstor.org/stable/40545917

Kamola, I., & Meyerhoff, E. (2009). Creating commons: Divided governance, participatory management, and struggles against enclosure in the university. *Polygraph, 21*, 15–37.

Kelley, R.D.G. (2016). Black study, Black struggle. *The Boston Review.* http://bostonreview.net/forum/robin-d-g-kelley-black-study-black-struggle

la paperson. (2017). *A third university is possible.* University of Minnesota Press.

Lorde, A. (1984). *Sister outsider: Essays and speeches.* Crossing Press.

Lorde, A. (1995). A litany for survival. In *The black unicorn: Poems* (pp. 31–32). Norton.

Martínez, E. (1998). *De colores means all of us: Latina views for a multi-colored century.* South End Press.

Matias, C. (2016). *Feeling white: Whiteness, emotionality, and education.* Sense.

Moraga, C., & Anzaldúa, G. (Eds.). (1983). *This bridge called my back: Writings by radical women of color* (2nd ed.). Kitchen Table, Women of Color Press.

Muñoz, S. M., Basile, V., Gonzalez, J., Birmingham, D., Aragon, A., Jennings, L., & Gloeckner, G. (2017). (Counter) narratives and complexities: Critical perspectives from a university cluster hire focused on diversity, equity, and inclusion. *Journal of Critical Thought and Praxis, 6*(2), 1–21.

Nieto, L. (2010). *Beyond inclusion, beyond empowerment: A developmental strategy to liberate everyone.* Cuetzpalin.

Patel, L. (2015). *Decolonizing educational research: From ownership to answerability.* Routledge.

Patel, L. (2016). Pedagogies of resistance and survivance: Learning as marronage. *Equity & Excellence in Education, 49*(4), 397–401. https://doi.org/10.1080/10665684.2016.1227585

Piper, D., Jacobe, J., Yazzie, R., & Calderón, D. (2019). Indigenous methodologies in graduate school: Accountability, relationships, and tensions. In S. Windchief & T. S. Pedro (Eds.), *Applying Indigenous research methods* (pp. 86–101). Routledge.

Richardson, T. (2011). Navigating the problem of inclusion as enclosure in Native culture–based education: Theorizing shadow curriculum. *Curriculum Inquiry, 41*(3), 332–349. https://doi.org/10.1111/j.1467-873X.2011.00552.x

Robinson, C. (2000). *Black Marxism: The making of the Black radical tradition*. University of North Carolina Press.

Rosa, J., & Bonilla, Y. (2017). Deprovincializing Trump, decolonizing diversity, and unsettling anthropology. *American Ethnologist*, *44*(2), 201–208. https://doi.org/10.1111/amet .12468

Rosas, G. (2018, September 26). Fugitive work: On the criminal possibilities of anthropology. *Hot Spots, Cultural Anthropology*. https://culanth.org/fieldsights/1529-fugitive-work -on-the-criminal-possibilities-of-anthropology

Salazar, M.D.C., Norton, A. S., & Tuitt, F. A. (2017). 12: Weaving promising practices for inclusive excellence into the higher education classroom. *To Improve the Academy*, *28*(1), 208–226. doi:10.1002/j.2334-4822.2010.tb00604.x

Severin, L. (2013, September 30). Doing "cluster hiring" right. *Inside Higher Ed*. https://www .insidehighered.com/advice/2013/09/30/essay-how-colleges-can-engage-cluster -hiring

Simpson, A. (2007). On ethnographic refusal: Indigeneity, "voice" and colonial citizenship. *Junctures: The Journal for Thematic Dialogue*, *9*. https://junctures.org/index.php/junctures /article/view/66/60

Simpson, A. (2014). *Mohawk interruptus: Political life across the borders of settler states*. Duke University Press.

Smith, D. G., Turner, C. S., Osei-Kofi, N., & Richards, S. (2004). Interrupting the usual: Successful strategies for hiring diverse faculty. *Journal of Higher Education*, *75*(2), 133–160. doi:10.1353/jhe.2004.0006

Smith, L. T. (2012). *Decolonizing methodologies: Research and Indigenous peoples* (2nd ed.). University of Otago Press.

Stanley, C. A. (Ed.). (2006a). *Faculty of color: Teaching in predominantly white colleges and universities*. Anchor.

Stanley, C. A. (2006b). Coloring the academic landscape: Faculty of color breaking the silence in predominantly white colleges and universities. *American Educational Research Journal*, *43*(4), 701–736. https://doi.org/10.3102/0002831204300470I

Tatum, B. (2017). *Why are all the Black kids sitting together in the cafeteria? And other conversations about race* (3rd ed.). Basic Books.

Tuck, E., Guess, A., & Sultan, H. (2014, June 26). Not nowhere: Collaborating on selfsame land. *Decolonization: Indigeneity, Education & Society*. https://decolonization.wordpress .com/2014/06/26/not-nowhere-collaborating-on-selfsame-land/

Tuck, E., & Yang, K. W. (2012). Decolonization is not a metaphor. *Decolonization: Indigeneity, Education & Society*, *1*(1), 1–40.

Tuck, E., & Yang, K. W. (2014). *Youth resistance research and theories of change*. Routledge.

Turner, C., González, J., & Wood, J. (2008). Faculty of color in academe: What 20 years of literature tells us. *Journal of Diversity in Higher Education*, *1*(3), 139–168. https://doi.org /10.1037/a0012837

Turner, C., & Myers, S. L. (2000). *Faculty of color in academe: Bittersweet success*. Allyn and Bacon.

Umbach, P. D. (2006). The contribution of faculty of color to undergraduate education. *Research in Higher Education*, *47*(3), 317–345. https://www.jstor.org/stable/40197402

Williams, P. (1987). Spirit-murdering the messenger: The discourse of finger pointing as the law's response to racism. *University of Miami Law Review*, *42*, 127. https://repository.law .miami.edu/umlr/vol42/iss1/8

Willinsky, J. (1998). *Learning to divide the world: Education at empire's end*. University of Minnesota Press.

Wilson, S. (2008). *Research is ceremony: Indigenous research methods*. Fernwood.

Young, A. M., Battaglia, A., & Cloud, D. L. (2010). (UN)Disciplining the scholar activist: Policing the boundaries of political engagement. *Quarterly Journal of Speech, 96*(4), 427–435. https://doi.org/10.1080/00335630.2010.521179

Youngbull, N. R., & Minthorn, R. (2018). Demystifying influences on persistence for Native American first-generation college students. In A. C. Rondini, B. N. Richards, & N. P. Simon (Eds.), *Clearing the path for first-generation college students: Qualitative and intersectional studies of educational mobility* (pp. 257–284). Lexington Books.

ACKNOWLEDGMENTS

Thank you to our families, who nurtured our dreams, shaped our trajectories, and continue to support us on our journeys, including our parents, Herminia Lachica Buenavista, Robert Abuan Buenavista, Surat Pyari Jain, Mahesh Kumar Jain, Josefina Ledesma, and Adalberto Ledesma; and our siblings, extended family members, coconspirator homies, Daniel Asres, and Iko Buenavista Gonzales.

Special gratitude to Jordan Beltran Gonzales, our editor extraordinaire, who taught us how to write in "proper" English and always made us feel confident in our voices; Alberto Ledesma, who created powerful imagery to make our stories come alive; and Lisa Banning, our editor at Rutgers, who supported this project to fruition.

We also want to acknowledge the contributors who made this book possible: José M. Aguilar-Hernández, Constancio R. Arnaldo Jr., Dolores Calderón, Patrick Roz Camangian, Rebecca Covarrubias, Alma Itzé Flores, Judith Flores Carmona, Nini Hayes, Norma A. Marrun, Samuel D. Museus, Cindy N. Phu, Omar Ruvalcaba, Darrick Smith, Ivelisse Torres Fernandez, Edil Torres Rivera, Verónica Nelly Vélez, Varaxy Yi, and Maria Estela Zarate. Thank you for entrusting us with your stories and practicing deep patience throughout the project.

Last, we want to especially acknowledge those who collectively mentored us and forged a path that hundreds have been able to travel, including Daniel G. Solorzano, Caroline Sotello Viernes Turner, Walter Allen, Ifeoma Amah, Rebeca Burciaga, Miguel Ceja, Mitchell J. Chang, Dolores Delgado Bernal, Kris D. Gutiérrez, David E. Z. Maldonado, Gina Masequesmay, Patricia McDonough, Nana Osei-Kofi, Don Nakanishi, La'Tonya Rease-Miles, Dean Itsuji Saranillio, David O. Stovall, Allyson Tintiangco-Cubales, Octavio Villalpando, Tara Yosso, and Eboni Zamani-Gallaher.

NOTES ON CONTRIBUTORS

JOSÉ M. AGUILAR-HERNÁNDEZ is associate professor at the College of Education and Integrative Studies at Cal Poly Pomona. He is the son of Esteban and María del Socorro, immigrant farmworkers from Zacatecas, México. Aguilar-Hernández is the youngest of nine siblings and the first in his immediate and extended family to enter higher education. He transferred from Moorpark College to UCLA, where he received a BA in history and Chicana/o studies, an MA in Latin American studies, and a PhD in education. His teaching and research interests include ethnic studies, critical race theory, higher education, student activism, and critical pedagogies.

CONSTANCIO R. ARNALDO JR. is assistant professor of Asian and Asian American studies in the Department of Interdisciplinary, Gender, and Ethnic Studies at the University of Nevada, Las Vegas. He examines the cultural politics of sport among Filipinx/a/o Americans in everyday sporting spaces and boxing spectacles. A second-generation Filipino American, Constancio is a first-generation college student and the first in his immediate family to earn an MA and a PhD. He is committed to helping first-generation college students and Black, Indigenous, and People of Color (BIPOC) students navigate higher education. He finds joy by rock gardening, hiking, cooking, and playing basketball.

TRACY LACHICA BUENAVISTA (she/her) is professor of Asian American studies and a core faculty member of the doctoral program in educational leadership at California State University, Northridge—although most of her family knows her as a "teacher." She is a "1.5-generation college student," second-generation Pinay/daughter of Filipino immigrants, parentscholar, and was raised in Hayward, California. In her research, she utilizes critical race theory to examine how race, (im)migration, and carcerality shape the educational access, retention, and experiences of students and educators of color. Her community work supports undocumented immigrant students and other justice-impacted individuals to persist in education and beyond.

DOLORES CALDERÓN is associate professor of youth, society, and justice at Western Washington University's Fairhaven College of Interdisciplinary Studies. She is from the El Paso/Juarez border region, where her family (Mexican and Tigua) have lived since the 1680s. Her research interests include coloniality/settler colonialisms, land education, and border issues as they permeate education. Some of her research projects include examining how settler colonial ideologies manifest themselves in social studies curriculum, teacher education, and teacher professional development. Calderón is a firm believer that theory is best illuminated by community engagement, valuing the work educators do to concretize critical perspectives.

PATRICK ROZ CAMANGIAN is associate professor and department chair of teacher education at the University of San Francisco School of Education. Against the wishes of his family, he left a job at United Parcel Service to become a teacher. Camangian was the first person in his family to obtain a bachelor's degree. Ten years later, he earned a PhD and pursued a career in academia as a teacher educator. Camangian has been working in schools since 1997, continuing in the tradition of teacher research, applying cutting-edge pedagogies in schools, and more recently, informing district-wide policy and practice through action research and collaborations in the San Francisco Bay Area.

JUDITH FLORES CARMONA is associate professor in the honors college and interim director of Chicano programs at New Mexico State University. Flores Carmona is the daughter of Josefina and Vicente (QEPD). She was born in Veracruz, Mexico, raised in Los Angeles, and is a first-generation college student and scholar. A sense of responsibility and commitment to social change guides her academic and community work. Her research interests include critical pedagogy, Chicana/Latina feminist theory, critical race feminism, critical multicultural education, social justice education, and *testimonio* methodology and pedagogy.

REBECCA COVARRUBIAS is associate professor of psychology at the University of California, Santa Cruz. Drawing from her own experiences as a low-income, Latina first-generation college student, Rebecca's research, teaching, and mentoring is dedicated to shifting practices in higher education to better reflect the cultural strengths of minoritized students. She collaborates with students, staff, faculty, community members, and families to develop culturally grounded initiatives that promote educational equity along the academic pipeline.

IVELISSE TORRES FERNANDEZ is associate professor of counseling psychology at Albizu University in San Juan, Puerto Rico. Born in Mayaguez, Puerto Rico, she is the first of only two women in her family to earn a doctoral degree and the only one to enter the field of academia as a professor. Her academic and professional career has been devoted to advocate for underrepresented populations with particular emphasis on immigrant children and families. Her primary research interests focus on issues of diversity, social justice, and trauma. She is the editor-in-chief of *Ciencias de la Conducta*, the oldest psychology journal in Puerto Rico.

ALMA ITZÉ FLORES is assistant professor in the Undergraduate Studies in Education department at California State University, Sacramento. As a Chicana feminist teacher-scholar, her research examines the educational pathways of Chicana/Latina first-generation college students, Chicana/Latina mothers, and the development and analysis of Chicana/Latina feminist pedagogies and research methodologies. Alma was born in Jalisco, Mexico and raised in Santa Barbara, California. She is the first in her family to receive bachelors, masters, and doctoral degrees. As a firm believer in the power of mentorship, she has dedicated much of her life to working with students of color as an educator, femtor, and coconspirator.

NINI HAYES is associate professor in the education and eco-social justice program in the environmental studies department at Western Washington University. They are the first person in their family to earn a bachelor's degree, a master's degree, and a doctoral degree. Nini was an environmental educator and then a fifth-grade teacher before moving on to higher education. They are drawn to the intersections of the historical, cultural, political, and social necessity of preparing critical and justice oriented environmental educators.

DIMPAL JAIN is professor of educational leadership and policy studies and a core faculty within the doctoral program in educational leadership at California State University, Northridge. She is the first in her family to earn a PhD and is proud of her family title of "Book Doctor." Her work centers on the relationship between community colleges and universities through a critical race framework, most notably how baccalaureate granting institutions can develop and maintain a transfer receptive culture for students of color. She values books, family, friends, community, cafés, classrooms, and sunshine.

MARÍA C. LEDESMA is professor of educational leadership and founding director of the higher education leadership master's program at San José State University. Born in Guadalajara, she grew up in Oakland, California and attended the University of California, Berkeley as an undergraduate. She entered the academy after earning postbaccalaureate degrees from Harvard University and UCLA. Her research interests focus on equity-minded critical policy analysis, including contextualizing and historicizing race-conscious social policy in higher education and examining the experiences of first-generation faculty. She is the daughter of Adalberto (a former bracero) and Josefina (an organic educator) of Huisquilco, Jalisco, Mexico.

NORMA A. MARRUN is associate professor of cultural studies, international education, and multicultural education in the Department of Teaching and Learning at University of Nevada, Las Vegas. She grew up in the San Francisco Bay Area and is a proud first-generation college graduate. She earned her doctorate in educational policy studies from the University of Illinois at Urbana-Champaign. Her research examines critical multicultural education, critical race theory, Chicana/Latina feminisms, recruiting and retaining students of color along the PK–20 educational pipeline. She is hella inspired by her students' brilliance, courage, and critical hope to create more humanizing educational *sitios*.

SAMUEL D. MUSEUS is professor of education studies at the University of California, San Diego (UCSD) and founding director of the National Institute for Transformation and Equity. He is the first in his family to earn a college degree and serve in the academy. Prior to joining UCSD, he taught at Indiana University–Bloomington, the University of Denver, the University of Hawaiʻi at Manoa, and the University of Massachusetts–Boston.

CINDY N. PHU is associate professor of speech communication at Pasadena City College, where she also served as the director/coordinator of the Forensics and Speech Center. As the daughter of Chinese-Vietnamese refugees, she is the first in her family to attain her bachelor's, master's, and doctoral degrees. Cindy has served on the executive board of the Pacific Southwest Collegiate Forensics Association and is now on the steering committee of the International Association of Maternal Action and Scholarship. She has spent fifteen years teaching, coaching, and empowering student voices in the classroom, at national competitions, and at academic conferences.

EDIL TORRES RIVERA is professor and director of Latinx studies at Wichita State University, Kansas. He is interested in multicultural counseling, group work, chaos theory, liberation psychology, technology, supervision, multicultural counseling, prisons, Puerto Rican studies, identity development, and gang-related behavior. He is the son of Iris Rivera Galarza, who was a single mother raising three boys in the public housing projects in Puerto Rico. He is the first and only person from his mother's side of the family to obtain an advanced degree and to teach at a university.

OMAR RUVALCABA is associate professor of psychology at California State University, Northridge. As the first in his family to receive bachelor's and doctoral degrees, he had to navigate academia's challenges while negotiating his passion for giving back to his community and pursuing research in tech and video games communities. Initially trained as a developmental psychologist, he employs a critical and liberation psychology approach to STEM and gaming research. He is the son of Felipe Ruvalcaba and Leticia Ruvalcaba of Amoxóchitl, Zacatecas, Mexico.

DARRICK SMITH is associate professor of educational leadership and codirector of the Transformative School Leadership program at the University of San Francisco. He has served as an educator, school leader, and consultant within secondary, post-secondary, and nonprofit spaces for over two decades. His commitment to social change has been recognized by a commendation from the California State Senate for his work in violence prevention and youth development. His research interests include culturally responsive discipline practices, equity in the community colleges, critical pedagogy, transformative leadership, and education for social justice.

CAROLINE SOTELLO VIERNES TURNER is professor emerita for the Doctorate in Educational Leadership program at California State University, Sacramento (CSUS), and Lincoln Professor Emerita of Higher Education and Ethics at Arizona State University (ASU). At CSUS, Turner served as interim dean for the College of Education. Prior to her appointment at ASU, she was professor of educational policy and administration at the University of Minnesota, Twin Cities, where she cofounded the national Keeping Our Faculties of Color Symposium. She is also past president of the Association for the Study of Higher Education. Her research and teaching interests include faculty gender and racial/ethnic diversity, leadership and organizational change, and the use of qualitative methods for policy research.

VERÓNICA NELLY VÉLEZ is associate professor of secondary education and the founding director of the Education and Social Justice program at Western Washington University. She is the first person in her family to earn bachelor's, master's, and doctoral degrees, and to enter the field of academia as a professor. Verónica's most recent endeavors aim to develop conceptual and methodological approaches that deepen a spatial consciousness and expand the use of geographic information systems in critical race research in education. She is the proud daughter of Nelly Vélez of Ciudad Guzmán, México, and Humberto Vélez of Colón, Panama, whose journey to provide her with a quality education fundamentally inspires her work for social justice.

VARAXY YI is a Khmer American assistant professor of educational leadership, coordinator of the higher education administration and leadership graduate program, and core faculty in the doctoral program in educational leadership at California State University, Fresno. She conducts research to advance equity, access, and opportunity for historically underserved communities, such as racially minoritized, Southeast Asian American, and refugee populations. She is a daughter of Cambodian refugees, firstborn in the United States, and the first to navigate the U.S. education system. While she may be the first in her family to earn postsecondary degrees, and now serves as a first-generation faculty member in academia, she will not be the last.

MARIA ESTELA ZARATE is vice provost at California State University, Fullerton. Previously, she was professor of educational leadership. Zarate is from San Luis Potosí, Mexico, and came to the United States when she was four years old. She was the first in her family to attend and complete postsecondary education. Her research addresses the trajectory of immigrant students in schools, including connecting between schools and families. More recently, she has written about and developed professional learning opportunities to improve teaching for first-generation college students.

INDEX

adjunct faculty, 82, 85; "freeway-flyer," 80
administrative leader, 107–108
administrative position, 20, 22, 47
advice: colleagues, 83, 107; family, 24, 93; financial, 135; job search, 21, 23, 33; mental health, 71; mentors, xiii, 70, 97, 99; service, 153–154; students, 18
advisor: departmental, 80, 99; faculty, 21–23, 69, 87, 119
affirmative action, 44–46, 143
allyship, 59
anxiety: alienation, 58–59; graduate school, 31–32, 69–71; mental health, 66, 71; pressure, 58
Anzaldúa, Gloria, 42, 49, 115. *See also* borderland *mestiza*
Asian American/s: American Dream, 79, 88; East, 30; futurity, 168–69; South, 17, 30; Southeast, 32; stereotypes, 29–30, 58, 79, 88, 143. *See also* Filipina/o/x; yellow peril
Asian American and Native American Pacific Islander-Serving Institution (AANAPISI), 92, 100
assets, 54, 102, 152–153, 157–158
autoethnography, 18, 21, 26, 54, 80

bachelor's degree, 3, 17–18, 142, 145
Baldwin, James, 106
banking model of education, 114, 116, 118
Black/s, 57, 103, 117–118, 129, 162; city, 55–56; community emphasis, 67, 102, 111; gendered experiences, 67; lack of representation, 45; legal training, 167; mental health, 66, 71; oppression, 56, 163; political activism, 61, 79; tokenism, 58–59, 166. *See also* conspicuous invisibility; multiraciality; racism: anti-Black
Black Lives Matter, xx, 10, 91, 98, 117
Black radical tradition, 164
borderland *mestiza*, 48–50
borderlands, 42, 139
Brown, Michael, 10
Burciaga, Cecilia, xiii–xiv, 140

California State University, Monterey Bay (CSUMB), 140–141
California State University, Northridge (CSUN), 68, 70

California State University (CSU) system, 93
campus visits, 23–24, 84
Chicana/o/x, 45, 48, 50, 92–94, 120, 140. *See also* Mexicana/o; Mexican American
Chicana feminism, 96, 115; Leisy Abrego, 120; Vicki Ruiz, 120
Chicana feminist epistemology, 42
Chicana/o studies, 116–117, 119–120. *See also* Mexican American studies
cisheteroaggression in higher education, 111
civil rights movements, 30
coaching, 24, 56, 80–81
collaboration: as emerging scholars, 35, 96, 98, 141, 152–153, 165–166; pedagogy, 97; research, 37, 155, 157
collective scholarship, 167
collectivist family, 4
collegiality, 107–108
colonialism, 61, 145–146, 163
coloniality, 114, 121
committee work, 68, 70–71, 86; graduate school, 87, 119; meetings, 47; search, 20–21, 46
community college: faculty, 7–8, 79–80, 82, 85; students, 18, 83–84, 93, 106, 119, 169
community cultural wealth, 18, 134, 141, 147
community-engaged research, 109, 157
competitive individualism, 8, 30, 37
conference: financial cost of, 82, 128, 135, 137, 156–157; microaggression, 65; youth, 93
confidence: as faculty, 24, 71, 90, 98; personal, 49; as undergraduates, 91
conocimiento, 50, 115, 117
consciousness: critical, 45, 122; racial, 32, 92
consejo, 142
conspicuous invisibility, 54, 58–60; Howard C. Stevenson, 55, 59
consumerism, 8, 30, 37
continuing-generation students, 18, 151
counseling services, 1, 68
counterspaces, 9, 48, 90, 99–100; ethnic studies courses, 91–92, 95–96; lab, 155–156; mentoring relationships, 97–98; office hours, 114–120; racial student organizations, 92–95; *testimonio*, 91
counterstories, 170